THE TEXTUAL SOCIETY

Semiotics – the study of the encoding of meaning – has so far been confined largely within the humanities, where it has forged a whole new way of understanding meaning and its construction. In this multidisciplinary study, Edwina Taborsky applies semiotic theory to her analysis of the organization of knowledge and therefore the organization of societies.

Taborsky looks at knowledge as a social construction involving two forces: stasis and variation, expressed within the group and the individual. These levels never merge, but exist in a state of continuous dialogical interaction, which transforms energy and permits meaning to exist. The unique, even tragic, nature of individuals is that they are the only means of expression for both realities, for the two opposing forces of energy – stasis and variation. Focusing on the nature of the dialogue between the two realities, Taborsky draws on key theoretical themes from the pragmatics and semiotics of Charles S. Peirce, the dialogues of Mikhail Bakhtin, and the fields of biology and quantum physics. As a whole, the book explores cognition as the social transformation of energy, and looks at different types of societies as differently organized forms of energy.

In this unique look at the social construction of knowledge, the dialogical framework of two realities, that of the group and that of the individual, provides a powerful analytic tool for the analysis of cognition and social behaviour.

EDWINA TABORSKY is Associate Professor and Director of the Anthropology Program, Bishop's University, Lennoxville, Quebec.

EDWINA TABORSKY

The Textual Society

UNIVERSITY OF TORONTO PRESS
Toronto Buffalo London

© University of Toronto Press Incorporated 1997
Toronto Buffalo London
Printed in Canada

ISBN 0-8020-0812-7 (cloth)
ISBN 0-8020-7180-5 (paper)

Printed on acid-free paper

Toronto Studies in Semiotics
Editors: Marcel Danesi, Umberto Eco, Paul Perron, and Thomas Sebeok

Canadian Cataloguing in Publication Data

Taborsky, Edwina, 1940–
  The textual society

  (Toronto studies in semiotics)
  Includes bibliographical references and index.
  ISBN 0-8020-0812-7 (bound)   ISBN 0-8020-7180-5

  1. Social perception.   2. Individuation (Philosophy).
  3. Cognition.   4. Sociology – Philosophy.   5. Semiotics.
  I. Title.   II. Series.

HM73.T23   1997   301'.01   C96-930800-0

University of Toronto Press acknowledges the financial assistance to its
publishing program of the Canada Council and the Ontario Arts Council.

TO MY SONS: PAUL, MARK, AND BEVAN

Contents

Acknowledgments

I should like to thank the members of TADAC, the Centre for Textual Analysis, Discourse and Culture, of Carleton University, for their ideological support over the years. Special thanks go to Dr Barry Rutland, the director, for having set up TADAC, with its interdisciplinary themes, its mixture of the sciences and the humanities, its commitment to the nature of semiosis as a basic action of life. I should also like to thank the members of the University of Toronto Semiotic Program for their interest and support. On a more personal level, I should like to thank my cousins, Charlotte Baker, Barbara and Eddy Levy, and Molly and Harry Shapiro, for being 'my family' and for their warm support for me and my work, over many years. Finally, I should like to thank my sons, Paul, Mark, and Bevan, for their years of support and acceptance of an 'academic mother.'

Introduction

This book is an examination of society as an organic entity, a 'text,' an active formation of a number of seemingly separate forces. It is also an examination of the human being as an author, reader, and multiple actor within that same text.

Most analyses of our social reality consider that we experience our lives within the conceptual domain of either the individual or the group. Either the one or the other is seen as the source of cognition, power, and decision-making. If we think of the individual we come up with such images as freedom, entrepreneur, hero, leader; at the other end of this parameter is selfishness, greed, corruption, tyranny. The collective will is expressed within such images as fairness, nurturance, protection and also domination, censorship, and repression.

In this same binary frame, the individual is often viewed as essentially pure until tainted by the instability of social beliefs and opinions. The whole Cartesian scientific method rests on this concept, along with the democratic ideology of the state, the economic idea of capitalism, and other images supporting the power of reason, the concept of privacy, the values of the heroic leader and inspired inventor. Philosophies based around these themes include rationalism, positivism, existentialism, phenomenology, deconstructionism. Against this purity of the individual, we find views such as those expressed by Durkheim, Hobbes, Locke, and Marx, which consider the individual tainted, imperfect, and that privilege the group or collective as the key activator of social life. These two forces, the individual and the group, are usually understood as either separate and adversarial, or from time to time facing each other in a fragile and vigilantic collaboration. Our political parties polarize themselves under the two themes of the individual or the group; we even write our history under the themes of which force wins – the freedom of the individual or the good of the collective. I should mention other forces that also seem to deprivilege the individual. We may from time to time feel that we have relegated biological causes of behaviour to the background, but these forces remain; they also wait for their voices to be heard. And there is yet another force, basic energy, explored by physics at one pole and by religion at another.

But what if this separation is an entire fallacy? What if these two, the individual and the group – indeed all four aspects – are actually parts of an organic whole? They can be analysed as separate parts much as we analyse an individual's heart, brain, genes, language. But would we ever suggest their separate existentiality? What if human existence is actually an organic complexity, made up not of the one reality of our individual existentiality but of four realities?

There exist, therefore, what I term four realities. I use the word *reality* with intent; they are real; they do exist; they order, guide, assist, and play havoc with our lives. However, they are not separately self-sufficient forces; none is privileged over the other. Let me give them names. There is individual reality, group reality, biological reality, and what I call generative energy rather than the reality of the gods. Our various hypotheses have separated them, pitted them against one another. In actuality, none of these forces operates alone but is existential only within a constant dialogical interplay with the other forces. That is why I refer to society as a 'text'; it is a constant interplay of multiple powers, voices, realities. Together, they form the social text.

There are two parts to this book. The first three chapters deal primarily but not exclusively with cognition as a factor of individual reality in dialogue with group reality. In the subsequent chapters, attention is given to the nature of the entire text, society as made up of those four realities: individual, group, biological, and generative.

The opening chapter, The Realities of the Social Text, introduces the textual society as a dialogical interaction between two realities, the individual and the group. Their natures, their differences, their interactions, and their various degeneracies are examined. The second chapter, The Action of Textuality, explores how these two realities interact to produce the sign as an action of meaning. Meaning is transformed from an open to an organized and therefore conceptual state within a dialogical act. The third chapter, Otherness in the Production of Meaning, continues the examination of the sign and introduces the theme of meaning as energy. Meaning is the transformation and therefore reorganization of energy; energy is understood to come from both old and new or 'other' sources.

With the fourth and subsequent chapters, we move into a closer examination of the society as an organic entity. In chapter 4, Dialogical Time, time is understood as a key factor in the establishment of a social text. Six different forms of temporal organization are examined to explain how they help define the nature of cognition. The fifth chapter, The Pattern of Cognition, focuses on the basic holding structure of any society – the syntax, the logical pattern of cognition that forms the fundamental stability of group reality. Two key syntactic patterns, called simply A and B, are explored both in their nature and their historic settings. Chapter 6, Textual Change, moves into a discussion of how societies, although seeming constrained within a syntactic structure, can actually change. Essentially, gradual evolution and therefore developmental and progressive social development is rejected, and punctuated evolution and catastrophic change is used as a basic theme. This explains that societies have long periods of stability and then suddenly undergo violent crisis periods during which they change their energy content and therefore their social organization. They emerge from this era of change not as a newer version of the old society but must be understood as a new 'species' within which a different cognition can exist. Chapter 7, Two Bodies / Two Powers, explores these two biological/physical forces of stability and variation in more detail. This chapter defines the interaction of these supposedly opposing and yet equally necessary forces and considers their interaction as the basic binary conflict in all human experience. It takes this binary frame further, considering these two forces as actual 'bodies' within the social text and examining them within the themes of gnostic and Lacanian analysis. The final chapter, Society as Text, summarizes the key themes of the book and concludes that human experience is a dialogical experience of multiple realities.

A key aim of the study is to move semiotics from its confinement within the humanities, where it has functioned primarily as a descriptive tool for codes, and bring its powers to the analysis of the organic and social nature of cognition. Key theoretical themes in this research come from the pragmatics and semiotics of Charles S. Peirce, whose analysis of the three categories of Firstness, Secondness, and Thirdness is indispensable to the understanding of cognition; from the chronotopic dialogics of Mikhail Bakhtin, which I expand from his use within the field of literary criticism to provide sociostructural insights; and from concepts within quantum physics and biology.

However, this book is intended not merely for those who are interested in semiotics and its broader application to the social sciences. It is also a suggestion that the humanities, the social sciences, and the natural sciences cannot maintain their isolation from one another. Our life as we experience it is operative within all three areas and we must use all three in our attempts to understand ourselves. We are disparate beings made up of multiple forces.

We are isolate and interactional; social and biological; we are forms of thought and thoughts are forms of energy. We are as variable as the gods who so easily transform themselves into multiple images and live their lives within the semiosis of duplicity and variation. But unlike the gods we are mortal and finite. Out of this very specificity of the mortality of our experiences have come signs, the basis not merely of thought but of existence. It is through signs and the logic and order they bring with them, signs whose nature is far broader than that envisaged by Prometheus who gave them to us, that we exist. It is hoped that this book can be used to broaden our use of signs and semiosis.

THE TEXTUAL SOCIETY

1

The Realities of the Social Text

Two Realities

I begin with an understanding that life is experienced within two realities, that of the individual and that of the group. Together they form the social text.

Individual reality (IR), the most immediate and perishable within our experience, exists only in current time and comprises the sensual as well as the conceptual experiences of the individual. Although both are existentially real in the sense that each is a distinct experience of the individual in current time, they differ greatly. Further, despite the influence of Cartesian rationalism, it is a contention of this analysis that one cannot move directly from the sensual to the conceptual. This interaction requires the mediation of group reality.

Group reality (GR) is without the sensual ground of individual reality and is made up of the pattern of social norms, the habits of behaviour and belief that have existed within this particular group in the past and must continue to exist in the future. It is less accessible than individual reality and I therefore term it the second level of reality. Group reality has no current essential nature, a vital factor that will be explored more fully in later chapters. Its role, if we may speak of it this way, is to provide a past and future logic to the existential reality of the individual. As such a law, it is structure only, a horizon of conceptual borders and limitations, acting as a potential to define and confine the reality of the individual experience. Unlike that of the individual, group reality has no sensuality and therefore no particular conceptual imagery. If we consider its nature as a logic, a law, which exists only as a habit of the past and a potential of the future, then we must further admit that it has no power to express itself. Expression is understood as a distinctive experience both in its sensual and conceptual nature that exists only in

Diagram 1: The Textual Society: Cognitive frame

S: Sensual (Firstness)	I___*_S_____*_C___I	Individual reality
C: Conceptual (Secondness)	I_____L_____I	Group reality
L: Logical (Thirdness)		

current time. Group reality therefore exists in current reality only by the expression, the existential experiences, the goodwill, of the individual.

Three Categories and Operations of Thought

I further refine these two realities in terms of the three Peircean categories of thought and the three intellectual operations of Thomas Aquinas.

The first category of Peirce, or Firstness,[1] 'comprises the qualities of phenomena.' This is immediate sensual experience without reason, understanding, or awareness of its nature. The category of Secondness 'comprises the actual facts' as distinct and individual concepts. It is a specific image or concept in the mind. The category of elements of Thirdness 'consists of what we call laws' (1:418–20) and can be understood as the habits of mind of a group. The important concepts in Firstness are both its conceptual unavailability and the force of its impact. It is a sensation of 'immediate consciousness ... yet, there is no consciousness in it because it is instantaneous.' It is raw physical experience in its forceful singularity, 'an instance of that sort of element of consciousness which is all that it is positively, in itself, regardless of anything else' and has in its openness 'the ideas of freshness, life, freedom' (1: 310, 306, 302). Secondness is that sensation understood in its distinct and existential signification. Here sensation moves into a specific conceptualization of its nature by also becoming aware of its singular finiteness such that 'we become aware of ourself in becoming aware of the not-self' (1: 324). There is an awareness of struggle with, of difference from, the existential actions of an other. Both Firstness and Secondness are part of the individual experience and therefore existent only in current time. The social laws of Thirdness are neither these qualities nor individual facts but are social habits developed by the group over generations of stability of behaviour and belief. These laws are 'the medium or connecting bond between the absolute first and last'; they connect the sensuality of Firstness to the specific rationalization of Secondness. 'Continuity represents Thirdness almost to perfection.' And 'law as an active force is second, but order and legislation are third' (1: 337). It is via Thirdness, that normative social power, that we move from sensual experience to knowledge of that sensuality.

Aquinas also refers to three aspects of cognition in his analysis of the nature of thought and intellect in *Summa Theologica* and *De veritate*. There is the experience of 'the form as it exists in corporeal matter.' This experience is via a 'knowing power [which] is the act of a corporeal organ, namely sensation' (*S.T.* 85 q. 1 a. 4c; in 1960: 9).[2] That is, we do indeed access 'knowledge from sensible objects through the senses' (*De ver.* 10 q. 6 a. 1; in 1995, II: 26). How do we move from such sensations to understanding? 'Our knowledge, taking its start from things, proceeds in this order. First, it begins in sense; second, it is completed in the intellect. As a consequence, sense is found to be in some way an intermediary between the intellect and things' (*De ver.* 1 q. 6 a. c; in ibid, I: 48). And further, 'the forms which are abstracted from sensed things become actually thought of – so that they can be taken into the passive intellect – in virtue of the light of the active intellect' (*De ver.* 10 q. 6 a. c; in 1988: 144) or in another translation, 'through the light of the agent intellect the forms abstracted from sensible things are made actually intelligible so that they may be received in the possible intellect' (*De ver.* 10, 6 c; in 1995: 28). The passive/possible intellect has the simple role of amenability, of openness 'to receive the forms which are abstracted from sensed things' (ibid; in 1988: 144). Sense or active/agent intellect is the key to conception; it 'causes a true or false judgment in the intellect' (*De ver.* 1, 11, c; in 1995, I: 48).[3] This action of mediation is no mere whim; it has the power of active composition and therefore it 'in itself is a thing; and it also passes judgment on other things' (ibid). Like Peircean Thirdness it is a social construct and therefore is not inherently true or false. 'It sometimes represents a thing to the intellect other than it actually is,' but the intellect will accept this social decision because 'in its relation to the intellect, sense always produces a true judgment in the intellect with respect to its own condition, but not always with respect to the condition of things' (ibid: 49). Within such a conceptual frame, there may therefore be a difference between what is true and what we believe is true. We do not have direct knowledge, for 'it is completely impossible for our mind to draw knowledge from things that are sensed' (*De ver.* 10 q. 6 a; in 1988: 141). We are human beings and not angels with that direct ability to reach 'more things with fewer intermediaries'(*De ver.* 10 q. 5 a; in 1988: 140); we therefore must live with our requirement for mediation; we must accept that 'sensed forms are only received in sensed matter through the influence of the active intellect' (*De ver.* 10 q. 6 a; in 1988: 142). In summary, 'things' are the immediate sensual experience, 'intellect' or 'passive intellect' is the individual conception, and 'sense' or 'active/agent intellect' is that group logic that moves between the two and unites them. As in Peirce, these three aspects of our knowledge operate discursively within two different realities. Things and the passive intellect are experienced by

Diagram 2: The Movement of Consciousness

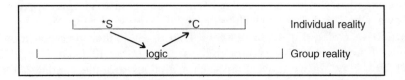

the individual in singular historial immediacy; sense or reason or active intellect provides the logical light of the group heritage. The movement of consciousness is from sensuality via group logic to conceptualization, or to use the terms of Aquinas: things to sense/active intellect to passive intellect.

Why have I put *intellectus agens* or Thirdness on a level of existence separate from that of the sensuality and rationality of the individual? Because, unlike individual reality, its nature is totally social; it has been created by and is owned by the group. As a social construct, it has a different temporality and exists only within past/future time.[4] The individual sensual experience is a completely Rabelaisian physicality without conceptualization, understanding, or even the desire for such. The rational understanding of this experience is part of individual reality in its immediacy and its confinement to individual experience, but it is also social and part of the long-term group reality, in that the individual must use the developed logic of the group to rationally understand that sensual experience. This unique interaction, which locates both sensuality and reason within the temporal and spatial immediacy of the individual, gives existence its intensity and its existential and intellectual violence, if one may use these terms for both experiences. However, to move beyond this first sensuality and into understanding of that experience in its rational nature requires mediation. This is group reality, the agent of Thirdness, Active Intellect, Augustinian memory, mediation, confinement, refinement, *compositio et divisio.* Group reality is a strictly social and non-sensual phenomenon. It can be considered as a habit of mind built from a logic developed within the experiences of the past, which establishes a logic for the experiences of the future. Essentially it does not, in itself, exist. Existence, whether sensual or conceptual, is only possible within individual reality, that reality of signs or distinct conceptualizations that are experienced and expressed only in current time.

Two Realities: The True Binarism

There are, therefore, at this point in our understanding, two realities within the social text: that of the group and that of the individual, two contrasting natures, each unable to live without the other. We can understand these two realities as existential within a dialogic interaction of a triad of contact points of three nodes; the sensual moves via the group logic to the conceptual. In Peircean terms, Firstness moves via Thirdness to Secondness.[5]

It is here in this dialogic interaction that the individual is both free and bound in chains – free because he alone of these two realities exists in current immediacy and therefore alone has the ability to interact with, experience, conceptualize, and even change physical reality. It is the individual who feels, thinks, acts, who is neither an object nor a thought but both. The sensual and conceptual realities of the individual can move, change, be born, and die. But all of these experiences are bound, because even to understand them as such, to recognize their distinct natures, to move from sensuality to rationality, requires the intervention of the group logic, with its boundaries and horizons of social norms of meaning. Such a dialogical frame necessarily sets up a confrontational structure. This is the real essence of our reality, this basic binarism that makes all other confrontations seem transient and irrelevant. The individual requires that Other even to experience his own life and yet, in order to retain some freedom of judgment, some capacity for analysis, he must constantly reject living as its vehicle. The group, seemingly bound to the individual as either assistant or dictator, is equally trapped because it cannot even express itself without the existence of and the cooperation, voluntary or not, of the individual.

The true binary frame in both its dialogical and its conflictual sense is therefore between two distinct realities. These two realities are real in that each has a spatial and temporal identity; further, they are existentially unique in that their spatiotemporal identities are different. They are two powers; they must be recognized as powers, in their differences, their oppositions, their readiness to invalidate each other, and equally their power of attraction for each other, the continuity of their intertwining bonds, their unconscious recognition that, like Zeus and Prometheus, neither could even think of an existence without the other.

I emphasize that these two realities are different from each other in the sense that each exists within its own distinctive nature. That neither can exist without the other is not to reduce the one to the other but is a comment only on their interactional nature and an understanding that these realities are alive and, like all living things, discursively interlocked within an interactional frame. It is more accurate to refer to their relation as organic, in the sense that each has a physical existentiality as well as a conceptual phenomenology and that these two forms of existence interact with each other as nodes within the existential actions of the social text. We could here use the metaphors of the physicist David Bohm, who, using the yet more historic imagery of Nicholas of Cusa, described the world as an ongoing action of logical orders actively enfolded within one another; of the *implicatio* (enfolded), which is a generative order, unfolding into the *explicatio* (unfolded); both these levels of reality are *complicatio* (folded together) in an even more basic superimplicate order (1980, 1987). As a generative whole, this basic order will 'unfold into ever more definite forms' (1987: 158) and 'explicate forms are generated in an order of unfoldment' (ibid: 184).[6]

Comparisons but not equivalences of the idea of two social realities can be made with such analyses as Vygotsky's speech and thought; Chomsky's performance and competence; the Freudian id, ego, and superego; Lacan's real, imaginary and symbolic (understood as Firstness, Secondness, and Thirdness), and many others. The point is, cognition is understood to operate on two existential levels. They differ from each other but both exist and neither is privileged.

Degenerate Binarism

To ignore the distinctive triadic nature and functions of these two realities leads to a defective or degenerate[7] conceptualization. There are two basic forms of degeneracy. One essentially ignores the existence of a group reality; the other collapses the two realities into one. Both forms are trying to retain the various functions of the two realities, but the infrastructure they establish for these functions is inadequate for the actions. In both forms one or more of the three nodes of cognition is either damaged or missing. True semiosis, as Peirce said, is an action that 'involves a cooperation of three subjects, such as a sign, its object, and its interpretant, this tri-relative influence not being in any way resolvable into actions between pairs' (5: 484).

To ignore the reality of the group removes one of the three dialogical nodes (Firstness, Thirdness, and Secondness) and inserts a binary rather than triadic interaction that exists only on the level of individual reality. Interaction between the sensual and conceptual experiences of the individual is necessary. However, without group reality, the actions of mediation between the sensual and the conceptual are lost; what remains is simply a movement between and not an intellectual interaction between these two nodes. The one can simply become a mimetic or inadequate copy of the other and as such is unavailable for rational examination; indeed, either the sensual or the conceptual form can completely disappear. Aquinas says exactly that: 'But if, by an impossible supposition, intellect did not exist and things did continue to exist, then the essentials of truth would in no way remain' (*De ver.* 1, 2, c; in 1960: 17). Another function of group reality that can be lost is its provision of a long-term stability that grounds the short-term existentiality of individuals and permits knowledge to exist over time.[8]

There are at least four types of degenerate binarism that attempt to provide mediation and stability without group reality. I term this reduction from the basic triadic structure degenerate because the mediation and stability their reduced frames provide actually harms the cognitive process.

External Form

One method transforms the long-term stability and dialogic mediating actions of the group to forms and locates them outside individual existentiality. Plato's dyadic structure removes group reality as a spatiotemporal action and transforms its functions of stability and mediation into ideal Forms that are existentially existent *per se* and do not rely on a social intellect for the establishment of their nature. These ideals that, as Aquinas pointed out, are already abstracted from the human intellect, become in the Platonic frame directly existential within the reality of the individual and never move through a mediating group logic. Such an interaction within the Thomistic analysis is only possible for God and the angels. An immediate result of this particular method is the creation of a framework amenable to fundamental and disassociated abstract truths. An authoritarian social and intellectual structure is an inevitable result. The individual essentially loses dialogical power and becomes only a passive receiver or dilettantic semanticist of objectified 'truth.' Truths as such pure forms obviously cannot fully exist within the inadequacies of human reason and are clearly asocial. Indeed, in this frame of cognition, individuals are existential only within the conceptual node of reality; their individual sensual experiences are not trustworthy. This ultimately leads to what I would term an emphasis on 'discourse' rather than dialogue, a state where the mind can only play obsessively with multiple descriptions of images, with the semantic nature of terms, and can only be saved from such chaos by establishing a monologic frame that reduces the individual to a passive receiver of images from whatever authorities, secular or not, are deemed their ultimate judge.

This form of degenerate binarism does not deny the requirement for a stability of past and future existence but it is made forever abstract, as in the Platonic architectonic ideals, or located within an equally inaccessible linear final cause, as in the Aristotelian frame. The abstract ideals that are the causality of the Greek world become universal and not creations of a specific social reality. This universality, this unavailability for dialogic argumentation, so against the themes of Socrates, is their totalitarian nature. With positivism, a material form of Platonism, existential reality is moved from being an external conceptual form and becomes embedded in an equally external physical world. Knowledge becomes understood as a reflection of this truth.

In this version, in contrast to the Platonic frame, the individual is conceptually existential in the sensual node; the conceptual is simply a mimetic copy of the sensual, and it is again only by reason of the inadequacies of the fallen human mind to mirror physical reality that the truth cannot be found in human knowledge. In the Cartesian-Baconian world of direct rational knowledge, there is no place for the mediatory actions of an imperfect intellect. The human intellect in this perspective loses that agential power of the triadic frame to define knowledge. In the thirteenth-century words of Jean de Meun, the human action, in this case in art, is fundamentally incompetent and 'Art, for all her representations and skillful touches ... may work as long as she lives and never catch up with Nature' for 'Art makes her models, but she does not make her forms as true'; the artist is only able to 'kneel before Nature and like a truant beggar, poor in knowledge and force, she begs and requests and asks of her. She struggles to follow her so that Nature may wish to teach her ... But her sense is so bare and feeble that she cannot make living things, no matter how newborn they seem' (1983: 271–2, ll. 16005–82). This degenerate binarism sets up reality, whether conceptual or physical, as authoritative Form, *sufficiens per se,* and then sits back and watches human beings as they struggle within the endless 'hope insubstantial' of eventual contact that equally destroyed Narcissus.

Dyadic Bond

Another example of degenerate binarism is the Saussurian binary frame of signifier/signified, which acknowledges both the sensual nature of the signifier and the conceptual understanding of the signified.[9] Both are within the existential reality of the individual. However, Saussure's *langue* is not a mediation of analytic reason between the signifier and signified and is therefore not the activity of a group norm but simply an abstract sense of linguistic totality. The Saussurian *langue* does not have the long-term formal reality of the Platonic architectonics nor the long-term energy of the Aristotelian causality. The result is that the relation between the two nodes becomes not an interaction but an empty rule, a prison sentence without cause. Further, such a frame, with its understanding that the sensual is bonded to the conceptual, can provide only a description of that image, not an understanding. As Peirce notes, 'the Sign can only represent the Object and tell about it. It cannot furnish acquaintance with or recognition of that Object' (2: 231). Aquinas, too, is opposed to this simple binarism, for 'it is completely impossible for our mind to draw knowledge from things that are sensed' (*De ver.* 10 q. 6 a; in 1988: 141). There is no dialogue, no movement between these two parts of the Saussurian sign, for they are bound to each other by convention; there is simply a mimetic 'toss' of an image between the sensual and conceptual sites. As Aquinas notes, 'a form which is already in a subject does not act on that subject' (ibid) and therefore reason cannot become active in this interaction. Lacking inherent durability, the bond between the two is unstable and any attempt to break it must be forbidden; the deconstructionists who have done so have created not an openness within which the dialogue of knowledge can exist but arbitrariness and the conceptual isolation of the schizoid mind. This form therefore lacks both the durability and the purity of the Platonic and positivist frames.

Semantic Discourse

Another form, resting on both the arbitrariness and resultant necessary bond of Saussurian semiology and the attempt to offset the stability of that bond seemingly provided by the monologic force of the external Platonic author, sees consciousness as based on a multiplicity of fleeting individual experiences. The discursive frame of many postmodern theorists of reception theory and deconstruction[10] sees social reality as an unbounded and unbonded totality of separate 'voices' within an amorphous spatiotemporal frame. Ongoing, perishable, microscopic, non-predictive, subject to constant interpretations, this social text lacks both stability and dialogue and is a denial of the existence not simply of group reality but of its functions. It is the 'world of fancy' of Peirce, where an individual need 'but to pronounce his fiat, and the thing exists' (1: 321). It can be likened to a form of Nietzsche's 'anarchy of atoms,' where, in terms of literary decadence, he writes that 'life no longer resides in the whole. The word becomes sovereign and obscures the meaning of the page ... the whole is no longer a whole' (in Kaufmann 1974: 73). Here, however, even the word loses any meaning. This degenerate form, like positivism, focuses only on the sensual node of individual reality, the signifier, the immediate quality of Firstness; the signified meaning is forever elusive. As Peirce said, 'the most degenerate form of Thirdness is where we conceive a mere Quality of Feeling, or Firstness, to represent itself to us as Representation' (5: 71). However, unlike positivism, this form denies long-term reality to any physical existentiality and thereby loses such stability. Cognition is impossible within this fragile isolation. As Eco too gently points out, 'the infinite drift of deconstruction' is not equivalent to the 'unlimited semiosis' of Eco (1994: 33).[11] Peirce, with his 'a sign is something by knowing which we know something more' (8: 332) and a sign is 'anything which determines something else (its interpretant) to refer to an object to which itself refers (its object) in the same way, the interpretant becoming in turn a sign, and so on ad infinitum' (2: 303), is not suggesting unlimited semiosis because the basic nature of a sign is its triadic inclusion of the contextual restraints of both Firstness and Thirdness. With Firstness, we have the requirement for the contextual intentionality, the external impulse from an object (not necessarily physical) such that 'a sign cannot even be false unless, with some degree of definitiveness, it specifies the real object of which it is false' (MS 7,000003–5) and 'all reasoning whatever has observation as its most essential part (2: 605). That is, there is a spatiotemporal context of a reality of origin that binds conceptual reality to definitiveness even if only for a conceptual instant. With Thirdness, we have that supreme limiting factor of conceptual continuity, for Thirdness 'is what it is by virtue of imparting a quality to reactions in the future' (1: 343). Removing this requirement of synchestic continuity results in degenerate Thirdness, where 'there is thought, but no conveyance or embodiment of thought at all' (1: 538). The *intentio operis* or intentionality of the text rather than that of the Platonic *intentio auctoris* or deconstructionist *intentio lectoris* is used by Eco (1992) in his rejection of open interpretation in literary works. I suggest that the group reality of a society has its own *intentio operis* that equally stabilizes human behaviour.

Binary Code

Another common form of this degenerate binarism, also only on the level of individual reality, functioning without the mediation of the group-reality logical interaction, focuses again on the conceptual node, the Saussurian signified. It classifies the variations of meaning on a polarized linear scale. For example, colour will become split into black/white; there may be various gradations between but the focus is on the polarities. Moving out of the physical world, human nature is split into gentle and violent; gender is polarized as male/female. Unlike Saussure, this binarism does not consider the sensual experience and the conceptual sign as the binary frame but uses only the signified and the values of a scale of measurement arbitrarily selected as opposite to each other. It then inserts the notion of struggle and difference to create a dialogue where none exists. In many cases, what happens is that this binary code will become arbitrarily asymmetrical and hierarchical, with one pole of the signified artificially seen as providing the long-term stability and mediation functions of a group reality. The oppositional binary codes of such as Barthes (1973, 1977) and Lévi-Strauss (1966, 1975) focus only on the signified, the conceptual half of the sign, and split the variations of meaning into two camps, two moieties. They are oppositional only in the mind of the observer and therefore so totally arbitrary that they lie within the power of the theorist to name and define. In this instance, they are removed not merely from the rational organization of group reality but also from the first node of consciousness, sensual contact; attention is focused only on the codes as defined by the individual theorist. Indeed, Rabelais has a whole chapter devoted to the 'innate' binary meaning of colours, and the simplicity of such analysis is well shown by his conclusion 'that blue definitely means heaven and heavenly things, according to the same exact processes by which we know that white means happiness and pleasure' (1990: 30). Irrational and yet definitive polarizations provide the framework for radicalism in all its forms. True binarism is much deeper and more basic than this arbitrary shuffling of codes.

There is another version of degenerate binarism that is not the establishment of an external and asocial law of normality, not the establishment of the sensual and conceptual experiences of the individual as binary, not the splitting of a code into polarities, but a form that collapses the distinct separateness of the individual and group realities into one existential level.

Collapse of the Two Realities

Unlike the first versions of degeneracy, where the properties of group reality did not fully exist within individual reality, this collapsed version sets up an existential frame wherein the distinct properties of both individual reality and group reality exist within the one level of individual reality, the level of specifics within current time. This transforms group reality from being a potentiality of past/future logic to an actuality of specific form. Group reality becomes a free-floating material existentiality that readily locates itself within the conceptual node of Secondness. The power of organization that is the basic nature of group reality will then become specific properties ranging from intellectual ability to codes of law. Such a frame destroys the harmonious balance of energy within individual reality between the two nodes of Firstness and Secondness, the sensual and the conceptual. These two nodes, which have become merged forms of the two realities, emerge as oppositional for the conceptual territory of the other, each vying for the same space, the same powers of control over the human being. A merger redefines the individual as potentially sensual *or* conceptual rather than a discourse of both. This is the neurotic form of the Freudian conflict between id and superego, with the superego taking the bodily form of some power figure. As material forms, the specific powers of this node become accessible to private ownership. Its qualities may become the property of different individuals or different classes or status groups, either by rights (or weaknesses) of biological or social heredity, or by force of physical or social power. In this degenerate form, the actions of the group become not a logic within which individuals can conceptually live as sensuous beings, as it was in the Thomistic contractual frame, but become a means to prevent this basic sensuality. The social contracts of such dyadic minds as Hobbes and Locke are a barrier to prevent the two realities from meeting and destroying each other, which they could easily do in this degenerate Manichaean form because of their unbalanced energies. When private ownership of these different functions by class, race, ethnic group, or profession is considered, then you have a society divided within itself and open to a hegemonic or totalitarian domination of oppositional powers.

A version of this form that also collapses realities and thereby increases the energy content of one of the two nodes of individual reality can be found in Le Bon's (1960) analysis of the nature of a crowd, with a crowd defined as lacking the logical habits of group reality. This analysis seemingly moves group reality into the sensuous rather than conceptual node, thereby increasing its power such that it overwhelms the conceptual node. Le Bon sees the human being in this format as an irreducible instinctive force of primitive emotion. More accurately, his analysis substitutes what I term 'biological reality' for the level of group reality; it is this force of basic biological needs that collapses into the sensuous node of individual reality to add its energies to that force and so establish his 'primitive horde.' A crowd is a short-term form of behaviour but the use of this degenerate frame to define non-European societies is outlined in chapter 6 under 'The Stages of Colonization.'

There are historic examples of the effects of the conceptual collapse of group reality into individual reality. The Reformation of the sixteenth century merged the two realities, thereby destroying the logic of the old order; it then set up a new group reality as specific codes and laws and gave their definition and control to a new elite, the middle class. With this action, the

Diagram 3: Collapsed Realities

Group reality / Individual reality	rather than	Individual reality
		Group reality

era denied the essentially fallible and short-term nature of individual existence and gave the individual powers that he in reality can never have, such
as the power of deciding his past and his future, setting up thereby a nation
of false yet immensely powerful kings. The twentieth century in its turn has
separated or 'deconstructed' the merger but has yet to develop a new group
logic of norms and has in this manner isolated the individual to an empty
existence of fleeting amorphous identities.

Both historic periods acknowledged a duality, yet both periods considered that this duality was merely between functions. They did not consider
that the true binary frame is not a simple Saussurian opposition of functions
but rather a relationship between two worlds that can never merge, can
never be friends, can never even be considered equal to each other; the
individual in his short-term profanity, the group in its long-term sacredness.
But such a merger happened, and it provided a tremendous surge of individual creativity and action by bringing the functional energy of the group,
the power of past and future time, within the control of the individual, who
then saw himself with powers to actually change and redefine the future. But
for how long? This coupled society existed for only five hundred years. It is
surely the shortest life span of any social group in history. It is this false
coupling that was so feared by Plato with his analysis of mimesis, where, if
the group and individual realities existed side by side, as equals in full view
of each other, then in time each could only copy the other and the future
would only be an empty copy of the past. 'Alas! experience of the world
teaches us the sad fact, strange but true, that union often dwindles into unity;
so it happens that "yesterday the Revolution was a religion; now it is becoming a policy" ' (Calasso 1994: 85).

It is what Marx saw when he recognized the worker as a powerless and
solely physical individual with all powers of conceptualization removed
from him, and the upper class transformed into the group reality and alone
invested with the power of mediation, the power to provoke thought and
decision-making. It was this collapse that thereby situated these two classes
into an open confrontation that was so different from the obligatory interrelationship of the medieval period. Such a social structure can be readily
seen, as it was by Marx, to be made up of oppositional individual and group
interests. Marx did not see this structure as it actually was, as two realities,
but as simply two power agencies. His goal was only to break up two
oppositional agents rather than that false marriage of realities. It was an essentially hopeless task, for it ignored the necessary existential differences
between the short-term reality of the individual (the worker), who exists

only in current time, and the long-term reality of the group (the owner), which has the power to continue life into the future.

Such a telescoping of the two locates group reality within the immediacy of individual reality and therefore opens it to unmediated, uncritical input from the senses, something that Aquinas pointed out was impossible, for 'there is no common matter between our mind and things which are sensed' (*De ver.* q. 6 a. 6; in 1988: 141). It is by such actions that a society will lose its temporal longevity and the stability of the logic of its conceptual heritage. I discuss time in more detail in chapter 4, but briefly, in the original binary frame of the two realities, time exists in two dialogical forms. The experiences of individual reality exist only in current time; group reality is a logic of the past and future. The dialogue between these two time frames permits conceptual reality. The collapse of the two realities reduces the nature of time to a one-leveled phenomenon understood as an external linear measurement rather than a discursive experience of two temporally different realities. This Newtonian time is measurable matter, and an older object has more time in it than a new object. The individual is given a false power of thinking that he can know his past not as a conceptualization, which he experiences only within his current reality, but as a true icon of that actual past. He is given the false power of thinking that he has the power to define the future, because time, like matter, seems to exist within his sensual nature, although if one thinks about it, no individual can experience reality in any other time than the present. But the collapsed frame redefines time in a linear sense of past, present, and future. Sensuality is devalued and equated with early time periods both within the individual experience[12] and within the group frame, where mature societies are considered more rational and more capable of control over sensualization.[13]

A further problem is that this compression of the two realities leads to a rejection of the conceptually finite universe (formed by the spatiotemporal bond between the individual and group realities) and the imposition of an infinite universe understood in error as either Origin or Future, both unattainable because they exist within linear time and are therefore beyond the current temporality of the individual. This means that there is no possiblity of accessing a force, which I term 'generative energy,' an energy existent beyond the frames of conceptual reality, because, in this degenerate world with its collapsed realities, there are no frames to reach beyond.

The Fourth Reality: Generative Energy and the Spatiotemporal Frame

There is another aspect of conceptualization that I call the fourth reality or generative energy (GE). It is simply potentiality, and I use the imagery of physics and scholasticism to explain its nature. It is discussed in more detail in later chapters, but I outline here some of its basic concepts. The third reality, biological, is referred to throughout this book within the physiological functionings of both individuals and the group. My numbering of these realities refers to the relative immediacy of their nature to our understanding and also the force of their power over us. Individual reality is that which is immediately and most briefly experienced by the individual; group reality is less instantly accessible and requires abstraction and thought to discover its more long-term nature. So, too, biological reality requires further examination to discover the nature of its organic powers over us; and the fourth reality, generative energy, is the least conceptually and materially accessible. In terms of their power over our individual experiences the linearity is reversed; individual contacts are effectually superficial, group reality is more powerful, the dictates of our biological reality still more powerful, and the power of generative energy is beyond measure.

Generative energy is an unlimited atemporal aspatial potentiality of existence, the chaos or free play of physics. We can understand it as basic energy that is potentially transformable into the sensual and conceptual forms of reality that exist in individual reality. In terms of the concepts of quantum physics of Heisenberg and Bohr, it is energy that is outside the boundaries of our actions of measurement. It becomes 'form' or sensual/conceptual reality only when it is enclosed; that is, when time and space are introduced, when it is 'measured.' The method of enclosing or 'entrapping' this basic energy is via a logical pattern. The logic establishes a horizon of dominance; it limits the amount of energy that, as a pattern, it can organize and keep stable. This horizon of its dominance is the spatiotemporal frame (STF). A specific amount and type of particles or units of both conceptual and material matter are able to exist within that frame and specific amounts and types of interaction between these particles are able to take place, according to the nature of the logical holding pattern. A biological reality accomplishes this holding of energy by its DNA pattern; in a similar manner a society has its syntax, a ground logic, its logical pattern of interaction developed within group reality and expressed within the actions of the individual. When energy is spatiotemporally enclosed by means of the dialogical interactions of the GR and IR levels, then the energy content becomes finite, stable, and functional, or capable of sustaining what we know as life. In terms of the principles of thermodynamics, a society as a finite amount of trapped energy within its STF must, using its basic logic, constantly reformulate its energy content into energy expressions, both material and conceptual. To put it another way, individual reality must, via the logic of group reality, reformulate itself all the time, or its existential nature as distinct units of material and conceptual existence, will entropically disappear into free energy. A second

Diagram 4: The Textual Society

GE: Generative energy   Individual reality

STF: Spatiotemporal frame   Group reality

aspect to consider is that, despite the retaining power of the syntactic logic, there is always a certain amount of energy loss from the STF, the spatiotemporal frame. This means that a spatiotemporal frame, be it of a physical or biological or social organism, must have regular access to the fourth reality, that basic or generative energy, otherwise its energy content will become so depleted that as a distinct system it will cease to exist. 'This world is fals, fikel, and frele, And fareth but as a fantasye.'

Because it lacks time and space in its nature, generative energy is not immediately accessible to the individual, who can sensually and conceptually interact only with spatiotemporal reality. Aquinas' *per se nota* argument about the existence of God supports this. If we understand God as generative energy, then His (its) existence is not self-evident, *per se nota*, because the human intellect acquires its knowledge via rational abstraction from the data of sensation. A wholly immaterial being or action such as God is therefore inaccessible when using the three-step format of consciousness of the two realities. 'It is connatural to know those things that exist only in individual matter ... the created intellect cannot see God in His essence' (*S.T.* 1, q. 12, a. 4; in Aquinas 1960: 26); in other words, the human intellect can only access knowledge from sensible things and is unable through itself to reach the vision of divine substance. Importantly, there is no specific intentionality to this force; 'it is not possible for God to enter into the composition of anything, either as a formal or material principle' (*S.T.* 1, 3 q. 8 a; in 1981: 20).

Quantum physics understands physical experience as arising within the spatiotemporal conceptual frame produced within a specific interaction, a concept commonly referred to as the Copenhagen (after Niels Bohr) analysis. This can be compared to the existential awareness produced by the dialogical interaction of the individual and group realities that establishes individual consciousness. Again, this existential awareness that appears in the dialogical interaction between the two realities is produced in a closed system.[14] The system is closed because it is functional only within a finite frame of space and time established in the interaction. However, reality is not confined to these phenomenological interactions, for many but not all followers of quantum physics also accept a reality that exists apart from that spatiotemporal conceptual reality; they accept it as real even if directly unknowable and not simply a phenomenon of the mind. This aspatial and atemporal reality is not, however, matter or things as we understand them in their concrete existence but the potentiality of existence, the possibility of existence, the reality of many universes that become defined into our singular reality by the limiting introduction of the spatiotemporal horizons of the interactions of the two realities. Within David Bohm's analysis of the generative order and the implicate order[15] we see that our conscious reality proceeds 'from an origin in free play which then unfolds into ever more crystallized forms.' Above all, generative energy as only potential and therefore indeterminate, is creative and completely 'open to the free play that is essential to creativity' (1987: 158).

In this sense, both Aquinas and quantum physics distinguish between the *esse ut verum* existence in the sense of the *true*, understood as potentiality but not actuality, and the *actual*, understood as the actual phenomenological existence. God or energy, to use the terminology of Aquinas and quantum physics for the same reality, is purely and simply the power of potential existence but not the actual existence itself, which is confined to the spatiotemporal interactions of the two realities.

Generative energy is an action and not a thing. Various comments from such diverse minds as Aquinas, Peirce, Lacan, and Bohm have explained this potentiality as a pure force of desire of existence without any sense of particular form, as eternal action with no internal *compositio* or *divisio*, such being the attributes of the group reality logic. It is 'something that initiates change without itself being in the process of change' (*S.C.G.* 1, chap. 13; in 1988: 141). It is the Peircean Evolutionary Love or *agape*, a force of an 'energetic projaculation' by which 'new elements of form are first created' (6: 300). Thus I define generative energy as the power of potentiality, the power of becoming a specific reality without the spatiotemporal confinement of any material or conceptual form. Although generative energy exists outside the spatiotemporal boundaries of a textual society, it is a necessary part of such a society in that access to its powers of regeneration are vital. Generative energy is the very basis of 'surplus,' and surplus is the impetus, the intentionality, of life. Literary access to generative energy is more accurately described by Vico's 'poiesis,' which was a direct contact with the mute and therefore conceptually open language of the gods that was expressed by humans in poetry as 'imaginative universals' (Vico 1948).

Degenerate Generative Energy

What generative energy is not is any deterministic guidance of form such as the Platonic patterns in the divine mind, a Thomistic impossibility since specifics cannot exist in the mind of God. Nor is it any guidance of action, such as those of Aristotle or Bacon, that explored causality in physical matter. Generative energy has no specific intentionality whatsoever in it and thus cannot act as foreordained form or cause of anything.

The necessity of this reality is a matter of opinion. My thesis accepts it and says that the other two realities cannot survive without it. Without this potentiality that is not initiated by anything outside it and is only the power to be, then all existence is a summation, a given. Existentiality becomes reduced to the simplicity of rearranging the Platonic content, or it falls into an entropic state where, in a finite system with a specific total of energy, the particular forms that energy takes will eventually break down and dissipate. The society in this state has abandoned its attempts to find meaning; it will only repeat its old definitions, for 'protocol is the last power for protecting abandoned symbols. It ensures that symbols, even when they are not perceived as such, can continue to act, often with an added touch of sarcasm' (Calasso 1994: 72).

Rejection of this prime mover or origin, understood in its generative sense, may lead to its acceptance in a linear sense and to the evolutionary linearity of Comte, Spencer, Morgan, Marx, and the many other believers in progressive evolution. Such an analysis is almost inevitable. These thinkers understood intentionality not as a source of pure energy but as an agency, a specific and goal-directed causality that can be controlled by some individual or group. The social movements of fifteenth-century Masonry and the sixteenth-century Reformation rejected the scholastic trinity of the three realities and retained only the spatiotemporal two, which they then easily telescoped into one by reason of what they considered the similar materiality of both. They thus lost all access to generative energy. Potentiality to be became located in a spatiotemporal 'spot,' either in the past, which meant that it was a set amount of cultural capital either currently held or potentially available for ravishing, or beckoning in the future, which meant that it was essentially unattainable because the future must always remain ahead of us.

Access to Generative Energy

As aspatial and atemporal action, generative energy is not existential in itself. How can the two realities, which are both spatiotemporal and therefore existential, access it? Group reality is a logic, a grammar that guides the experience of individual reality. As an action, not an actor, it cannot make contact with anything. Individual reality has two forms: sensuous experience, which is immediate, physical, and not conceptual; and the conceptual, rational understanding of this experience. The latter exists via the organizing logic of group reality. Full conceptualization has three parts, which I explain in more detail in chapters 2 and 3 but whose nature I briefly outline here. First, the sensuous experience of the actor; second, the introjection of the guiding logic of group reality, which guides the sensuality into the third, a conceptual experience of this action. These two realities, although different, are tightly bound to each other in conceptual experience. How can access to generative energy, which exists beyond the spatiotemporal frame of the individual/group realities, occur? The answer is that the actor of individual reality must forcefully bypass or break the tie between the two realities. This is where I bring in the terms of modernity in literature, carnival in everyday life, and revelation in the religious sense.

The experience of generative energy begins in the sensual and remains as such. This experience is a sensual action, which is never conceptual because it does not move from sensuality to conceptualization via the guidance of the group logic. In order for the Actor to access this generative energy, the conceptual path is changed. Instead of the regular path (Individual Sensual → Group Logic → Individual Conceptual) the path is: Individual Sensual 1 → Generative Energy → Individual Sensual 2. This Individual Sensual 2 is not the same experience as Individual Sensual 1. Generative energy moves into the nodal locality of the Peircean Firstness of sensuality and combines its powers with it, thereby increasing its force beyond the grasp of immediate reason. This we know from the stories of so many of the gods who moved into the bodies of humans, mingled their desires, and thus drove men mad. There is more energy, more emotion, more sensual phantasms, and thus a requirement for a different logic to even begin to conceptualize it. Such an experience, if it brings enough energy into the entire social text by moving into the bodies of many people, has the power to force the entire syntactic logic to change and so enable it to conceptualize and thereby retain that energy. This ability to provoke change is the functionality, the pragmatic reality of generative energy. It is equally possible that if the syntactic logic cannot grasp and retain it, all that new energy will be lost; even worse, its contact, brief as it is, may destroy the individual or society; thus did contact with the gods destroy Psyche, Daphne, and Semele.

It is always more understandable when discussing theories to locate them within a pragmatic experience. I locate these three realities within the experiences of literature, carnival, and revelation.

Literature and Generative Energy

I understand literature to be the linguistic expression, oral or written, of a group. It is created by individual reality, guided by a logic of group reality, and expressed by, read by, used by, individual reality. Literature therefore is both a sensual and a conceptual experience and is a dialogical interaction between the two realities. Given this dialogue, can we consider that there might not be a need for any contact with a generative reality? Literature could exist simply as an individual-group interaction that expresses the past/future group logic within the experience of the current reality. But this would be to ignore the pragmatic nature of literature, which is not simply to repeat what is, the rubric of a mirror, but to permit what is. That is, it should provide a conceptual frame, a group logic that has the power to conceptually express the individual sensual experience. The only way to develop a group logic that is active and has the power to keep up with the variations of individual reality is to provide a means for this group logic to change. The means of changing a group logic is by the input and subsequent organization of more energy, obtained via the individual's contact with generative energy. Therefore, literature must be considered a method of both expressing current reality and accessing generative energy. As such, it must be capable of expressing the normative and using those same norms to bypass its regular meanings. Literature must provide the means to reveal the arbitrariness of the conceptualization of experiences in the very act of using those symbols as codes of normalcy.

De Man speaks of this experience that accesses a different reality as 'moments of genuine humanity ... moments at which all anteriority vanishes, annihilated by the power of an absolute forgetting.' He refers to 'Nietzsche's ruthless forgetting, the blindness with which he throws himself into an action lightened of all previous experience.' Such action, whatever the name, 'exists in the form of a desire to wipe out whatever came earlier, in the hope of reaching at last a point that could be called a true present, a point of origin that marks a new departure' (1983: 147, 148). What we have here is the rejection of group reality by some action that permits forgetting it, that refuses its existence. Certain literature, defined by de Man as modernity but not confined to this, thereby hopes by severing itself from the past to also sever itself from the present conceptualization founded on that logic. Only then can new energy be admitted to individual reality and then also to group reality. It is here that the past/future logic can be forgotten and wiped out. Whatever exists is only in the 'true present,' the site of individual sensual experience.

A key problem with both deconstruction and modernity is that they have become trapped within that first step of bypassing the logical frame and thereby accessing generative energy. The vital second step of moving the accessed energy into group reality, so that the logical patterns can organize it to be used in new cognition, has been ignored. As I previously mentioned,

the reason is that both methods have been operating within a frame of degenerate realities; there is no group reality in such semantic discourse. The
result is not merely that generative energy is continuously accessed and also
continuously lost, but such pointless interactions further drain the society of
whatever cognitive energies it might still retain.

Carnival and Generative Energy

Bakhtin defines this same action in everyday life as carnival, a time of feast-
ing, festivity, laughter, the breaking of normative boundaries. It too is a time
of access to generative energy, for 'the feast is always essentially related to
time, either to the recurrence of an event in the natural (cosmic) cycle, or to
biological or historic timeliness. Moreover, through all the stages of historic
development feasts were linked to moments of crisis, of breaking points in
the cycle of nature or in the life of society and man.' These were not official
feasts to celebrate the norm, as described by Freud in *Totem and Taboo*, which
'did not lead the people out of the existing world order and created no second life.' Carnival is special in that it 'celebrated temporary liberation from
the prevailing truth and from the established order; it marked the suspension of all hierarchical rank, privileges, norms and prohibitions. Carnival
was the true feast of time, the feast of becoming, change, and renewal. It was
hostile to all that was immortalized and completed.' It is the true sensual
existentiality of the individual, for 'all were considered equal during carnival.' And 'people were, so to speak, reborn for new, purely human relations.
These truly human relations were not only a fruit of imagination or abstract
thought; they were experienced' (1984b: 9, 10).

Literature, used as carnival, is a vital social action. Simply because of the
basic laws of thermodynamics, group reality with its norms, its habits, its
static human relations and stable human thoughts will gradually become
entropic, will become anti-life, inhibiting, and even dangerous to the con-
tinuation of life beyond a few generations. The individuals within this
sociostructure of individual/group reality absorb all the conceptual energy
within that frame and the society starts to wither from within. Carnival,
which is opposed to the 'ready-made and completed,' is an experience of
the individual that 'demanded ever changing, playful and undefined forms.
All the symbols of the carnival idiom are filled with this pathos of change
and renewal, with the sense of the gay relativity of prevailing truths and
authorities.' The carnival experience is a recognition of both the confining
and withering authority of the definitions of the group and the necessity for
their strictures. Carnival permits a fresh perspective, the absorption of the

new, the different, and therefore 'the entire world is seen in its droll aspect, in its gay relativity' (1984b: 11). Carnival is a recognition of relativity, and this alone is the right of the individual. To realize that the laws one has created are arbitrary, are actual creations and recreations of beings who, equally, are born and who die, is a power that cannot be neglected, because without this realization it leads to an arrogance of self-absorbed righteousness. Therefore the Dobe !Kung will insult a successful hunter to prevent his arrogance, for 'this way we cool his heart and make him gentle' (Lee 1984: 156); and the Masai moran warrior, when leaving this phase of his life, will mock and demean his mother because in his new adult role he must abandon both his early dependence on her and his freedom as a warrior, to assume the new role of care-giver and provider. Carnival is an action that acknowledges that group reality is created and can be recreated. Carnival 'actually offers a description of the world's metamorphoses, its remodeling, its transfer from the old to the new, from the past to the future. It is the world passing through the phase of death on the way to birth' (Bakhtin 1984a: 412). Prometheus, the 'fore-thinker' who plans ahead, can be bound to his rock, his very abilities to live nightly destroyed, but he still has the power to develop new organs of law and so continue with his life.

As a footnote, it should be stressed that this Bakhtinian carnival is not the ritual 'otherness' of what I term illusionary mirror carnivals, where carnival is simply a reversal of roles, a momentary experience of the not-self, with this Other not being generative energy and its powers, but simply the Otherness of another person or class. Freud's analysis of carnival experiences as 'nothing less nor more than excesses provided by law and which owe their cheerful character to the release which they bring' (1955: 131) is the opposite of the Bakhtinian carnival, for these experiences are considered only in terms of the individual psychology. A Freudian carnival exists only to provide an emotional release from the inhibitory pressures created by social dictums; these rules are understood as similar to the compulsion prohibitions of neurotics in that both are 'unmotivated and enigmatic,' both are repressive, both deny the basic 'pleasure to do the forbidden,' and both must be relaxed from time to time in carnival festivals to prevent both individual and group neurosis. Such an analysis reveals a complete misunderstanding not only of the ecological relationship between human beings and their environment that led to the development of taboos and social laws, but also of the cognitive relationship between the individual and the group. As Bakhtin notes, 'the carnival spirit with its freedom, its utopian character oriented toward the future, was gradually transformed into a mere holiday mood, the feast ceased almost entirely to be the people's second life, their temporary renascence and renewal' (1984b: 33). The illusionary carnival, operational in the era of collapsed realities, no longer provides an access to energy but becomes a means to waste energy, to free the individual from the stresses of living without contact with the unconscious logic of group reality and in contact with only the irrational rules of an inhibitory Other. Carnival became a release, a safety valve for individuals, a means to create vitality where none existed. The mirror carnival as a ritual, proscribed and pre-scribed, simply permits the individual and group realities to exchange cur-rent images but provides no access to pure energy, permits no new energy to enter into the society. True carnival has nothing to do with this binary frame of dominant/repressed, this simplistic reversal of the structure of society.

Revelation and Generative Energy

To consider another means of accessing generative energy, we may turn to Aquinas, who speaks of revelation as an experience that introduces a knowl-edge beyond the capacity of the individual conceptual experience. These things 'are not to be sought after by man using his reason, they are neverthe-less to be accepted on faith when they are revealed by God' (*S.T.* 1 q. 1 a; in 1960: 298). This knowledge or sacred doctrine is 'knowledge proper to God and the blessed' (ibid 2 a; 300). If I translate the term God to understand it as a form of potentiality or energy, then when I read Aquinas' comments that sacred doctrine provides information 'about God principally and about creatures as they are related to God as to a source or an end' (ibid 3 a; 301), and also that 'sacred science is chiefly concerned with God, Whose works men are' (ibid: 4 a; 302), I understand by this that the revelatory actions are concerned with energy, with the potentiality of life, which creates all living things, including human beings. The knowledge proper to this science comes through revelation, an action that belongs to the individual in his sensual existentiality, and that bypasses the group logic and therefore, nec-essarily, the reasoning of the individual.

Revelation as a force of potentiality is not to be understood, which means that it does not originate in or even use Secondness, the realm of reason, for 'truth is found especially in the first, rather than in the second, sense; for its reference to the divine intellect comes before its reference to a human intel-lect' (*De ver.* 1 q. 2 a, c; in 1994: 11). It is simply to be accepted, in its basic sensual, material existentiality, which means that it is first experienced within the individual realm of Firstness, of sensuality. The experience gained via revelation is not social; it does not pass through the judgmental logic of the group, for 'these things are so revealed to man as, for all that, not to be understood, but only to be believed as heard, for the human intellect in this state in which it is connected with things sensible, cannot be elevated entirely to gaze upon things which exceed every proportion of sense.' (*S.C.G.* 4, 1, 2, 26; in 1960: 319). Only later, possibly in the next generation or even the one after that, will the individual with this new knowledge at first existent only in its sensual nature 'have been freed from the connection with the sensibles, then it will be elevated to gaze upon the things which are revealed' (ibid). In this third generation, the individual will have created a new group logic and only then will the new knowledge be understood in its conceptual nature.

Again, Aquinas reminds us that revelation is not 'something made clear to be seen, but to be believed.' This knowledge, or rather energy that has the potentiality to be knowledge, moves directly into the immediate experience of the individual; it becomes part of his sensual reality. In order for it to be experienced in itself, even as a sensual experience, it must be made conceptual. Since this movement to conceptualization is never direct but via the conceptual logical horizons of group reality, then for one to rationally experience this, group reality must be changed to accommodate it. This means that revelation, as a movement that ignores and denies group reality and yet thereby leads to its change, is a necessary social action.

Conclusion

What we have here, with the reality of generative energy, is a social text wherein creativity is a fundamental concept. In the words again of David Bohm, 'the extent to which society is no longer creative in its basic generative order, it becomes destructive to itself and to everything that it touches' (1987: 209).

I have earlier suggested that the degenerate forms are static; they do not operate in a dialogical format. Can access to generative energy occur when the two realities are combined into one? My answer is negative. When the two are combined into a monadic frame, you cannot deny or destroy group reality without also destroying the individual. They both exist in the same spatiotemporal conceptualization and cannot be separated by any action. De Man says that 'modernity invests its trust in the power of the present moment as an origin, but discovers that, in severing itself from the past, it has at the same time severed itself from the present' (1984: 149). It has destroyed the individual, who is unable to experience his own existence because he cannot move from sensation to conception.

In the collapsed realities, the individual and the group are set up in a confrontational frame. This simply tosses a set amount of energy back and forth between individual and group, lower and upper class, or whatever terms one uses for the individual/group confrontation. Within the collapsed realities the individual can do nothing with energy except waste it. The group exists not as a logic but as a summation of individuals and therefore cannot absorb this energy and reformulate its logical frame, its DNA format so to speak, so that the new experiences can be not simply sensual but also conceptual. The very format of this collapsed reality has prevented any access to generative reality. As Aquinas notes, 'if, by an impossible supposition, intellect did not exist and things did continue to exist, then the essentials of truth would in no way remain' (*De ver.* 1 q. 2 a. c; in 1994: 11). I would compare his term 'intellect' with generative energy and therefore a society without access to such can only decay of and in itself.

Could the Oedipal myth be interpreted within this framework in a way different from Freud's? Living within an era of collapsed realities, Freud in his analysis privileged the individual, interpreting interactions solely within the sensual and conceptual existence of the individual. Interpreted within the frame of these four realities, could the myth be understood as the creative surge of a new unfocused generation trying to kill the logical frame of the old generation, the socially created group reality (the Father), and uniting with the third reality, the biological force of life (the Mother) to come up with a new '*explicatio,*' a new order of experience? If we understand that group reality must change to accommodate new energy gained by contact with the generative forces of life, then we must consider whether the degenerate forms of reality are able to change. If we come to the conclusion that they are unable to, as I am suggesting, then we must develop methods that will 'de-construct' this merger in all its forms within our sensual and conceptual experiences, so that we may formulate a new social logic, a new group reality.

Within the literary world, deconstruction is playing the role of separating the individual and group realities from each other. In itself, deconstruction is not a logic, a theory; it is rather a means of constructive destruction to separate the collapsed group and individual realities. That is all it can do. It cannot create these two realities as separate and distinct; it can only destroy their former connuptial joining. We are currently experiencing this new, or rather this renewal of, the conceptual frame of the two realities. We are destroying the merged format and experiencing the new existentiality of the two realities. We have not yet settled on the exact nature of the metaphors that will permit us to conceptually understand our two realities. That will be our next task.

The true binary reality that has haunted human beings for millennia is between the individual and the group, each with a distinct nature and each unable to exist without the other. What we can do is recognize the fallacy of their collapse, recognize their real nature as different identities, and therefore permit their separation. This will allow both dialogue in the social text and access to the potentialities of change. Individual reality and group reality exist as separate realities; the continued differentiation between the two, the constant dialogue between the two, and those brief explosive contacts with generative energy are actions that are absolutely necessary within the textual society.

2

The Action of Textuality

Introduction

The action of textuality is a specific part of the total action of making meaning. It originates within individual reality and is a cognitive frame of action that exists only in current time. This frame sets up an interactional frame enabling the two IR nodes, the IRS and the IRC, to dialogically interact with the GR ground logic.[1]

As has been discussed, knowledge is not directly reflective of physical reality but is socially defined, developed, and agreed upon as a limited definition of reality and so used by all its members as authors, readers, and actors within the social text. Actual meanings occur within the individual cognition and are created in dialogical interactions based within this text. A social group embodies both individual and collective behaviour, each aspect enfolded in the other.

Basic Reality

I accept that there is what can be termed a 'physical reality,' what Peirce defined as 'Real Things, whose characters are entirely independent of our opinions about them' (5: 384), what Bakhtin described as 'the actual world as source of representation ... we must never confuse ... the represented world with the world outside the text' (1981: 253). There is a 'real world' but the nature of this real world can only be known within a textual scheme. There is only one conceptual world and it is social. Meaning can be analysed as *actions of textuality.*

Key Points

Let me provide an outline of the main points of my argument regarding the nature of meaning in a society.

When I refer to the *textual reality* of a society, I see it as a *potential conceptual energy*, a finite amount of energy already bound within an STF, which is a spatiotemporal frame that is tied to a basic *ground* or *syntactic logic*. Particular meaning or *actual conceptual energy* (IRC) becomes such when individual reality interacts with group reality logic in a dialogical interaction. This means that the potential conceptual energy is organized into an actual existential unit of meaning, a sign. In order to have such a dialogical interaction with GR logic, the individual level of organization operates within a frame called the action of textuality. This AOT exists only in current time and within the spatial experience of the individual. This frame is, like the larger (in terms of energy content and organization) STF, a spatiotemporal horizon. It provides boundaries to energy content and therefore establishes a frame to hold and organize that energy. Meaning can only exist when it is bound and organized. The STF frame of the society binds and organizes a certain amount of 'loosely organized' energy. The STF frame of the individual within that society further binds and organizes energy. The AOT frame, which is really an action-of-framing or bonding energy of the individual, further refines this energy and organizes it into specific existential signs or units of meaning.

The AOT frame is made up of the IRS, GR, and the IRC *nodes* or articulation points, which are sites of energy organization of an individual (not the society).[2] However, the individual exists within the STF of a society, the GR syntactic logic is a factor of that society; therefore, the individual's AOT is an expression also of that society. The AOT frame becomes existent only when an initiator/activator energy 'activates' the STF frame of an individual. When this happens, a smaller STF frame is set up – the AOT frame, operative only within current time. Cognition, the action of the IRC, the action of the sign, takes place within this smaller frame of experience, within this AOT frame, which helps to refine and organize potential energy to a specific unit of meaning, a sign. As Davies points out, 'we can never, even in principle, observe *things* , only the interaction between things. Nothing can be seen in isolation, for the very act of observation must involve coupling of some sort' (1990b: 57). This is Bohr's 'complementarity principle,' where nothing exists in isolation, where both momentum and position form complementary and yet mutually exclusive aspects of reality. It is Heisenberg's uncertainty principle, which supports Bohr's interactional perspective, where the introduction of the action of observation between observer and observed introduces a finite and specific spatiotemporal frame between the two poles of the interaction, which produces a finite and specific (and only for that interaction) 'observed.' This interaction, which establishes (1) the spatiotemporal frame of current individual existence, (2) the dialogical interaction between the IR and GR levels, and (3) the sign as action, I call: 'the action of textuality,' the AOT.

The Potential of Meaning: Logic and Energy

Let me begin this analysis with the syntactic logic that is based in the group, whether this be a group of humans, insects, or atoms. The potential to mean, *potential conceptual energy* (PCE), can be understood as basic energy bound within the logical pattern of a specific group. It is, because it is within a specific social STF already finite, limited, and partly organized. I may speak of a human being or a winged horse. Because I have spoken/written them, these are now existent as singular meanings but they were existent as the potential to mean before I moved them into existent meanings. I do not mean that they existed as discrete units; rather, the group logical pattern that could accommodate such images as meanings already existed. They existed as cognitive potential within this STF.[3] There are two points to consider: logic and energy.

Logic

We can consider the logic of a text to be its patterns of organization, which guide and define the interactions of current experience. This logic should not be understood as a stock of meaning, such that meaning would simply be understood in the Platonic sense of existence prior to expression, whether in an empirical or ideal form, and the expression as simply mimetic. Meaning does not exist on its own (that is, external to the individual in interaction) either in actual or potential form . The descriptions of Peircean Thirdness can be applied to this logic, for Thirdness is an essential ingredient of reality, yet does not by itself constitute reality, since this category, which appears as 'the establishment of habits' (1: 392) can have no concrete form in reality. The real nature of this logical ground is that 'it is that which is what it is by virtue of imparting a quality to reactions in the future' (1: 343), and 'the being of law that will govern facts in the future' (1: 23). It is a long-term logic of conceptual order that is basic to a whole society. It is not the actual themes and values of the group, but rather the *logical order* of conceptual existence. In a similar reference to a logical format, Heidegger refers to the nature of Dasein or Being as existing in a structure of 'fore-having, fore-sight and fore-conception' (1962: 191). This suggests that this logic with its organizational power acts as the potential to define, rather than the finality of a full-fledged concept. The logic, as a pattern of past and future organization, can take potential energy and organize it. It does this within the dialogical action that takes place within the spatiotemporal frame of the AOT, the action of textuality frame.

Energy

Meaning moves from a state of potentiality to a finite sign via dialogical interactions within the spatiotemporal frame of the AOT. This is a frame of action in current time that unites the three nodes of the two realities (IRS, GR, IRC). Potential meaning as IRS energy exists in a form similar to Peircean Firstness, where something is not yet 'an event, a happening, a coming to pass, since a coming to pass cannot be such unless there was a time when it had not come to pass' (1: 307). The point is, as Aristotle said, 'no one can ever learn or understand anything without sensing anything' whether that sensual contact be material or image (*De Anima*, G, 432a: 7). The tie with a sensual impulse is vital; however, the potential in this sensual Firstness is unavailable to us as meaning until it has been dialogically united with a syntactic logic. In this interaction potential energy is transformed into a particular meaning, whether that be a cell or a sign. The AOT interactional frame is activated into existence by a sensual stimulation of intentionality that adds energy to the individual STF and so sets up an 'instance of disequilibrium of self-organization.'[4] The slightest brush of energy moving into the STF frame of an individual can activate the formation of an AOT. The action of textuality restores equilibrium by transforming this disorganized energy into a unit of meaning. The energy of intentionality can be a spoken word, an unspoken image, a sense of heat, a sound – any sensation, any unit of energy that enters and *is accepted* within the STF, via the IRS node, of an individual. Thus, energy that is potentially meaningless or even harmful is not held or retained in the STF. This means that an AOT may not develop to transform it into an existential unit. (Energy may sometimes be held, but an AOT may only transform it at a later time as in memory, and in dormant or latent viruses.) Uncaptured energy is not part of our reality. Intentional energy can also arise from within the STF of an individual; an individual may start the cognitive process himself by, for instance, a flash image that will start the energizing action of thought.

Group reality is organized within a logical pattern, the syntax, grounded within the development of the group as a society and expressed within a variety of socially developed genres (Bakhtin) or code systems, such as language, interactional behaviour, economic behaviour, and so on. But the logic is not itself any one of these social systems. Castoriadis refers to 'the first natural stratum' and says that 'the institution of society leans on the organization of the first natural stratum,' but it 'does not reproduce or reflect this organization' (1987: 234). David Bohm's concept of enfolded *implicatio* orders, which 'appear in what is called the explicate or unfolded order' (1980: xv), express this theme of basic substratum orders of organization binding and patterning energy into conscious existentialities. The systemic codes of a society, such as its language and behavioural codes, are existential within the IRC node; they are organized via the patterning of the syntactic logic; they themselves are not the actual logic. In summary then, the GR logic is a long-term socially developed pattern of organization bound within a specific pattern of continuity. In order for energy, understood as the 'potential to mean,' to move to actual meaning, several things must happen.

1. Immediately after the introduction of intentional energy or energy accepted by the spatiotemporal frame of individual reality, a spatiotemporal *frame of textuality* appears. This frame links the two realities and thereby permits a dialogical interaction between them. Specific or actual meaning (IRC) can come into existence in this interaction.

2. Within this interactional frame between the two realities, space and time can be brought into discursive existence *in current time only*. Space exists by the awareness of differentiation or Secondness between one unit and another unit, the individual and the other (the source of Intentionality). Space then, exists within an action of interaction; it is created within the action of textuality that sets up the awareness of a sign, a unit of meaning discrete from other units. Time exists or, more accurately, is expressed, in the AOT interaction that sets up a conceptual relation between the two phases of time: past/future and current.

3. Within this spatiotemporal reality of the AOT, the two realities can logically interact. This interaction, which I stress is an action, permits the finite expression in space and time of the sign (IRC). Meaning exists only as an action; the IRC sign is not a mimetic reproduction of an object or a thought but a mediating single action that expresses a meaning in a current spatiotemporal existence. This action moves the potential energy to

mean into a current existential meaning. This interaction of the two realities is what I refer to as dialogical.

Time and Society

Two concepts should be clarified at this point: time and the nature of the group/individual.

Time

Time can be understood in two forms, which I term *current discourse* and *potential discourse.* Current discourse/time is an action, expressed within a unit of existentiality, a sign, located in the immediate current 'now.' It provides a sense of immediate and conscious existence. Potential discourse/ time is the logico-conceptual pattern of past and future experience. (I do not distinguish between past and future time). It is the intentionality of the past and future, but not the experience, because the experience can take place only in current time. Time therefore is not uniplanar and linear (past, current, future); it is bipartite and functional on two levels. Current conceptions exist within a 'deeper' long-term logical ground of past/future potentiality as illustrated below. Potential discourse does not store images in any clear form; it provides a logical pattern that, in the bonding action of the AOT, is used to define images within current discourse.

The Group and the Individual

As Voloshinov writes, 'No utterance in general can be attributed to the speaker exclusively; it is the product of the interaction of the interlocutors, and, broadly speaking, the product of the whole complex social situation in which it has occurred' (1976: 118; quoted in Todorov 1984: 30), for 'there is no human being outside society ... to enter into history, it is not enough to be born physically ... a second birth, social this time, is necessary as it were' (ibid: 37; 31).

The point I wish to make is that the syntactic logic for meaning is not in the possession of the individual, for 'thought is not necessarily connected with a brain. It appears in the work of bees, of crystals and throughout the purely physical world' (Peirce 4: 551). Whether it be a chemical, biological, or social logic, it exists in the form of a spatiotemporally bound particular pattern of organization and it is held within the entire genre, species or society, the entire group. The criterion of a society as existentially 'real' is its development and possession of a syntactic logic, this long-term 'habitual logic.'

The Action of Textuality Frame

When we refer to meaning, we must introduce the concept of confinement, a spatiotemporal entrapment of energy that limits the potentiality of meanings.

The action of confinement requires a relation with something else, the acknowledgment of an end to one unit by the awareness of a 'not-this-unit.' Peirce's Secondness is described as a 'mode of being of one thing which consists in how a second object is' (1: 24). By this awareness of there being something else (the Second) in the environment besides us, we develop a sense of 'struggle.' And 'by struggle I must explain that I mean mutual action between two things regardless of any sort of third or medium, and in particular regardless of any law of action' (1: 322). Meaning develops from that unfocused and amorphous potential energy existent within Firstness by our development of an awareness that this sensation has a specific definitive or measurable existence. The awareness of such a spatiotemporal existence can only be done in a state of closure, a confinement of energy and its organization. Therefore, the first step in meaning, of moving from potential to actual, is the creation of the cognitive frame of the AOT, which is made up of a spatiotemporally limited 'action of interaction' between the IRS, GR, and IRC nodes. Intentionality, or 'new' energy, activates the creation of this AOT, by making the agent aware of 'otherness,' of an energy that is not existentially bound within the agent's current STF. This sets up an instance of instability within the entity; the new energy must either be absorbed or rejected.

The Agent of Intentionality

Todorov notes that 'concretely, one always addresses someone, and that someone does not assume a purely passive role ... the interlocutor participates in the formation of the meaning of the utterance' (1984: 30). A key point to remember: the interlocutor or agent of intentionality 'participates in the formation of the meaning of the utterance.' Intentionality introduces energy as an activator into the STF of a closed system, and is therefore a requirement in the establishment of the AOT spatiotemporal frame. Voloshinov/Bakhtin argue that 'the utterance is constructed between two socially organized persons (whether that person be there or not) ... discourse is oriented toward the person addressed, oriented toward what that person is' (Voloshinov 1973: 101; quoted in Todorov 1984: 43). Importantly, 'it is not necessary then to be actually addressing someone else: even the most personal act, becoming conscious of oneself, always already implies an interlocutor, the other's glance upon us' (Todorov 1984: 30). The action of intentionality therefore only exists in a discursive relation with an other,[5] but the organization and therefore sign-potentiality of intentionality and the organization and therefore ultimate nature of the resultant sign are not necessarily the same. The final IRC sign is not the property of the agent of intentionality, with cognition understood only as a copy. The rejection of total author-authority follows this concept. Indeed, as Peirce points out, such an iconic relation is really degenerate, for the dual relation between the sign and its object is degenerate if it 'consists in a mere resemblance between them' (3: 362). Rather, intentionality should be understood to arise in an action of disequilibrium within one STF. Such a disorder of energy is dealt with by a *focused* action of intentionality within the individual that reorganizes this energy and thereby stabilizes the individual. A baby's cry may arise when the baby's current normative state destabilizes; the cry is an action of focused intentionality to restore order by releasing the tension developed within the system by the destabilization. When I see someone on the street and then recognize him, this can be understood within the actions of intentionality. My perception of this person changes my current normative state of energy organization; my organization of this new state of energy is focused into my action of recognition. Bakhtin points out that 'the word in living conversation is directly, blatantly, oriented toward a future answer-word: it provokes an answer, anticipates it and structures itself in the answer's direction ... the word is at the same time determined by that which has not yet been said but which is needed and in fact anticipated by the answering word' (1981: 280). We may understand the 'word' here as the IRS, the sensual stimulus from the agent of intentionality and the 'answer-word' is the IRC, the conceptualization of the intention. This is a dialogic action, 'the word is shaped in dialogic interaction with an alien word that is already in the object' (279).

The relationship between the cognitant self and the agent of intentionality has been defined in a number of ways that, despite their contradictions, have certain important similarities. The self/other exists as a Hegelian concept of the relation of self to self, where 'the self-relation is a negative self-relation'; for, 'if we express identity in the form A is A' then the A which is subject is different from the A 'which is predicate. Hence identity necessarily involves difference' (Stace 1955: 184, 185). However, Hegel does not put this difference into an action involving both self and intentionality of the other but only in the eye of the observer. I insist on the interaction. I also include here Gadamer's 'prejudice,' for 'all understanding involves prejudice' (1975: 239), and we can understand prejudice as the Other, as that which we are not, which helps therefore to define what we are. Peirce uses the concept of Secondness, the notion of Struggle. Here the Other is a realization of a 'not-me.' I refer to Heidegger's *angst* or dread as an Other and acknowledge its importance in establishing a horizon, a periphery of what we are not. It is only in this frame that meaning as *Dasein* can exist. The term *Dasein* suggests the necessity of an other separated in space, for *'da'* means 'there,' which also establishes a 'here.' Brentano's usage of intentionality establishes a link with an Other, a channel, as it were, between the agent and the other. Bakhtin's Other is the potentiality of response, for 'understanding and response are dialectically merged and mutually condition each other; one is impossible without the other' (1981: 282), and 'the limits of an utterance are marked not by the sentence structure but by the ability of other speakers to respond to it' (1986: 218). The action of intentionality, therefore has its origin in otherness, a frame of energy that is not currently existent within the spatiotemporal reality of the agent. It is other to the agent. The agent of intentionality introduces some of this energy into the spatiotemporal frame of the individual and destabilizes its current order. Importantly, the introduction of this new energy is not necessarily 'intentional' or in the conscious control of the agent; and it is not received as a 'sign,' a unit of Secondness. It is received as Firstness, and therefore must be accepted as 'fresh and new ... it must be initiative, original, spontaneous and free; otherwise it is second to a determining cause' (1: 357).

The Spatiotemporal Frame

With the establishment of the AOT, space and time can exist. Both exist only in a current interaction that is expressed as a meaning. Even a memory of the past or hope of the future is only existent in our consciousness in current existentiality. Space exists within the action of Secondness, by the awareness of differentiation between one unit and another unit, the agent and the not-agent, and time exists as a specific and current pattern of energy. We do not live 'in time' as if it were an external measurement; we live 'as a particular time.'[6] Space and time as contextual references are an essential part of the meaningful interaction. As Kant noted, they are not external aspects of the observation (as in the Newtonian-Cartesian frame) but lie within our own perceptual frame. Space and time are not reified entities but play an indispensable part in the intellectual ordering of experience, not as causal factors, for they cannot be treated as a ground in themselves, but as part of the essential structure of meaning.

Interaction: The Sign as Action

Within this spatiotemporal frame, an action of cognition can take place. This action, which I stress is an action , is ultimately expressed in the finite form of the sign. The minimal unit of meaning of a human, or any group – and I include biological, chemical, and physical groups – is not a word, a sentence, a phrase, it is not grounded in language or any one systemic form of behaviour, but is an *action*, developed within a spatiotemporal interactional frame (even if there is no response), that exists within a group-based logic of reality. Meaning does not result from the transference of an image from site to site but from the creation of one unit of meaning within a spatiotemporal interaction. As Peirce notes, 'we perceive objects brought before us; but that which we essentially experience ... is an event' (1: 335). And this event, this sign-as-action, is 'a quality, relation, state of things' (unpublished text, cited in Deledalle 1990: 51). It is not a 'thing.' Heidegger's *Dasein* or 'being' is not an entity but a meaningful action, existent within a dialogic frame; *Dasein* needs a space and a time in order to appear, 'a space established for the appearing in entities' (1959: 145).

The sign focuses the interaction of the action of intentionality into a single cognitive experience. The mediation of the AOT uses the group-based ground logic in its actions and therefore unites current and potential discourse.

The Action of Textuality

I stress that this action of textuality, this interaction, is not simply a linear format, a movement from site A to site B, but an interactional movement. It is what Gadamer would refer to as an 'episode,' an 'event of being' (1977: 50), based within a sociocultural frame. Meaning does not exist in what Heidegger refers to as *vorhanden* or neutral objects that exist 'present-at-hand' in a linear sense, but within what he defines as a three-dimensional state of 'disposition' (*Befindlichkeit*). This is an action that involves all three cognitive nodes and both realities.

A society or group is an expression of a textual structure of meaning that exists only within that group and therefore also provides its horizon of understanding, its manuscript boundaries. As a socially developed system the text is governed by the law of habit, which provides a long-term logic that explains the past and defines the future. Groups of people, in order to live as a society – which can simply mean to exist in a coherent form-of-meaning for several generations – require a stability of meaning for their interactions among themselves and with their environment. The text as a logic of knowledge provides a structure, a concept of past and future identity, within which current sensation can be measured and interpreted.

I now briefly explore this action of textuality within a number of modern research frames: the cognitive scheme of Jacques Derrida, the speech act theory of John Searle, the translinguistics of Mikhail Bakhtin, and the unit of meaning in quantum physics. These four methods of defining reality in modern society share a basic approach to the nature of meaning. First, they set up an interactional area measured by an agent and an other, or self and intentionality. Then, a conceptual area within space and time, which I refer to as the textual area, is established by the boundaries of this interactional area; that is, by the participants, real or imaginary, human or particle. Meaning as an action, expressed within the sign, arises within the discursive (not dialogical) interaction of these participants.[7] I call this approach textual, for it acknowledges (1) that meaning is not inherent in the agential force or perceiver; (2) that meaning as a potential (but not specific) force exists within the cognitive logic of a specific group or text; (3) that particular meaning is created from this potential, using that logic, within a spatiotemporal interaction; (4) via a system of coded signs.

Jacques Derrida

Derrida argues that writing is not to be understood in the customary (Aristotelian) sense as the visual form of language but includes 'all that gives rise to an inscription in general, whether it is literal or not and even if what it distributes in space is alien to the order of the voice: cinematography, choreography ... but also pictorial, musical, sculptural "writing."' Writing is a means of creating meaning; it 'comprehends language'; it is a means of order and 'the contemporary biologist speaks of writing and pro-gram in relation to the most elementary processes of information within the living cell' (1976: 7, 9). I should at first glance compare his Writing with a group reality, a generative order of logic that also seemingly functions within a textual interaction to create meaning.

A common understanding of meaning is that it follows the pattern of Reality → Meaning (Plato, Descartes). This analysis accepts that there is such a
thing as a permanent and directly knowable reality that can be accessed,
even if imperfectly, within the individual mind. It considers that a medium
that does not affect this replication is superior to one that does; speech is
(arbitrarily, it must be said) considered to answer this need. Speech is seen to
be a more natural and less social creation (belonging to the vagaries of the
individual rather than the conformity of the group), and therefore better
able to mirror reality than Writing. A brief look at oral interactions shows,
however, that they are as much a social creation bound within the group
perceptual horizons as is Writing (Whorf, Bernstein, Lord). Another pattern
is Reality → Social Horizons → Meaning, as expressed in various semiotic
mediums such as language and other symbolic systems.[8] Here we understand that material reality exists, but we cannot have direct knowledgeable
access to it. Instead, we define an understanding of our interactions with
reality using a group-based conceptual frame within which symbolic entities, signs, exist whether in visual *or* oral form. This is the Kantian frame,
clearly in opposition to the previous frame.

Using this latter frame, Derrida focuses on the sign and its nature as a
social belief rather than a natural truth. As a social belief, it is a Saussurian
dyad, made up of a signifier and signified (IRS and IRC). Derrida's introduction of the action of *différance* (with an a̲) is the key act of deconstruction,
breaking the quite arbitrary and also quite firm bond between the signifier
and signified. He uses the term *différance* to indicate an action that includes
both difference and deferment; that is, the imposition of a spatial separation
and a temporal gap of differentiation. He considers '*différance* as temporaliz-
ing and *différance* as spacing' (1973: 137). It is 'neither a word nor a concept'
(130) but, in my terms, a spatiotemporal interaction that deconstructs the
degenerate bonding of the individual and group realities. By separating
these two realities, it can supposedly create 'the structured and differing origin of all differences' (141); in other words, it can possibly permit the interaction of dialogue, which can only take place within differentiation. As noted
earlier within the context of Secondness, for meaning to exist, differentiation or 'an interval must separate it from what it is not' (143). This interval,
this gap that permits differentation, is created within the action of *différance*,
which is 'time's becoming-spatial or space's becoming-temporal' (ibid).

Différance is an action that 'makes the presentation of being-present possible' (134), because its separation of the two realities (individual and group)
permits an interaction that is based on 'difference' as a sense of the other (the
spatial reality) and 'deferment' or a sense of time (the temporal reality). That

is, as an action, it does two quite similar things. First, it destroys the dyadic bond between the signifier and signified, a degenerate form of the sign, as previously discussed. For Derrida then, following Lacan, the resultant freed signifier becomes floating, elusive, and indeterminate of a conclusive signified meaning. But the Derridean deconstruction of the Saussurian sign is not simply within the one level of individual reality but is also a deconstruction of the more degenerate form of collapsed realities. Therefore, this same action destroys the collapse of group reality into individual reality. It thereby re-establishes the sense of space by separating the two realities; it re-establishes the fact that time in its current experience (individual reality) and time in its 'not-now' experience (deferred in group reality) are not the same and must be separated. *Différance* thereby separates and decentres both the individual and the object;[9] they are no longer separate units each attempting to be privileged centres of meaning. The action destroys the power of the external referent (the signifier), whether it be an object or individual, and equally destroys the power of the internal referred (the signified) as specific meaning. This destructive interaction itself cannot be exposed, for its logic is not separate from the action. In itself, since it is neither a spatiotemporal 'word nor a concept,'[10] it can supposedly never be represented as a methodological tool. This seems to be a form of generative energy, but I think we will find that its isolation as destroyer and not creator prevents its inclusion within that force. Essentially, *différance*, by its acknowledgment of the variable forms of space and time, sets up a spatiotemporal frame (where none before existed) within which Writing as potential meaning can exist.

In Derrida's analysis, Writing has a greater ability to provoke meaning than the fleeting nature of speech not because, as Derrida suggests, it can absent itself from its speaker/author (as Searle notes, you can write a note to your companion and the electronic tape can speak without its speaker) but the written symbolic unit (novel, film, sculpture) exists outside the spatiotemporal level of individual reality. It is 'more exterior to speech, not being its "image" or its "symbol" and more interior to speech, which is already in itself a writing.' In this sense, Writing is outside the synchronic, iconic, subjective individualism of the Saussurian frame. Writing 'constitutes the absence of the signatory, to say nothing of the absence of the referent. Writing is the name of these two absences' (Derrida 1976: 41, 46). It exists as a basic other, a diachronic form with a more long-term potentiality to incite intentionality. The written form as other can repeatedly provoke an action of textuality. The actual written form is not meaning but only a potential to mean that provides a repetitive impetus to establish an interaction and so 'make meaning.' It is the procedures, the actions of making meaning, which are 'iterable,' not the writing or the meaning. Is Writing similar to the logic of group reality? Is Writing similar to the potentialities of generative energy?

Meaning is not found in the space between the signifier and signified (as Saussure found it in the sign), both existent on the level of the individual, but within the deconstructed realities. Writing appears within this frame of *différance* and establishes a frame of origin or contact with a force that is beyond the individual author. However, as I discuss in more detail in chapter 3, this Writing is not a syntactic logic of group reality but has more similarities to a Platonic ideal form or, based on this theme of pure other, a Jungian archetype, a 'collective unconscious' of 'universal images' of primordial ancestry, such that 'the unconscious contains not only personal, but also impersonal collective components in the form of inherited categories or archetypes' (1966: VII, 138). Rather than a semiotic system that uses the creativity of the dialogic individual to develop signs to define his experiences of the natural world, these basic a priori forces act as the formative agents in the definition of the human experience of reality. 'All the mythologized processes of nature ... are in no sense allegories of these objective occurrences; rather they are symbolic expressions of the inner unconscious drama of the psyche which becomes accessible to man's consciousness by way of projection – that is, mirrored in the events of nature.' And 'the psyche contains all the images that have ever given rise to myths' (Jung 1966: IX, 1, 6, 7). Writing is the unconscious that defines individual comprehension; it is not similar to group reality because it is universal rather than group based; it is not a pattern of interaction but a collection of specific formative forces. Nor can we say that the deconstructive actions of *différance*, as carried out by the individual, in combination with the universality of Writing, together act as generative energy enfolding within group reality, because Writing maintains both a power of intentionality and an aloofness from dialogic transformation of that intentionality. Such intentionality is the opposite of generative energy, which is only the power-to-be. The key factor of generative energy is that, as potentiality and not actuality, it can only exist within transformative actions. What Derrida has set up, after forthrightly separating both the signifier/signified and the collapsed realities, is a frame that lacks a group reality and instead links itself directly with generative energy as archetypal form. He has set up the first type of degenerate binarism, that of the external form.

John Searle

John Searle's concept of the speech act can also be understood as a spatio-temporal action of textuality, but it functions within a frame different from that of Derrida. Searle uses two particular terms that seem at first to imply concepts quite different from Derrida's action of writing, namely 'intentionality' and 'speech.' He notes that 'the unit of linguistic communication is not, as has generally been supposed, the symbol, word or sentence, or even the token of the symbol, word or sentence, but rather the production or issuance of the symbol or word or sentence in the performance of the speech act.' Moreover, Searle's speech act can be both verbal and written, such as 'a noise or a mark on a piece of paper' (1969: 16). I note the stress on meaning not as a unit but an action. The speech act is not to be understood as the simple articulation or rather re-articulation of a prior given, a word, a sentence, which exists intact in the mind of either the author, reader, or object. The speech act is not a movement of a definite meaning from site A to site B, but is the creation of meaning within an action, it is 'the basic or minimal unit(s) of linguistic communication' (ibid); it is an action of textuality.

Searle writes that 'no speech act is performed in isolation ... [but is] organized within a certain variable discourse pattern,' and 'an adequate illocutionary logic is essential to an adequate universal grammar' (1985: 293, 8). Therefore, the 'phenomenological episode' of the speech act functions within a deeper logic, related to the group . By this I understand that speech acts exist within a group logic, because 'speaking is a rule-governed form of behavior' (1969: 17). Intentionality has an intent, a focus on the other-as-horizon, on the boundary of the self where the other begins, whether this other be another person or an object. Intentionality is not located as a concept in the sender or receiver but is really the establishment of a spatiotemporal frame, an 'other than the self,' which therefore provides a horizon for meaning but is not meaning itself. The key factor is the establishment of a frame of spatiotemporal interaction by the intentionality of the speech act; this is very similar to the function of *différance*.

Intentionality should not be confused with subjectivism, with psychological intentionality, but should be understood as the establishment of an interactional frame by the 'injection' of the energy of the potentiality of meaning. This interactional frame includes three actional nodes: the agent, the other, and the intermediary activator, the sign/representamen, expressed in any media system, speech, or writing. The media system has no value in this analysis. The speech act is not the movement of a message, but the creation of a meaning, and this can only be done within a contextual, spatiotemporal action. The intentional speech act is made up of an illocutionary force and a proposition. I understand *force* (as expressed in the mood, the intonation) to be the temporal facet of the action of textuality, which reaches out in time to an other; and the *proposition* as providing the spatial component with its symbolic forms. Both are activated by intentionality, which is the potential to mean. Essentially then, Searle's speech act is setting up an action of textuality; it keeps the two realities separate and understands meaning as an action produced within a movement of energy (understood as intentionality) that uses a shared conceptual logic or proposition. Intentionality can be understood as the action of the agent of textuality within the action of textuality.

With Derrida, meaning is also created within a current spatiotemporal frame that is established by the action of *différance*. Derrida's *différance*, like Searle's speech act, establishes a spatiotemporal frame. However, it does this only by the destruction of previous bonds, an action that is necessary because Derrida's analysis lacks a separate group reality. Derrida's 'habits' exist within the bonded sign of the individual reality level rather than the normative patterns of group reality. At first glance, with this acceptance of the need for a spatiotemporal frame and intentionality, Derrida and Searle may have more in common than either would care to admit. The difference, and it is an important difference, is that Derrida's spatiotemporal frame is the result of a necessary destructive act and both his logic and his agent or intentionality are focused in a Writing which exists beyond the group reality, within what I have defined as a false generative energy. Searle locates his speech acts within a logic that exists within a community, within a social text, and gives intentionality to a member of that community.

Mikhail Bakhtin

Bakhtin uses the term *chronotope* (literally, time-space) and defines it as 'the intrinsic connectedness of temporal and spatial relationships that are artistically expressed in literature.' He argues that 'the image of man is always intrinsically chronotopic' (1981: 84, 85); that is, it is meaningful only within a specific spatial and temporal frame of reference. I compare the chronotope, not with the action of textuality but with the syntactic logic of a group. It is a socially based conceptual logic particular to a society. As a social text made up of a logic and potential to mean, it must find a spatiotemporal site wherein actual meaning can exist. Bakhtin finds a number of distinct chronotopes clearly expressed in the novel. The interactional frame is itself situated within the 'text, written or oral ... the text is the immediate reality ... of thought and experience within which this thought and these disciplines can exclusively constitute themselves. Where there is no text, there is neither object of inquiry nor thought' (1979: 281; quoted in Todorov 1984: 17).

The dialogical interactions that generate specific meaning are found in the novels, as operative in those chronotopes. 'The fundamental condition, that which makes a novel a novel ... is the speaking person and his dis-course.' What does this do? It establishes a frame where interaction can take place. Meaning is generated in such an interaction, and meaning is 'always a particular way of viewing the world' (1981: 332, 333). To Bakhtin, a novel, set in a particular chronotope or social reality (which provides that basic social logic), awaits the completing act of the reader, who establishes an action of textuality, a spatiotemporal frame of interaction. Bakhtin also sug-gests intentionality as a requirement for establishing this interactional frame when he states: 'the word in living conversation is directly, blatantly, ori-ented toward a future answer-word: it provokes an answer, anticipates it and structures itself in the answer's direction. Forming itself in an atmosphere of the already spoken, the word is at the same time determined by that which has not yet been said but which is needed and in fact anticipated by the answering word. Such is the situation in any living dialogue' (280). This frame includes both the agent and the other, existent or not: 'discourse is oriented toward the person addressed.' And 'even the baby's crying is "ori-ented" toward the mother' (Voloshinov 1973: 101, 104; quoted in Todorov: 43, 44). Meaning exists only within a discursive frame, for then 'the speaker populates it with his own intention' (Bakhtin 1981: 293). This utterance, like the speech act of Searle and the *différance* of Derrida, 'is a considerably more complex and dynamic organism than it appears when construed simply as a thing that articulates the intention of the person uttering it, which is to see the utterance as a direct, single-voiced vehicle for expression' (355). Again, the medium is not the prime factor here. Meaning is created within an ac-tion, an utterance, that exists in a spatiotemporal frame of interaction in a contextual or group-based logic. 'In its naive and realistic interpretation, the word "understanding" always induces into error. It is not at all a question of an exact and passive reflection, of a redoubling of the other's experience within me ... but a matter of translating the experience into an altogether different axiological perspective, into new categories of evaluation and for-mation' (1979: 91; quoted in Todorov: 22). As Gadamer notes, 'understand-ing is not a reproductive procedure, but rather always a productive one' (1975: 280). This spatiotemporal frame is created within the intention of the utterer: 'All true understanding is active and already represents the embryo of an answer ... *All understanding is dialogical*' (Voloshinov 1973: 122; quoted in Todorov: 22). By this he means that understanding exists in this interactional frame, not in a unilinear path, and that intentionality is a form of energy, an intent, a potential to mean, that finds existence in the interac-tion. For Bakhtin, the dialogical frame can be termed the 'utterance' and it is a frame that includes 'the *space* and *time* of the enunciation ("where" and "when"); the object or *theme* of the utterance (that "of which" it is spoken); and the *relation* of the interlocutors to what is happening' (Voloshinov; quoted in Todorov: 42). Simply, we have here the spatiotemporal context, the meaning, the self, and the other, all operative within an action of intentionality.

Niels Bohr

Let me now move on to my last example of an action of textuality, the Bohr quantum frame.

The EPR perspective (Einstein, Podolsky, Rosen 1935) argued that 'the atom of matter must necessarily have a complete description, independent of any measurement that may or may not interfere with it' and 'all of the atoms of a material system have a complete description, independent of measurements' (Sachs 1988: 156). This analysis suggests that there is a frame of measurement (which is also an action of description) that is independent of the units themselves. In the terminology of this paper, there is a basic physical reality (the atom), and its meaning is a direct measurable copy of this. There is no interactional frame, no action of textuality. What is measured in research *is* reality, not as an area for an agreed-upon interaction but as material content. But the so-called Copenhagen interpretation (Bohr 1935) that is modern quantum physics analysis says that 'all the canonical variables of an atom of matter (momentum/position, energy/time, and so forth) are not precisely prescribed, simultaneously, to arbitrary accuracy, because a measurement carried out by a macroapparatus to determine one of the canonical variables automatically interferes with the knowable values of the associated conjugate variable of that atom' (Sachs 1988: 155). In other words, the action of measurement becomes part of the identity of the unit of meaning (atom). This interpretation can be expressed in terms of textual reality by the statement that the action of measurement is the action of textuality, or that the introduction of a spatiotemporal frame that creates a finite frame for an interactional development of a unit of meaning, the atom, is particular to that cognitive logical text, namely physics. This frame of meaning includes the observer and the observed (atom), and the meaning is the action of existence when that which is observed is existent as a particle. The meaning of the atom is not existent within the atom, nor within the observer, nor within the text of physics, but, using textual logic, an interaction permits a unit of meaning, a particle, to exist. The meaning of a unit comes into existential reality in the action of observation, and 'the act of observation influences the meaning of the observed.' And 'the idea of an underlying, objective reality, independent of an observation, is rejected as a meaningless concept' (Sachs: 129). The action of observation or textuality sets up a frame that incorporates both the observer and the observed. Energy exists in a potential or intentional state in potential discourse, to be a wave or a particle, and the interaction that can be called a measurement or an action of textuality provides a specific spatial and temporal frame and moves the entity into a particle state. Bohr felt that this measurement interaction must be the main area of future interest. Therefore 'if we're to talk about reality, it's always within the context of a specified experimental arrangement; you've got to say precisely what you're going to measure, and how you're going to do it, before you can say what is going on' (Davies and Brown 1986: 72). The unit of meaning is created by the interaction of an agent with the other, as intentionality.

Summary

To summarize the concepts offered in this chapter, I suggest that a group, any group, be it a human society, animal, biological, chemical, any logical conglomerate of interactive units, can be understood as a text. In the case of the human society, it is a cohesive structure of socially created knowledge, operative within a long-term group-based logic of interaction. This social logic is particular to each society and exists harnessed to the energy of potential discourse. Together, they provide the potential or intentionality to mean and the logical form that meaning can take. Meanings, however, exist in current time and within a particular spatial area, and are created within a contextually based interaction, which is therefore spatiotemporal. The action of making meaning is called an action of textuality. This action is created within the introduction of energy or intentionality. This disturbance of energy sets up a spatiotemporal frame, the action of textuality, between the two realities (individual and group) and permits a dialogical interaction between them. This moves the sensual energy or IRS into a specific meaning called the sign or IRC, that appears as an act of meaning, operative within the group logic.

Briefly, this textual reality and the AOT are *not* similar to the symbolic interactional frame, conversation analysis, or ethnomethodological interactions, for these analyses are all operative on only one level. Their analysis is focused on what happens on the immediate level, which I term the individual reality level. They do not use a deeper analytic level that consists only of a logical pattern nor are they involved with the concept of bound potential energy. I insist on the bileveled nature of cognition. Further, their interactions are between two agents and not between an agent and an other, which other exists only in the actual interaction.

There are other analyses, particularly those with reader-response themes, which may seem to belong to the AOT frame but do not. Iser refers to the 'implied reader' who is written into the text by the author and may wander through the text helping to define the meaning. This is not what I would refer to as an actual action of textuality, for Iser is not referring here to the establishment of a current interactional frame, but to the inclusion of another agent besides the author within the text. Like the sociological frames above, this is simply the usage of another agent to 'play ball.' Throwing a sign back and forth is not a dialogical interaction. Fish writes that there is a prior perspective to the text, and the reader 'fills in the gaps' as it were, and thus gives it actual meaning. Here, I would also consider that this action of 'filling in the gaps' is not the creation of a current interactional frame, but the inclusion of another agent (albeit not yet existent) within the text. There is no interactional frame permitted. One simply steps in where one is told.

What has been accomplished by relating these concepts of difference/deferment in writing, intentionality of the speech act, dialogical interaction in the novel, and quantum interaction? Apart from the substitution of different analytic worlds, what does such a comparison do? The point I am trying to make is that meaning in both what we understand as the physical world and the social world has a similar generative base. All meaning arises within a dialogic interaction using a group-based logic of meaning that exists within a spatiotemporal frame. The interaction within this framework is an action of meaning, which appears as the sign or unit of meaning. Meaning exists within the establishment of a spatiotemporal frame by means of an interaction of different forms of energy, where energy particular to that textual logic (physics, society, novel) can become focused into a particular action of meaning.

3

Otherness in the Production of Meaning

'The very essence of living things ... is order.'
Davies 1990a: 65

The basic framework I am developing here for the analysis of societies is the interaction of the two realities. The level of individual reality consists of the IRS, the sensual experience, and the IRC, the conceptual experience.[1] Group reality (GR) is the logic or the conceptual organization of the group within which the individual exists. There are therefore three 'contact points' or nodes: the IRS, the GR, and the IRC. These nodes are sites for actions – the transformation of energy from a simple to a highly organized state, from the meaningless to the meaningful.

Meaning is energy that has been transformed from an unorganized to an organized state by a series of transformations that take place at nodes. These transformations organize and reorganize energy; they involve both a loss of original energy and an input of new energy. The changes in energy content and its organization continue until we, as neurological and conceptual beings, can understand this energy as a conceptual entity, a sign, a meaning. Each nodal site is functional within a different type of organization and therefore a different type of organization of energy occurs at that node. The IRS site organizes energy, using its bioneurological codes; these will accept and hold only the energy that can be organized within this code. A fly will 'see' differently than a cat does because their biological natures accept and encode energy in a different way. The next site, the GR logic, organizes that energy in a more explicate and ordered pattern, using what I have termed a syntactic logic. (The specific patterns by which the syntactic node organizes energy is discussed further in chapter 5.) Finally, the IRC site organizes energy within a semantic code; this too is discussed in chapter 5. Essentially, each node site accepts energy and organizes it using a different method; this is a dynamic action that takes 'raw' energy and transforms it by these multiple types of organization until we experience it as meaning. Each nodal point permits an increasingly complex organization of energy.

Energy as Meaning

Energy is the basic matter of life, with 'life' understood as an existentiality or action of meaning. Energy exists in two forms, potential and actual.

Potential energy exists outside a spatiotemporal frame; it is unorganized and chaotic and has no meaning in our sense of the word. In the terms of quantum physics, its 'subatomic uncertainty ... is inherent' (Davies 1990b: 120). In order to be meaningful, energy must be organized and bound within a spatiotemporal frame. As we now know, space and time are not physical matter but *relations* or a means by which matter organizes itself. As I have suggested in previous chapters, for both Charles S. Peirce and quantum physics, 'constraint plays a crucial role' in the development of meaning. Until this free energy is spatiotemporally bound it remains unavailable for work, which is to say, it is unavailable for physical/conceptual existentiality. These boundaries are Bakhtin's 'conceptual horizons,' which are found within the individual, the group, the society.

Actual energy is meaningful because it exists within a spatiotemporal frame. A spatiotemporal frame is an action of restriction; the extensional realities of space and time limit both the amount of energy held within such a frame as well as its movement. It is only within such a frame that organization, as a logic that binds a finite amount of energy within its patterns, can exist. If we understand meaning as such a bound system of 'organized energy,' then we see that meaning can never be completely open but can only exist within a specific organizational structure. How does meaning, by which I mean not simply comprehension, but a unit of existentiality that is itself an action of comprehension, come into being?

Let us consider the three nodes, the IRS, GR, and IRC, as sites for the transformation of energy from the potential to the actual form, from uncertainty to meaning. Potential energy has an inherent *intention* to become spatiotemporal. This does not mean that it carries any specific meaning; it only carries the potential to become spatiotemporal, to be constrained by organization. It is moved into this spatiotemporal frame, which I have previously explored as the action of textuality (AOT), by the introduction of the intentionality of an observer; 'the translation from a quantum phenomenon to knowledge or meaning depends on the existence of conscious observers'

(Davies and Brown 1986: 63). Intentionality should be understood as a specific and therefore already bound and limited pattern of organization or logic. Simply put, the action of the observer or agent introduces a spatiotemporal frame to free energy and thereby sets up a *first horizon* to limit indeterminacy and permit the evolution of meaning. I will term this action that introduces the spatiotemporal horizons of intentionality, the action of intentionality (AOI). It permits the action of the action of textuality (AOT).

Intentionality is 'captured' within the user's first node, the IRS node. This first bound energy becomes located within the STF frame of an individual[2] at the IRS node. Not all intentionalities are accepted within the IRS/STF node. Many are ignored, are considered 'noise.' The existent energy of the IRS node is already 'refined' and organized within the biological frame of that individual; it has less potentiality for variation of meaning than basic open energy. Its refinement, its less open capacity for variation, comes from its existential nature within the spatiotemporally finite neurological and physiological capacities of that particular individual. Energy that is actually accepted within this node becomes bound to the organizational pattern of that particular IRS and is thereby already transformed from its former state.

The second site is the group conceptual reality, the GR logic. At this site, the potential energy continues to lose more of its original open or loose energy, and also, to add more refined or organized energy, coming from the long-term conceptual infrastructure of the GR syntactic logic as experienced within the socialized habits of the individual. That original potential to mean as activated by the action of intentionality (AOI) is thereby further transformed at this second node via the individual experiences of socialization.

At the third site, the IRC, more potential energy is lost and actual energy, specific to that particular individual's current spatiotemporal reality, is added. At this site, the stock of energy is given a final reorganization within the semantic frame of the individual's current reality. All of these actions are part of the AOT,[3] where cognition as a particular sign relevant to that individual's sensual and social existentiality finally comes into existence.

The original content and organization of energy as free and unfocused and the final content and organization as meaning are therefore not the same. Each of these three sites uses a different method of organization, biological, syntactic, and semantic, and changes and reorganizes the nature of energy, such that one basic energy source or action of intentionality will necessarily have different meanings according to the nodal codes within the STF frame that accepts that potential energy within an AOT action. This is Bakhtin's heteroglossia, the potential for the multiplicity of meanings. It is

Kant's heteronomy of ends, and quantum physics' overlapping of worlds. That these three nodal sites function within different patterns of organization is vital; if any site becomes too similar to the other then the individual and social textual meanings will become degenerate. The importance of variation is discussed in chapter 7.

Otherness and Dialogue: Energy as Other

Energy is transformed and reorganized at each node. However, it must be emphasized that this energy is not totally new at each site; it is in large part shared with a previous node. This sets up a situation where part of the energy of the second site is shared with that of the first site and yet, because it is being organized in a different way, it is different from that first site. It is *other to its previous form*. It is similar because much of it is shared; it is different because at the new site, some energy is lost, some is added, and a new organizational pattern deals with the totality of this new energy content. Similarily, the energy of the third site is other to that of the second site. Otherness then can be defined as the *interaction of shared energy* situated at sites that are spatiotemporally and therefore organizationally different from each other. 'No particle is elementary or primitive, but each contains something of the identity of all the others' (Davies 1990a: 48).

The other does not exist in itself, in the classical Cartesian and Saussurian sense of a binary differentiation or in the Hegelian and Marxist sense of organized opposition. Otherness, as a different organization of a shared energy, originates from and also currently exists in interaction with, another state of energy. In terms of Peirce's concepts, cognition exists within an immediate experience of continuity, expressed within a 'succession of points of the series each at a distance' and 'every continuum contains its limits' (Peirce 6: 121, 123) such that the interactional frame is finite. Within this interaction, the nodes are related to each other such that a 'beginning is the middle of the former, and whose middle is the end of the former' or 'the present is half past and half to come' (6: 111, 126).

Even though I have outlined these actions in a linear format, these transformations are not linear and sequential but immediate and dialogical. What we have here is a defined amount of energy, shared between the three nodes of the two realities. At each node site, a dialogue occurs with another node site. This dialogue involves a recognition of shared energy, a recognition of new or not-shared energy, and a reorganization of the combination of the two, the shared and not-shared energy. Such a dialogue transforms this shared energy into an other of its 'former' self. This 'openness' of each nodal site to interaction is a key aspect of Bakhtinian dialogue. 'The word is born in a dialogue as a living rejoinder within it; the word is shaped in dialogic interaction with an alien word that is already in the object' (Bakhtin 1981: 279). What I am defining in this study is an understanding that dialogue is not simply a factor of openness to other energies but that the 'other' is a different organization of energy; dialogue is an interaction of 'different energies.' Cognition can therefore be understood as the transformation of energy via 'states of otherness,' as the creation of meaning wherein 'the variant is the origin' (Calasso 1993: 147).

These nodes are not other in the sense of independent or alternate realities; they 'overlap each other'; both energies are mixed together. The concepts of quantum theory explain it well, for a 'wave describes not one world but an infinity of worlds, each containing a different path. These worlds are not all independent – the interference phenomenon shows that they overlap each other and "get in each other's way"' (Davies 1990b: 103). This analytic frame of three nodes therefore rejects the binary rivalry of the image and word, of the IRS and the IRC, of the signifier and signified. It rejects any form of oppositional otherness, where the other is 'a reflection which the subject is unable to recognize as its own' (Tiffany 1989: 211). Rather, otherness in the textual society is understood as that which is shared and reorganized. Using Merleau-Ponty's terms, it is a 'remainder,' something that is not totally part of the other nor totally part of the agent.

Cognition as Evolution

We can consider the development of meaning in the pure sense of evolution as the increased complexity of organization. This evolutionary action is not mutational chance nor mechanical necessity.[4] Rather, meaning as an evolutionary action can be considered as 'the agapastic development of thought [which] is the adoption of certain mental tendencies, not altogether heedlessly, as in tychasm, nor quite blindly by the mere force of circumstances or of logic, as in anancasm, but by an immediate attraction for the idea itself ... by the power of sympathy, that is, by virtue of the continuity of mind' (Peirce 6: 307). As such, the action of textuality increases the original intentionality, narrowing and defining purpose, leading to the final confinement of the sign as a unit of meaning, for the 'agapastic development of thought should, if it exists, be distinguished by its purposive character, this purpose being the development of an idea' (ibid: 315).

Consider the interactional frame of two people, known as the sender and receiver. Energy, organized by the action of intention within the sender, may enter the STF of the receiver. Bodies and minds are not accessible to all forms of energy. Any human being or other living entity has a specific energy organization or 'energy content typology.' Energy with an 'alien' organization cannot enter that individual's STF; we already understand this in terms of the biological immune system, and surely the conceptual system has its own immunities. The sender, by his expression of his IRC as intention, has framed energy into an organized form of *potential* energy. As such, it breaks free of the STF of the sender and may enter the STF of an accessible person, locating itself first at the node of the IRS. It carries an organizational pattern from its previous state, that of the sender's IRC. The receiver's three nodes or sites of organization make a hybrid of this 'original' energy, and so, 'the word in language is half someone else's. It becomes "one's own" only when the speaker populates it with his own intention, his own accent' (Bakhtin 1981: 293).

Each node is a frame of energy, understood as both energy and a particular organization of energy. Each node, by its sharing of energy and also by the interactional nature of its different methods of organization, is other to another node. Bakhtin refers to language as a medium and says that the meaning carried in this medium is not transferred from site to site (speaker to listener) but is carried only within 'the intentions of others. Expropriating it, forcing it to submit to one's own intentions and accents, is a difficult and complicated process' (1981: 294). Peirce too says the same, for if each node were iconically identical, then 'it would instantly crystallize thought and prevent all further formation of habit' (6: 23). And certainly, the concept that meaning (as existentiality) emerges within an interaction and as such prevents entropic dissipation of energy/meaning is equally the basis of quantum physics. Each nodal site does not simply accept energy in its former nature; instead it shares this energy, adds new energy in the form of its particular organization, and thereby transforms it. The transformation of energy at each node site induces energy (and meaning) loss, includes energy (and meaning) addition, and by the reorganization of this energy according to the code structure of that particular node site, it transforms the energy into an other to its former state of being. Thought, therefore, 'is an action, and ... it consists in a relation' (Peirce 5: 399). Meanings are actions of relationships with otherness.

Davies writes, outlining Bohr's principle of complementarity, that the 'electron simply does not possess a definite position and momentum simultaneously' (1990b: 62). I translate this to mean that the conceptual unit does not exist both as an IRS sensual stimulation(momentum) and an IRC sign-unit (position) at the same time/place. Each is a transformation of the other and this transformation is only possible within the action of textuality that adds organization (as energy) within the interaction with the group reality. These three nodal sites do not exist as separate entities in themselves, potentially confronting and opposing. Rather, they are always other to each other, with otherness understood as an action of shared differentiation.

These separate node sites, with their separate 'actions of meaning,' are not really separate from nor independent of each other but overlap, interact with, and are in that sense other to each other in a continuously interactive sense. Energy moves from node to node; its existential shapes and meanings are changed by the reorganization of this energy, by the loss of energy, by the input of new energy. Is this not chaos? No, for the binding principle is that there is a relationship of intentionality between each node site, with such shared intentionality understood as a particular and yet interactive, and therefore shared, organization of energy. Each node, the IRS, the GR, and the IRC, are cognitively linked; they exist within the same STF, that spatiotemporal frame or organizational infrastructure that establishes the necessary horizons by which reality is made meaningful, is engaged, captured – for that particular being in that particular society. Thus, although the potentiality of meaning may be infinite, the actuality is operative within a finite and ever narrowing horizon.

Such an interaction of energy is what Bakhtin refers to when he is speaking of the novel as polyglossia, 'where languages and cultures interanimated each other, language became something entirely different, its very nature changed: in place of a single unitary sealed-off Ptolemaic world of language, there appeared the open Galilean world of many languages, mutually animating each other' (1981: 65). Meaning is not static, it does not move, as in the Process communication school, intact from site to site, from speaker to listener, from author to reader. The monologic text, where 'the author proceeds by following a plan given at the outset,' like the monologic physical world, cannot conceptually exist as such. Rather, a text and a textual society is 'an open process that seeks "surprisingness" at almost every step of the way' (Morson and Emerson 1990: 244). Or, 'subatomic uncertainty is not just a result of our ignorance about microforces but is inherent in matter – an absolute indeterminacy of the universe' (Davies 1990b: 120). This is heteroglossia, those actions of 'another's speech in another's language, serving to express authorial intentions but in a refracted way' (Bakhtin 1981: 324). Bakhtin is here referring to the novel, but I use the same concept to refer to the production of meaning within the social text, where there are 'two different intentions: the direct intention of the character who is speaking and the refracted intention of the author. In such discourse, there are two voices, two meanings and two expressions. And all the while these two voices are dialogically interrelated, they – as it were – know about each other (just as two exchanges in a dialogue know of each other and are structured in this mutual knowledge of each other); it is as if they actually hold a conversation with each other' (ibid).

When any node or site of the transformation of meaning is damaged or non-existent, we have a reduced capacity to create meaning. The final sign of Secondness is not an understanding but may be a total distortion or a mere reproduction of an original impulse, something regurgitated but not conceptualized. Such discourse can be found in a totalitarian state, where the transformation of energy at nodes is not permitted. A cognitive structure that does not permit energy transformation or true dialogue cannot last beyond one generation, because no new energy enters the system and entropic decay will so deplete the system that it will collapse. Each node, as in Bakhtin's novel, must be active in its nature, must act as a '*subject* for the engaged, practical transmission of information, and not as a *means* of representation' (1981: 340). Therefore, 'no living word relates to its object in a singular way: between the word and its object ... there exists an elastic environment of other, alien words about the same object, the same theme' and 'any concrete discourse (utterance) finds the object at which it was directed already as it were overlain with qualifications, open to dispute, charged with value ... It is entangled, shot through with shared thoughts, points of view, alien value judgments and accents' (276). This is the vitality of heteroglossia, the key means of bringing new energy into the closed spatiotemporal frame of the society.

'The word, directed towards its object, enters a dialogically agitated and tension-filled environment of alien words, value judgments and accents, weaves in and out of complex interrelationships, merges with some, recoils from others, intersects with yet a third group: and all this may crucially shape discourse' (ibid). This heteroglossia, this polyphonic creation of meaning is the same within the textual society, though Bakhtin is here referring to language and the novel, the author and the reader. As Peirce has also said, in speaking of intention, and as Bakhtin concurs, 'every word is directed towards an answer and cannot escape the profound influence of the answering word that it anticipates' (280). So, too, every unit of energy, situated at each node, is directed towards another node; each entwines with the other, affects the other. Wheeler points out that 'the quantum principle shows that there is a sense in which what the observer will do in the future defines what happens in the past – even in a past so remote that life did not then exist, and shows even more, that 'observership is a prerequisite for any useful version of "reality"' (in Davies 1990b: 126).

Being or meaning is an event. Bakhtin's analysis is that 'the activity of the world comes to each of us as a series of events that uniquely occur in the site I, and only I, occupy in the world' (Holquist 1990: 24). The site 'I' is the STF of the individual and also of the textual society. Even though these sites are unique, 'they are never in any sense of the word "alone"' (ibid). Bakhtin's term of *sobytie* or event 'is formed from the word for being – *bytie* – with the addition of the prefix implying sharedness' (25). Meaning is not an entity in itself but is an action of shared otherness. The textual society is an entity in itself, a unique organic species, but as an organic text, it is alive and exists only in a state of the constant transformation of energy.

Degenerate Otherness

There are a number of analyses that view otherness not as a constant reformulation of energy but as a reification of energy. I refer to these forms as 'degenerate otherness.' They acknowledge, correctly, that meaning requires stability, something that I consider available in the syntactic horizons of group reality. They usually acknowledge that meanings may and even should change and therefore that there is some action by which this can be accomplished. However, they do not see energy as a potential form of an *implicatio* order that unfolds and folds into an *explicatio* form of an actual form of existential energy. They do not see energy as an action and otherness as simply a spatially or temporally different moment of that energy. Instead, these analyses remove other energy and reify it as an isolate entity, a separate agent. As such, energy becomes associated with separate and private powers of stability and action, as found within the Hegelian master/slave analysis of power. Otherness may become a deviant opponent to stability, may be defined as malicious to the secure lives of human beings, much as Ares, forever involved in intrigue and wars, was a 'most hateful' being. Equally, stability may become reified as antipathetic to progress and swept away with the heads in revolution. Or stability may be combined with action and merged into a singular god-like force of totalitarian decision-making that deals, often arbitrarily, with both stability and change. An obvious further danger when dealing with these forms of reified otherness is the mystification of its powers. I shall examine three examples of degenerate otherness within the frames of structuralism, Saussurian semiology, and deconstruction. Each of these analyses combines a number of the problems of otherness within its nature.

Structuralism

Structuralism considers a society to be made up of systems as structures that seemingly provide the stability of habit within which meaning can exist; that is, the GR syntactic logic is vested within a specific system rather than a logic of interaction. These systemic structures are group-based in that they last longer than any individual and are dominant over individual behaviour. One of the most well-known examples of this system is Lévi-Strauss's establishment of 'social statics or communication structures' that appear in the 'precise and stable forms' of 'communication of women, communication of goods and services, communication of messages' (1963: 296). The deterministic sociolinguistics of Bernstein (1971), the reductionist social typologies of Benedict (1934), the dyadic metaphors of Barthes (1967, 1973), the epistemic structures of Foucault (1972, 1973b) are other examples. Structuralism can lead to a variety of degenerate forms of otherness because the tendency in this analysis is that the GR moves from being a syntactic pattern of organization that is necessarily interactional with the IR level of reality and becomes reified on the IR level as a particular IRC system, such as the language, the cultural metaphors, the economy, the political system, the kinship system, the religious system, the genetic structure. This is a situation of 'collapsed realities,'[5] where the GR logical level merges with the IR level of existential experience. As such, the logic becomes a discrete metaphysical entity of singular causality. As with merged realities, the result of that merger provides a society with a powerful agential force for stability and/or change. The fundamentalism of many religions, the coded determinism of structural analysis in both myth and genes, the polarization of the Marxist and other goal-directed patterns of social history – these are examples where otherness as generative dialogue has essentially disappeared and has become a singular force of intentionality. As we saw previously,[6] a situation of collapsed realities is powerful but cannot last over time; simply put, it 'uses up its energy content' too quickly and is unable, by the very nature of its collapse, to access more energy; it quickly falls into social chaos.

A binary frame of opposition, whether it is developed within the dyadic bond of the two nodes of the individual reality[7] or within the collapse of the two realities, sets up a frame wherein these two existential[8] realities, the sensual and the rational, become fixed in a confrontative isolation rather than interactional frame. Energy, rather than being shared in the interactions between them, is polarized and defined in its opposition. Since these two nodes are existential their energy content can be measured on a quantitative scale. The systems of the sensual node may be considered less organized (either within the simplicity of Rousseau or the mechanics of Durkheim); as less organized it may also mistakenly be taken for the unfocused potentiality of generative energy. This form of degenerate otherness, found within collapsed realities, can be seen in a variety of feminist analyses that see woman as goddess, innately in contact with generative energy or the familiar images of the purity of the non-industrial lifestyles and peoples. The systems of the conceptual node may be considered more organized (the organic of Durkheim, the civilized of Lévi-Strauss). In these forms of degenerate otherness, the other is not a site for actions of reorganization of both shared and different energy, but is a static other engaged in an ongoing battle to maintain its own stock of energy and self-identity.

With this collapsed infrastructure, with energy understood as enclosed rather than interactional, a key problem in structuralism is to identify a source of action, a source of intentionality. Since energy is focused within a specific node, this node is understood as causal. Action becomes understood as either positive or negative. The positive, understood as 'progressive' action, may become located in the reified IRS, the sensual node. It can be located within the genetic forms of gender, race, sensuality, non-industrial imagery. It may be located within the reified IRC, the 'civilized' node. It can be a cultural code, cultural images, a language, a religion, a system of laws, an historic hero, an historic date, technology. The energy of the reified node becomes the motivating force for all social actions. Whatever it is, as a set of inviolable norms it confronts individuals to both activate and guide their experience of reality. The negative form is understood as regressive and deviant. It can be the mixing of races, the other gender, the industrial technology, or instead, the inherently deviant sensuality of the individual, the savagery of the primitive, the superstition of devilry, the denial of the hero, the rejection of technology. Deviance is considered dangerous because it is a threat to the hegemonic power of the dominant node that is alone understood as capable of moulding a valued life. Within this situation, individual experience, rather than being an expression of both stasis and an infusion of new energy, becomes a means only of reproducing the static nodal codes. A society that can only reproduce itself and cannot introduce new energy is doomed. It cannot maintain itself because it has lost its adaptive power; it becomes trapped in entropic decay.

One seeming way out of the static nature of this confrontational frame is to consider that the interaction between the two nodes is not a stable hegemony but is developmental. Platonic analysis establishes ideal forms as the intentionality of the earthly existential forms. This romantic idealism is temporally linear; the rational or ideal form is first and the human sensuo-rational experience is a weak and flawed version of the original ideal. We should remember that in the degenerate forms of the two realities, either one or the other of the IR level nodes may disappear, may be combined with the other, or may have the GR node take the role of the missing node. The Platonic form would have the GE as a degenerate GR, as a generative force that is also organizationally (acting as the GR) intentional; and the IRS would be combined with the IRC. The resultant social being lacks the GR nodal infrastructure for the dialogical interaction of the triadic frame. Rousseau's sensual purity is temporally first in origin and value; the human sensuo-rational is second. Goddess feminism confines contact with this external purity to women, who are thereby both temporally and socially first in origin and value. In all these cases, temporal 'firstness' is privileged because it is mistakenly assumed to be generative energy[9] and the interaction between these two nodes is not a true shared interaction but a hegemony of a mythic energy experienced in a linear rather than current time frame. New energy becomes located in another temporality, either the past or the future. This, as mentioned earlier, is a degenerate form that, because of the static trap of missing or collapsed realities, necessarily sees the first node as equivalent to or directly tied to generative energy. This may seem to provide energy to the society in the form of a strong emotional attachment to the social or mystic heritage or a strong attachment to the 'hope' of a new future, but this type of energy can only be found in metaphors that are confined to either past or future time. The nodes, within missing or collapsed realities, can only move energy from site to site; they cannot share and transform energy.

Therefore, according to the analytic frame of nodes, the energy of this type of society remains locked into a node and cannot be used within transformation but only within the mechanics of reproduction. Individuals in this society are unable to conceptualize and thereby introduce new organizations of energy. They can only reproduce the past or future.

Hegel also follows this developmental path of action; the thesis is the ideal truth, exterior to the individual; the antithesis (IRS) is a stage in coming to this truth. The final result is not an organization of both shared and new energy, but a new term for the original thesis. These two nodes seem to be involved with each other; 'consciousness finds that it immediately is and is not another consciousness' for 'they not merely do not contradict one another, but ... one is as necessary as the other.' But this involvement has a

Newtonian linearity, for 'the bud disappears when the blossom breaks through, and we might say that the former is refuted by the latter; in the same way when the fruit comes, the blossom may be explained to be a false form of the plant's existence' (1967: 231, 68). These stages are not spatiotemporal transformations of a shared and new energy; they supplant one another as incompatible; the second node as antithesis involves the destruction of the first node. Is this dialogue or monologue? Only one voice speaks and it is a voice with a single intentionality, the expression of the original thesis. This is comparable to Peirce's analysis of anancastic evolution, a theory that attributes 'all progress to an inward necessary principle, or other form of necessity' (6: 298). I can only here repeat what Peirce said about the Hegelian philosophy; namely, 'living freedom is practically omitted from its method. The whole movement is that of a vast engine, impelled by a *vis a tergo*, with a blind and mysterious fate of arriving at a lofty goal' (6: 305). Bakhtin too has said of such a theory that 'what happens in all these cases is that the living, compellent, and inescapable uniqueness of our actual life is diluted with the water of merely thinkable, empty possibility' (1993: 51). There is neither sharing of energy nor input of new energy and therefore no transformation of reality.

Marx used a similar frame of inherent intentionality, but 'filled' the individual reality level by having both the IRS and IRC nodes as separately existential. The two nodes were located in current rather than linear, supplantial time. The lower class was one node; the upper class the other node; they were other to each other. In this degenerate form of otherness, energy is considered private rather than shared; their relation is confrontative rather than interactive. The way out of the endless pendulum of this non-dialogical frame is a revolution, where the one supplants the other, eventually to destroy the binary form. A problem, however, is that although Marx does destroy the static frame of binary structuralism by his revolution and sets up a final system of a communism of shared energy, it becomes, like all structural systems, static because it rejects nodal otherness in any form whatsoever. With his famous statement that 'religion is the opiate of the masses,' he quite rightly rejects the external form frame with its Platonic activator-other of religion; he rightly rejects the dyadic frame of the master/slave class structure by his revolution to destroy that bond; but his final system of communism excludes all otherness. Otherness, as a sharing and reorganization of a basic energy that is spatiotemporally located in a different node, is a necessary action for all living organisms. The Marxist attempt to deal with the idealism and hegemony of structuralism leads to a single-node organism where there is no otherness. Marxism sets up a trap; it creates a system that, without the dialogical transformations of otherness, can only result in the entropic dissolution of the society.

Saussurian Semiology

Semiology must be distinguished from the semiotics of Charles Peirce, whose analytic frame of the three cognitive states is a very real expression of dialogical action. Saussurian semiology uses only one level, that of individual reality. Unlike structuralism with its collapsed realities, the semiology frame completely ignores GR, the continuity of habit, and considers only the experiences of the individual. However, as in structuralism, to create stability it uses a binary format that inevitably set up an oppositional interaction. The Saussurian frame consists of the IRS (the signifier), and the IRC (the signified). The tie between them, at first arbitrary chance, becomes a mechanical bond. This bond provides the semiological stability, unlike structuralism, where stability comes from the long-term hegemonic power of the GR as an IR-level system. Bonded together, there is no interaction, no mediation between the two Saussurian elements. Together, they are the sign.

Semiology can be considered a form of Cartesian rationalism. Semiology considers that the tie between the two nodes, IRS and IRC, is tychastic chance, while rationalism puts it down to mechanical anancastic necessity. But in both cases, the tie is vital; stability comes from the long-term bond of each node to each. There is no mediatory action via a node of conceptual habit, the Thirdness of group reality. Rationalism considers the IRC, if understood properly, to be an exact copy of the IRS, physical matter. As in semiology there is no dialogue, no action between the two. Similarly, this interaction between the two nodes can happen only in current time. There must be no intentionality of a past or future heritage to mediate and possibly 'corrupt' the tie between the two nodes. Such a static frame removes the potential for change. Barthes also suggests that the signified can be a duplicate of the signifier. In 'denotation' there is no need for a socialized learning phase; you know the meaning of an entity directly through its physical nature. His analysis of 'readerly' texts sees them using an IRS in this way as a direct sign. The reader can, as in the Cartesian frame, accept it in its own nature as truth. Barthes' 'writerly' texts, however, permit a conceptual creation of meaning. The 'writerly' text supposedly involves the reader as co-author, supplying imagery so that both the writer and the reader are 'born simultaneously with the text' (1977: 145). However, Barthes ignores the necessity of group reality, the logic of habit. His frame locates the individual, whether reader or author, as existent only in the immediate, with no contact whatsoever with a continuity of habit. As he says, 'myth is discontinuous. It is no longer expressed in long fixed narratives but only in "discourse" at most, it is a phraseology, a corpus of phrases' (165). As a structuralist, Barthes has no dialogical group reality, only a current collectivity of signs.

It is a mistake to transform the GR into an abstract corpus as Saussure did with 'langue,' and an even greater mistake to transform it to a code system and restrict it only to current time as Barthes did with signs. Barthes uses words or signs as 'floating' codes whose code meanings can be added on to existing objects, supposedly adding their former meanings to these objects, for 'semiology ... is part of linguistics' (1967: 11). Such a system rejects the controlling frame of long-term habit and permits an arbitrary movement of meanings from site to site. I call this 'taxonomic translation,' a slippery substitution of meanings that are essentially without meaning because they function without a spatiotemporal frame, without the restrictions of a syntactic horizon. Signs as IRC (meanings) are taken from their spatial bond with one IRS (a physical object) and added on to another IRS, another physical object. Barthes suggests that this added meaning is actually a hidden aspect of this second physical object, a meaning that we have somehow failed to see. He further mystifies this 'translation,' thereby removing it from our being able to logically analyse this new meaning, by bonding the two IRC terms into a binary frame. Whereas Saussurian semiology bonds an IRS with an IRC (signifer and signified), the binary frame of Barthes is strictly IRC bonded with IRC; signified with signified.[10] So, in his *Mythologies*, he says that milk is 'now the true anti-wine ... milk is the opposite of fire by all the denseness of its molecules, by the creamy, and therefore soothing, nature of its spreading. Wine is mutilating, surgical, it transmutes and delivers; milk is cosmetic, it joins, covers, restores. Moreover, its purity, associated with the innocence of the child, is a token of strength, of a strength which is not revulsive, not congestive, but calm, white, lucid, the equal of reality' (1973: 60). He takes meanings from a variety of signs and applies them to another, as in the creaminess of milk somehow bonded to 'soothing,' 'cosmetic,' 'purity,' 'child,' 'strength,' 'lucid.' Wine is bonded to 'mutilating,' 'surgical.' These two new signs, with all their newly tacked-on meanings, are then bonded to each other in a degenerate opposition. That all Barthes' associative terms are simply chance and without any inherent biological or social intentionality is obvious but difficult to refute, because all sign terms are social creations and therefore amorphous. The intentionality that supposedly set up their binary nature (milk versus fire) is not shared in our current experience but is lost in some long-gone mythological past. In taxonomic translation, intentionality becomes as in structuralism not an infusion of new energy and an interaction of shared energy, but a linear monological hegemony of a static and unreachable other, an other totally unavailable for dialogue.

The Saussurian frame is amenable to such distortions, for the two nodes, the IRS and the IRC, lack true otherness (with otherness understood as the sharing of energy); they are arbitrarily related and isolate from each other. The stability that they have is one of a permanent bond created without any intentionality or any possibility of a dialogical interaction. It therefore lacks any possibility of action, a requirement in the production of meaning.

Discourse or Dialogue

I should like at this point to clarify two terms and two cognitive situations to support my insistence that cognition is an action. A clear differentiation should be made between discourse and dialogue, for the two terms are often confused. Discourse is a mechanical action between two units that are not different entities, but two forms of the same thing. Because they are, to our perception, spatiotemporally distinct, they may seem to be unique in themselves. They should rather be considered two units within one organism.

Essentially, a discursive situation exists on one level of reality, the individual reality. The key problem in the discursive frame is that both nodes are identical. Discourse is not an interaction between different organizational structures. It involves no transformation; it is simply the short-term preservation of energy by its being moved from site to site, each site having the same organizational structure and thus preventing entropy by 'adding' more of the same energy at each site. It is an action between units that are similar in energy content and organization and remain similar; there is no dialogical action, which means that there is no sharing of a basic energy and no addition/loss of *other* energy and a resultant *reorganization.* Discourse can be likened to a pendulum swing from side to side. Discourse cannot change or add meaning. It has been variously called 'idle chatter,' 'empty speech,' or 'insignificant bagatelles' (Lacan 1977: 150) and is the tedium of many social evenings, political rhetoric and, of course, academic conferences.

The individual reality is made up of two dissimilar nodes, the IRS and the IRC. The group reality, the logic of habit, dialogically acts as the mediation between them. In the discursive frame, there is only one reality, the individual reality, and both nodes are identical to each other. They may both be IRS, as in two parts of a computer, or they may both be IRC, as in two role-players in a routine drama. Entropic decay is inevitable in a discursive frame precisely because it cannot organize energy differently and is thus susceptible to the gradual loss of energy and therefore meaning. Discourse can keep an energy content in spatiotemporal existence for a short period of time but entropy is inevitable. If you call a machine and are answered by a mechanical voice, at first the voice will have meaning but gradually it will simply be noise. You will no longer listen to it as a message but will consider it a barrier to meaning.

In the discursive frame, found within structuralism and semiology, codes become degenerate forms of the group reality logic. Individuals reproduce roles whose authorship is completely external to them. Dramaturgical role-playing models and social reproduction themes set up a framework that turns individual existence into reproductions of a static stored original. Rather than being involved interactionally, as in Bakhtin's concept of 'knowledge *of*,' which also involves a 'knowledge of it *for me*' (1993: 49), and therefore a concept of interactional obligation, the individual operates essentially out of contact with knowledge. The origin of such roles, their intentionality, is shrouded in an inaccessible mystique of genetics, repression, and latent purpose. Because intentionality is inaccessible, because the codes are static, the discursive frame is destructive to the individual. It denies individual sensuality, denies variation and new energy, and therefore is entropically destructive to the society.

Derrida and Deconstruction

Deconstruction recognizes the problems of single level and collapsed realities and has attempted to break their static cognitive frames. Derrida, the key figure of the deconstructionist movement, agrees that the classical or Saussurian analysis sees the sign as 'put in place of the thing itself' (1973: 138). He admits that there is, external to the sign, a 'thing-in-itself' of which the sign is a 'representation.' However, rather than maintaining some form of relation via the mediation of a syntactic social logic as in the Peircean triadic frame of cognition, Derrida uses a very different infrastructure. The sign is secondary to the origin, but in Derrida's case, to an origin defined not as Peircean object but as a presence, for 'it is second in order after an original and lost presence, a presence from which the sign would be derived' (ibid). This lost *présence* seems to be a key component in his thought. If one can break the current bond between the signifier and signified, or more broadly, between the two nodes within the binary frameworks of structuralism, semiology and discourse analysis, this action of deconstruction may permit contact not with the external object (to which Saussure and Derrida are equally indifferent) but with the more basic aura of this *présence*.

Derrida's *présence* arises within the powerful action of *différance*, an action that separates the previous bond between the signifier and signified by differing their natures and deferring their contact. *Différance* ensures their separation and non-identity, for 'in order for it to be, an interval must separate it from what it is not' (143). *Différance* as an action thereby permits the traces of *présence*, it ensures that each now separate element is 'related to something other than itself but retains the mark of a past element and already lets itself be hollowed out by the mark of its relation to a future element' (142). We read that 'the trace is not an attribute; we cannot say that the self of the living present "primordially is" it' (85) and can thereby consider that our current life is neither the 'primordial' trace nor its copy. Let us continue with 'this trace relates no less to what is called the future than to what is called the past, and it constitutes what is called the present by this very relation to what it is not' (143). It is 'primordial' (85–7) in the sense that its origin is aspatial and atemporal; it is 'not now. *Différance* therefore creates a profound 'gap' between the previously bonded signifier and signified; it permits actual experience to come into existence by permitting a contact with this lost *présence*. Without *différance*, consciousness is a black hole, 'a voice without differance, a voice without writing, is at once absolutely alive and absolutely dead' (102). In this gap between the two nodes, set up by the action of *différance*, *présence* can come into existence. As in the Peircean triadic framework , we seem to have some mediation between the two nodes of the individual reality. But is *présence* actually mediation?

Derrida's 'gap,' the point where *présence* may make contact with us, is filled by Writing, which is 'in the metaphoric sense, natural, divine ... it is equal in dignity to the origin of value, to the voice of conscience as divine law'; it is 'the divine inscription in the heart and the soul'; it is 'natural, eternal and universal'; it is 'that forgetting of the self, that exteriorization, the contrary of the interiorizing memory' (24) and 'what Writing ... betrays, is life' (1976: 17, 15, 24, 25). Writing, the essence of *présence*, is asocial, universal, and importantly, external to the commonality of everyday life. It is 'more exterior to speech, not being its "image" or its "symbol."' I understand this to suggest that the current sign is not an image/symbol of this purity of force. It is 'more interior to speech which is already in itself a writing.' The purity of Writing seems to enter speech without an action of social mediation. Derrida certainly says this, for writing seems to 'give us the assured means of broaching the de-construction of *the greatest totality* – the concept of the episteme and logocentric metaphysics – within which are produced, without ever posing the radical question of writing, all the Western methods of analysis, explication, reading, or interpretation.' He offers Writing as a form of generative energy, for 'there is no linguistic sign before writing' with Writing understood as 'natural, divine ... living writing is venerated; it is equal in dignity to the origin of value, to the voice of conscience as divine law, to the heart, to sentiment, and so forth,' and 'writing is that forgetting of the self, that exteriorization, the contrary of the interiorizing memory, of the Erinnerung that opens the history of the spirit' (1976: 46, 14, 17, 24). It is essentially non-individual, and with overtones of the Jungian archetype, 'when fantasies are produced which no longer rest on personal memories, we have to do with the manifestations of a deeper layer of the unconscious where the primordial images common to humanity lie sleeping' (Jung 1966, VII: 65). What has Derrida given us with this Writing? It seems at first glance to follow the themes of Aquinas and the Divine Word more than the Platonic architectonic form. The vocal or exterior word of Aquinas is comparable to Derrida's speech and is of equally little importance; the interior or incarnate word, the Saussurian sign, is also unimportant. But is the Divine Word, the word of the heart which is the intentionality of an existence, actually comparable to Derrida's Writing? He has, importantly, removed the IRC from functioning as a bonded signifier/signified (the vocal/exterior word as equivalent to the interior word/sign) and thereby removed it from its former privileged role of supplying epistemic intentionality in the collapsed reality frame of structuralists. But has he, via these actions of deconstruction, opened up the dialogical interaction of the realities of individual, group, biological, and generative energies so that otherness can move between them? If not, then his Writing follows the Platonic form, because the act of understanding in Aquinas 'is called a motion' and, as has been earlier discussed, this motion is triadic, social, and therefore dialogical.

Dialogism insists on constant interaction and says that spatial and temporal distinctions not only do not prevent this interaction but are a condition of it, for 'the world in which an act or deed actually proceeds, in which it is actually accomplished, is a unitary and unique world that is experienced concretely' (Bakhtin 1993: 56). A spatiotemporal world is singular, unique, concrete; it is particular to itself and no other. The Copenhagen interpretation of quantum physics explains that there is no 'deep reality,'[11] and the only reality we can conceptually know is existential within a spatiotemporal interaction. That is, for generative energy to even enter into a dialogical form, you must also introduce a spatiotemporal dimension. Derrida does exactly this with his deconstruction, an action that forces a spatial and temporal distinction between the nodes. However, the next step, that of the actual dialogic interaction, the action of textuality, the act that transforms the various forms of energy in their otherness, is completely missing within Derrida's theory.

What we are given within deconstruction as separation of the signifier and the signified and Writing as archetypal *présence* is the introduction of a spatiotemporal force that is separate from an interactional action. Jung defines his archetypes as the 'contents of the collective unconscious' and 'so far as the collective unconscious contents are concerned we are dealing with archaic or – I would say – primordial types, that is, with universal images that have existed since the remotest times' (1966, IX, 1: 5). Derrida's Writing appears as 'presence,' as 'traces' in the gap; this 'presence' is not in interaction with the nodal energies but is a direct and isolate movement into the space between nodal energies. This is the contrary of the quantum interaction, the Bakhtinian dialogue, the Peircean cognitive act, the action of textuality. In all these forms, the cognitive act is a dialogic sharing and transformation of energies within a specific and finite spatiotemporal frame. Certainly deconstruction introduces space and time and thereby separates the various nodes and permits their differentiation, but there is no subsequent dialogical interaction within these now separate nodes; there is no transformation of shared energy. All that happens is that, in this spatial gap, traces of the eternal *présence* as expressed in Writing move into these now vacant spaces, and touch these now separate nodes. Such an input of energy can happen irrespective of the intentionality of an action of textuality, but such energy cannot be utilized and transformed into a new entity, a unit of meaning. This movement of Writing is merely a tychastic or anancastic act; that is, an action of energy movement based on either chance or determinism, an action that grabs hold of a sudden gap, an opening in the otherwise bonded net or plots, and waits for that gap to appear. But as the research of quantum physics points out, without an interaction, there is no existential reality. Writing is a movement, but not an interaction. Further, its goals of using *différance* to separate the nodes and then move its energy into the resultant gaps, betray an intentionality of purpose that is foreign to generative energy. 'There is then no need to attribute the cosmic order ... either to the activity of a Deity or to the input of organization at the initial singularity' (Davies 1990a: 52). There is primal energy, which I term generative energy, but there is no primal order as intentionality. The Divine Word of Aquinas, understood as the Father's knowledge, exists within a triadic interaction that permits particular reality by its spatiotemporal variations. The Derridean order of *présence* is not the interactional and dialogical agapastic form that is initiated by individual intentionality, that is contextual, local, and operative within the limitations of a particular spatiotemporal reality. It is therefore more akin to the Platonic purity of forms, functioning as a degenerate form of Jungian archetype intentionality (without, however, the specific metaphors of the Jungian biological reality). The trace structure of Writing as ultimate order cannot be compared either with the syntactic logic of the group reality, for 'the concept of trace is therefore incommensurate with that of retention, that of the becoming-past of what had been present' (Derrida 1973: 152); that is, it is atemporal, aspatial, and therefore asocial – all factors that are the opposite of both the Jungian archetype[12] and the group-based syntactic logic, and also, I suggest, the opposite of any logic whatsoever. Trace writings are simply flecks of primordial energy attaching themselves to the now separate nodes. But primoridal energy has no order, for 'the primeval state was not one of maximum organization but one of simplicity and equilibrium' (Davies 1990a: 50). Order only arises within the establishment of spatiotemporal boundaries.

Deconstruction becomes a conceptual structure without any mediation between the two nodes of the individual reality. They are prevented from their arbitrary Saussurian bonding by the ongoing actions of the *différance* of deconstruction; however, to deal with the resultant isolation and confrontational separation of sense and thought, Derrida has given us an agent, Writing, that can supposedly make contact with both nodes. This contact is not an action of interaction, is not a sharing and subsequent transformation of that which is shared. In the action of textuality, each nodal site is different; therefore, the nature of energy is different at each node. Within the frame of deconstruction, the two now separate nodes of sense and conception are quite similar and the energy they receive from the mystic *présence* of Writing is equally similar. There is no reorganization specific to each node, no sharing and also adding, no transformation and reorganization. Derrida, with his purity of Writing moving into our individual reality, has done the Thomistic unthinkable of giving God an intention when God can only have the potential of intention, 'the word of the heart.' As Bakhtin points out, the 'incarnated flesh and blood living human being' is 'declared to be valid only as a moment of infinite matter (1993: 51). In such a situation, the interaction has lost its 'answerability,' its bonds with otherness.

Différance, that force that permits the emergence of this universal intention of Being, that supposedly permits its local existentiality, 'the historical and epochal deployment of Being' is nevertheless profoundly anti-social, it is 'even the subversion of every realm. This is obviously what makes it threatening and necessarily dreaded by everything in us that desires a realm, the past or future presence of a realm' (Derrida 1973: 153). Generative energy, on the other hand, is asocial in the sense that its energies are not bound within the spatiotemporal frame of the society, but these energies are not anti-social, they do not threaten the dialogical society but are vital for its constant regeneration. The traces of *présence* that become existential within deconstruction are not actions of sharing but rather the transportation of a deadly and mystically non-existent artefact that points to, that reminds us, of something other, but is not itself also other. Derrida's trace is the Hegelian mark of the *absence* of a presence. Otherness in my terms is the mark of its *presence* within the spatiotemporal frame.

Writing becomes not a concrete logos, the false IRC frames of semiology and structuralism, but an equally degenerate IRS, understood in the Platonic sense as basic origin, force, intentionality. The key problem is that Derrida has quite correctly separated the IRS and IRC, has separated the collapsed realities of the IR and GR. But he has completely ignored the required development of a group reality with its necessary syntactic logic; he seems to scorn such structures as 'epistemic.' His stability of cognition, his intentionality of life come directly from his version of generative energy; however, generative energy is by its very nature inherently unstable and without intention. Therefore, his Writing is a degenerate form of group reality by being also a degenerate form of generative energy. This is not dialogue but a monologic intentionality, a hegemonic control by a primordial force.

What is a dialogical action of intentionality and how does it differ from the *présence* of deconstruction? First, there is the requirement for an infrastructure that permits the sharing of energy. Shared energy is by its very nature found only within an interaction, and an interaction can take place only within a specific spatiotemporal horizon. Therefore, the infrastructure enabling that sharing must act as both an enclosing action and a promoting action. It promotes the movement of energy from node to node. And second, importantly, it must permit the transformation by reorganization of this shared and old energy at each node site. The communication structures of Lévi-Strauss that operate 'on three different levels: communication of women, communication of goods and services, communication of messages' (1963: 196) fulfil the first requirement. They enclose these interactions within a particular society and permit the movement of energy, understood as women, goods and services, and messages. However, as Lévi-Strauss himself points out, this communication infrastructure consists 'exclusively of the study of *rules*' and has 'little concern with the nature of the partners (either individuals or groups) whose play is being patterned after these rules.' Such a structure certainly helps lay 'a foundation for prediction and control' (198, 199). But this is an anancastic interaction, deterministic and mechanical. It is a structure in which 'the whole is built out of the parts ... in which the whole emerges through accumulation of detail' (Bohm and Peat 1987: 158). There is no provision for the transformation of energy at each node, for the unpredictable adaptive power of the organic entity. This is where analyses that are based solely on structure fail us in trying to understand organic reality. The Derridean attempts to break this structure with its confinement of the movement of energy to mechanistic rules do not provide us with the second step that permits the reorganization and transformation of energy within the communicative interaction. Instead, his new energy comes, not from an action of reorganization that uses both the new shared energy and also the old, private energy, but from an external Platonic font of wisdom, the *presence* of Writing. It is therefore other to *all* nodes, regardless of their differences; it does not set up each node as other to another node. It removes what I will later call the notion of desire, the requirement for contact with the similarity/differences (otherness) between the nodes. The separation of the nodes of signifier and signified within the act of deconstruction does not encourage or even permit them to relate to each other. As Bakhtin writes, 'since theory has broken away from the actually performed act and develops according to its own immanent law, the performed act itself, having released theory from itself, begins to deteriorate' (1993: 55). Without a syntactic logic that relates the nodes of the individual reality, that permits those nodes to fulfil their desire to relate to their otherness, the textual reality becomes degenerate; it falls prey to the empty chaos of overinterpretation. Again, Bakhtin: 'if we take the contemporary deed in isolation from self-contained theory, we end up with a biological or with an instrumental act' (56). That is, if we separate the existential nodes from the syntactic logic, we end up with the irrelevance of the tychastic or anancastic interaction. As Pushkin says, 'you have fallen asleep forever' and this is a betrayal of life.

Conclusion

In all these analyses, there is indeed a provision for long-term stability. Nodes are set up as stable sites for the development of meaning within these structures. In all these analyses, a distinction is made between sensual and conceptual meaning. However, these frames of stability permit only one type of interaction between the nodes. All are operative in terms of a Newtonian linear analysis of energy, which sees matter as conserved and

moved from site to site, rather than shared, added to, lost, and also transformed. This will not permit cognition as creative conceptualization but
only mimetic imagizing.

Cognition exists within the transformation of shared and new energy at
different nodes in dialogical interaction. Energy, in its pure form as generative energy, moves into a spatiotemporal frame by various interactions via
the realities of biological, group, and individual reality. Within this spatiotemporal frame, it dialogically interacts with nodal points that have the ability to transform their stored energy and take new energy from the interaction. The result is a new formation of energy. This movement of energy can
be explained within David Bohm's 'generative order,' where 'the generative
source of the idea' unfolds 'into ever more definite forms.' Actuality 'proceeds from an origin in free play which then unfolds into ever more crystallized forms' (1987: 158). And from the definite form, from the crystallization,
from that quantum interaction, energy is released to move yet again into the
implicatio/explicatio interaction. The whole point of otherness is both the
dialogical action of sharing energy located at different nodal or organizational points and the transformation of this energy. 'In science as in art it is
necessary that what is done with more definite forms should continue at
each stage to be open to the kind of free play that is essential to creativity'
(ibid). Otherness then is an infrastructure within which energy can constantly organize and reorganize and so permit life to exist in all its multiple
variations. As Mauss pointed out, 'a gift always looks for recompense' and in
the action of exchange, 'the person who receives the thing takes it in his
hands. He does not merely recognize that he has received it, but realizes that
he himself is "bought" until it is paid for.' The interaction of energy is a
bond, the 'contracting parties are bound in perpetual interdependence'
(1970: XIV, 51, 62), and so we must recognize that the exchange of energy
provides a foundation for the existentiality of life.

4

Dialogical Time

Space and time organize energy and are vital aspects of the textual society. The action of textuality both establishes and functions within a spatial boundary (the observer-observed) and both establishes and functions within a temporal frame. This chapter specifically focuses on the nature of time as a factor of conceptual reality.

Two Forms of Time

Time is a means of organizing energy. There are two types of temporal organization, current and past/future. Current time represents immediately accessible energy, whether sensual or conceptual. It exists in individual reality. The second form is a logic of past/future and is therefore not immediately accessible. I make no distinction between past and future time; they are similar in that both can only be defined as 'not-now.' This form of time as a pattern of continuity exists in group reality. A final aspect to consider is our cognitive reliance on signs; we think only in signs. However, a sign has a finite existentiality, it has both spatial and temporal boundaries. The AOT, which produces the sign by its bonding of the two levels, combines the infrastructure of current time with past/future time. This prevents the spatial dissipation of the IRS and forms a current spatiotemporal existentiality, an IRC.

Individual Reality and Time

Individual reality exists only in current time and is the sensual as well as the conceptual experiences of the individual. We have already established that there is a difference between the sensual and the conceptual experiences, and this is readily expressed within such diverse research fields as quantum physics and literary criticism. Quantum physics says that 'our thinking about the universe creates ... a description' of that universe. As conceptual beings, we live within these descriptions (Peierls, in Davies and Brown 1986: 75). Bakhtin points out that 'there is a sharp and categorical boundary line between the actual world as source of representation and the world represented in the work' (1981: 253). The sensual is the immediacy of the felt experience and, as described by Peircean Firstness, it is a 'sensation of immediate consciousness, yet, there is no consciousness in it because it is instantaneous' (1: 310). Peircean Secondness is our understanding of that sensual experience in its specific conceptual nature as a sign. What is evident about both these nodes is their immediacy, the immediate impact of their energy on our experience. Current time can be understood as an interactional 'string,' an action of linking the diverse formats of the energy of the nodes. I would consider it comparable to the quantum sense of the 'graviton,' the 'messenger particle of gravity' that, by its holding property, links quanta to each other to permit the development of a specific existentiality. Current time as an interactional string of immediately available energy provides an avenue to otherness, to those nodal points both within the semiotic realities of the self and those of other entities. Current time provides a link between nodal points, thereby permitting the introduction of this new energy for further reorganization. As previously discussed in the action of textuality, we move from the sensual to the conceptual via a dialogical interaction with the logic of the group reality. Essentially, therefore, current time permits the introduction of energy into a spatial area; such energy, if accepted, must be reorganized. This happens within the organizational actions of the nodal points, tied to each other by the linking action of current time.

Group Reality and Time

Group reality has no discrete sensual and conceptual units of experience. It is a long-term logic, a pattern of experience and expression that has existed within this particular group in the past and must continue to exist in the future. It is preserved, not in 'the unconscious, not even a collective one, but in the memory of languages, genres, rituals; that is where it comes from to enter into people's discourses and dreams' (Bakhtin, in Todorov 1984: 33). It is Peircean synechism, the concept of enduring habits that is the basis of Thirdness. Explaining its nature, Peirce writes that 'there are three characters which mark the universe of our experience in a way of their own. They are Variety, Uniformity, and the passage of Variety into Uniformity. By the Passage of Variety into Uniformity, I mean that variety upon being multiplied almost in every department of experience shows a tendency to form habits. These habits produce statistical uniformities.' He notes that when the instances are small, the laws of habit so produced will be 'rough,' but when the number of instances is large 'there are no departures from the law that our senses can take cognizance of' (6: 97). Such a law will enforce continuity. However, this law is a structure only, a patterned horizon of conceptual borders or limitations, not any specific thought or form. If we consider its nature as a logic, a law that exists only as a pattern of the habits of the past and a potential of the future, then we must further admit that it has no power to express itself. Expression is a distinctive 'felt' experience of current immediacy, both in its sensual and conceptual natures, and therefore a part only of individual reality, that reality found only within current time. Group reality as a pattern of logic and not an actual expression of law does not exist on its own in current time; it exists in current reality only via its mediating actions on the existential experiences of the individual.

Neither form of reality and neither form of time can exist on its own, and each is differentiated from the other by the nature of its organization of energy. The action of textuality unites the two forces of time; it does this by its establishment of a spatial infrastructure that permits the two forms of time to interact. The immediate sensation, the introduction of intentionality from an other, is a force that functions only within the string-ties of current time. This energy is instantaneous and immediately lost; it becomes existential by bonding to the syntactic habit of past/future time. Equally, the syntactic habit can only become existential by the vitalizing infusion of the enormous power of the energy found within the packed particles carried within the stringed actions of current time. What I am setting up is an understanding that current time is an interactional link; it exists as an action between nodes of organized energy; its function is to move energy from node to node. Past/future time is an ongoing habit of organization and as such limits the potentialities of organization. I am here reminded of the paintings of Francis Bacon, whose intertwined bodies and portraits become immediate existentialities when their amorphous past/future existences and movements are trapped, are bonded together by the fusing power of a single immediate action. These two forms of temporality decrease the randomness of energy and provide finite boundaries such that the energy within these boundaries becomes organized.

Linear Time: Absolute and Relative

Let us now consider the variations of our understanding of time within the textual society.

The conceptual heritage that Western society developed from the thirteenth century considers that time is a physical phenomenon; it exists as such in two forms. Time is a measurable content of itself and also a system of measurement of other content; it is three hours and three hours-of-waiting. Newton called these two forms of time absolute and relative. The absolute form functions as a linear, mathematical, and measurable entity. As a neutral system of measurement it is uninvolved with the conceptual variations of individual experience. 'Absolute, true and mathematical time, of itself, and from its own nature, flows equably without relation to anything external, and by another name is called duration.' However, 'relative, apparent, and common time, is some sensible and external (whether accurate or unequable) measure of duration by means of motion, which is commonly used instead of true time; such as an hour, a day, a month, a year' (Newton (1729 [1947], 6). Relative time is given names, such as an hour, a long time, a jiffy, an aeon; these names are social and without the detachment of absolute scientific measurement. It can be seen that these two forms of time are quite different from past/future and current time as I have described them above. Newton's absolute time as an asocial scale of measurement cannot be found in my analysis of time as a means of organizing energy within a particular, not absolute, horizon of time and space. His relative time is a social definition of duration and not, as I am suggesting, a link between nodes.

The concept of 'duration' is important to both the linear definitions of Newton. Time is understood as successive moments of 'duration,' whether their measurement is by an absolute or a relative scale. In this sense, time fills space, and it is possible to measure the amount of time-as-content a thing or action has gathered in its 'moments of duration.' Equally important is the requirement for a sense of the 'absolute,' an insistence on a scale of measurement quite apart from the individual's relationship with the world, an anti-positivist idea that 'we ought to abstract from our senses, and consider things themselves, distinct from what are only sensible measures of them' (ibid: 8). A final aspect of this era's definition of time is its infinite linearity; there are no horizons to the ongoing movement of time and the gathering of time-as-content.

Put together these three concepts: time as an absolute and neutral scale of measurement; time as duration or filling in space; and time as infinite, and the result is that societies and their conceptuality can be measured for the

Diagram 1: Newtonian Time

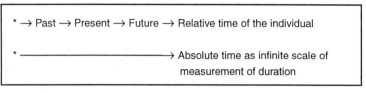

* (origin)

amount of time they have in them, and therefore, their place on the scale of progress and development. A society in A.D. 1600 had more time-as-content in it than a society of A.D. 100 and was more developed. When Europeans met aboriginal peoples who did not use linear time they understood them to be 'chayned under the bond of Deathe unto the Divell';[1] the time frame of the devil and hell was pre-linear, post-linear or even alinear. This meant that these peoples did not have the content of thoughts and technology that the Western societies had acquired via their experience of linear time. Time as content meant cumulative progress, and 'what good man would prefer a country covered with forests and ranged by a few thousand savages to our extensive Republic, studded with cities, towns and prosperous farms, embellished with all the improvements which art can devise or industry execute ... and filled with all the blessings of liberty, civilization, and religion.'[2] Aboriginal time and aboriginal societies seemed to lack any sense of linearity and accumulation.

When faced with the very real signs of developed learning, elaborate buildings, furnishings, and other concrete goods of the Chinese, Indian, and other Eastern peoples, the Western mind considered that these peoples lived within linear time, but defined it as having finite rather than infinite boundaries and following a cyclical rather than one-way pattern. Being on a cyclical linear time scale, these societies repeated their time as content over and over again, which explained why, to the Westerners, they remained with the same thoughts and technology and were not 'progressive.' Supporting this perception, the Durkheim school of sociology saw one-way, infinite linear time as mathematical and scientific, while cyclical time locked social behaviour into repetitive, rather than progressive and developmental life actions.

However, to the Eastern and Aboriginal mind, linear time, whether circular or progressive, was unimportant and referred only to the small realities of personal life, that time that Newton saw as 'relative' and idiosyncratic. True time, if we still want to use that word, is, to these people, alinear; the Brahman is the 'one-without-a-second' (Zimmer 1956: 306). This alinear time is comparable to what I define as generative energy. It is potentiality; it is pure energy; it is the force that provides the basic energy that will be organized as a specific existentiality. Once that force of generative energy meets up with an agent of intentionality and can move into an action of textuality, then a temporal existentiality is possible. The Eastern-Aboriginal saw anything existential as merely a finite and not very important expression of potentiality. Simply put, 'there are, assuredly, two forms of Brahman: the formed and the formless. Now, that which is formed is unreal, while that which is formless is real, is Brahman, is light' (ibid: 361). The formless, the chaos, is basic energy and, as the source of the 'stuff' that the action of textuality moves into life, it is timeless. The spatial entity, the living being, exists within linear temporality. As temporal, imperfect, and transient forms (in the plural), it is 'unreal' and much less important. Such an understanding permits a serenity of indifference.

Diagram 2: Eastern-Aboriginal Time

Present individual life	Relative time of the individual
——————————————————	Generative force of life

Two Forms of Power

Both perspectives of time, Newtonian and Eastern-Aboriginal, see the need for more than one agential force for life to exist. One form seems to be a necessary generative force; the other form is specific to an individual's experience of life. However, there is a vast difference in the analysis of these two time forms. In Newtonian analysis, both absolute and relative times are linear and measurable. They differ only in the terms of measurement. Absolute time is measured by abstract and universal means; relative time by individual idiosyncratic definitions. The Eastern and Aboriginal societies understood only relative time as measurable; the other force is understood as the atemporal generative power that permits the linear time experience to exist. The key difference between these analyses seems to lie in the definition of absolute time.

If we translate the basic power of Newtonian absolute time as evidenced by its being duration and see it as functional to existentiality, we might reconsider the Newtonian definition to also mean 'potentiality,' the power to make time-as-content, to make that material reality within which relative time exists.

These three societies, Western, Eastern, and Aboriginal, agree that there are necessarily two forms of power required in order for existential forms to exist. One form provides potentiality; the other form provides the framework for the current experience. In the Eastern-Aboriginal frame, potentiality is atemporal; the current experience of both a society and its individual members are understood to be an expression of this basic potential of generative energy. However, the Newtonian definition of time, operating within a frame of collapsed realities, changes this open and indifferent potentiality of generative energy; it moves it into the spatiotemporal frame of the collapsed two realities. As such, generative energy becomes not pure intentionality but very specific intentionality; it acquires an exact and singular agenda of progress and change. Any society without such an agenda will be viewed as depraved and deprived, any peoples (for without an agenda they are not viewed as a society) that do not follow the agenda of progress, that do not 'till and improve' the soil, that reject 'the gifts of education, agriculture and the gospel' – such a group is aligned with whatever metaphors Western society understood as antithetical to progress, 'slaves of the divell,' like 'our English Witches.'[3] It is interesting that the images defining those people living without Newtonian linear time are also used within European society to define those atemporal beings (devils and witches) that seek to upset the careful linear plans of both God and men.

Newtonian infinite linearity changes potentiality from being an atemporal 'power to make temporal' and , by being linear, by having a goal of movement, it provides it with 'intentionality.' Intentionality is already an existentiality; it already operates within a spatiotemporal horizon. From the discussion of both the action of intentionality and the concept of otherness, we should remember that the energy forces of the Thomistic God, of quantum physics, of the agapastic evolution of Peirce, have no intentionality and no linearity of purpose. Both forms of Newtonian time must therefore be considered material because they are spatial; they are measurable and cannot be compared to the Eastern-Aboriginal definition of potential energy and relative time. A key result of both forms of time (absolute and relative) being measurable is that it removes the necessity for dialogical interaction as part of the basic action of 'making reality.' We shall discuss this shortly.

Time in Language

The Whorfian analysis of language can be considered a study of the two different forms of this absolute time, Newtonian and Aboriginal, located within two languages. The SAE (Standard Average European) is a language developed by a society with a sense of linear time, a past, present, and future linearity. 'Our objectified time puts before our imagination something like a ribbon or scroll marked off into equal blank spaces, suggesting that each be filled with an entry' (Whorf 1969: 153). Therefore, the language provides a three-tense verbal frame that can express such linearity. In comparison, the Hopi have 'no general notion or intuition of TIME as a smooth flowing continuum in which everything in the universe proceeeds at an equal rate, out of a future, through a present, into a past; or, in which, to reverse the picture, the observer is being carried in the stream of duration continuously away from a past and into a future' (ibid: 57). The 'Hopi language is seen to contain no words, grammatical forms, constructions or expressions that refer directly to what we call "time," or to past, present or future, or to enduring and lasting, or to motion as kinematic rather than dynamic (i.e. as a continous translation in space and time rather than as an exhibition of dynamic effort in a certain process), or that even refer to space in such a way as to exclude that element of extension or existence that we call "time," and so by implication leave a residue that could be referred to as "time"' (ibid: 57–8). Hence, according to Whorf, the Hopi language contains no reference to 'time,' either explicit or implicit. However, Whorf is defining time only within the Newtonian frame, as a progressive, measurable linearity of duration, and he fails to see that the Hopi do refer to the basic power of time, the power to 'make things temporal' and therefore existential; however, they define it as the potentiality of existence rather than a specific heritage and future.

A key principle in all concepts of time, to which we shall return, is the notion of this power or potentiality to become a unit of meaning. Whether this force is a linear motion or non-linear energy, it contains within it the potentiality to be a spatiotemporal unit. The exact nature of this unit that ultimately appears is not, in my analysis, predetermined in any linear sense; we can compare this with the quantum concept of a wave motion becoming a single existential unit with the 'collapse of the wave packet' (Peierls, in Davies and Brown 1986: 73). It could have become, as is well known within the complementarity theme of Niels Bohr, either a particle or a wave; its spatiotemporal life has no predetermination. Newton's absolute time, which ensures the specific potentiality of life, sees that life as progressively cumulative and definitive, while that of quantum physics sees it as indeterminate and variable. And therefore Whorf can accurately say:

[the] Hopi actually have a language better equipped to deal with such vibratile phenomena than is our latest scientific terminology. This is simply because their language establishes a general contrast between two types of experience, which contrast corresponds to a contrast that, as our science has discovered, is all-pervading and fundamental in nature. According to the conceptions of modern physics, the contrast of particle and field of vibrations is more fundamental in the world of nature than such constrasts as space and time, or past, present and future, which are the sort of contrasts that our own language imposes upon us. The Hopi aspect-contrast ... practically forces the Hopi to notice and observe vibratory phenomena and furthermore encourages them to find names for and to classify such phenomena. (1969: 55–6)

Without going into the deterministic view of Whorf and language, which said that language determines the concepts of time and matter, rather than understanding that the linguistic structure is a part of the whole social cognitive structure, we may still concur that he is actually describing two forms whereby spatiotemporal reality can come into existence. In the Western form, based around linear development, spatiotemporal reality includes time as matter; among the Hopi, time is understood to be generative and spatiotemporal reality existent simply as transient 'particles' of this energy.

Dialogical Time

If we redefine time and consider it as still existent in two forms, but which, rather than existing separately in themselves, come into existence only within a dialogical interaction, then we come up with an analysis of time, which I have earlier outlined, that is different from both the Newtonian and the Eastern-Aboriginal time frames.

Space and time come into existence only within actions of interaction (and I stress the plural) that provide ever more specific, narrow and complex horizons of existentiality, as expressed within the *implicatio / explicatio* unfolding metaphors of Bohm and the 'transformations to higher levels of complexity' of Prigogine. A dialogical interaction both sets up and functions within a frame of finite sensual and conceptual experience. It establishes horizons of space and time whereby spatiotemporal realities or 'things,' whether objects or thoughts, can exist. Space and time as existentially real come into existence within the limitations established by the interactional event, that action of textuality. The AOT and space and time come into existence together and thereby set up the horizons of their existence and the limitations on the meaning(s) that can exist within that AOT. Actions of textuality or dialogical interactions occur within the frame of the four realities, each of which has a different temporal and spatial horizon, and together act to confine and organize energy and thereby permit an action of existentiality or meaning.[4]

There are a few basic assumptions to this analysis of dialogical time. First, space and time do not exist on their own as absolute entities. Therefore, I am removing the Newtonian understanding of absolute time as a singular material reality. Peirce clearly outlined two forms of time: 'I do not question Time's being a *form*, that is, being of the nature of a Law, and not an Existence; nor its being an Intuition, that is, being at the same time a single object; nor its having a special connection with the internal world' (6: 97). There are two forms of time in this analysis, one being a law, the other being a particular. One has a power of definition that is valid within an existentiality that exists over a long period; the other is valid within an existentiality that exists only for the immediate interaction. However, both are social, both are aspects of cognitive interaction and not absolute in themselves.

Diagram 3: Dialogical Time

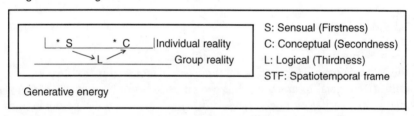

S: Sensual (Firstness)
C: Conceptual (Secondness)
L: Logical (Thirdness)
STF: Spatiotemporal frame

The Dialogic Interaction within the Social Text

We live in a text, a social reality created within the actions of conceptualization. It is here that I bring in the Bakhtinian emphasis on the social or group identity of the individual. 'No utterance in general can be attributed to the speaker exclusively; it is the product of the interaction of the interlocutors, and, broadly speaking, the product of the whole complex social situation in which it has occurred' (Voloshinov 1976: 118; quoted in

Todorov 1984: 30). And 'the entire verbal part of human existence (external and internal discourse) cannot be charged to the account of the unique subject, taken in isolation: it does not belong to the individual but to his social group (his social environment)' (128; 30). There is a strong sense here that there is a physical individual who must also become, and I stress the word become, a social individual. 'To enter into history, it is not enough to be born physically ... a second birth, social this time, is necessary as it were' (37; 31). This is what has been defined by Lacan as the 'mirror stage,' when the child becomes aware of the reality of its identity as a separate being and thereby ready for its entrance into the social reality of the symbolic order. If we consider only the action of textuality, then we can see that the sensual immediacy of the first contact must be transformed by the social logic, to permit, to enable, an action of conceptualization, the IRC. The sensual first experience is a simple one. But in order to conceptualize that experience, one must undergo a 'second birth.' Such a birth is necessarily of a different time period from the first. This second birth, via the logic of the group reality, infuses duration, which I understand to be 'time-as-content' into the simple sensuality of the first experience. It is the addition of this durational time, carried within a logical pattern, that enables human beings to be conceptual beings. This action of adding time, in its second nature as it were, as a logic of past/future duration, is carried out within the dialogical action of textuality, an interaction between two realities, which are temporally and spatially distinct from each other. This joins the two 'forms' of time, past/future and present, together.

Bakhtin gives the name 'chronotope' or time/space to 'the intrinsic connectedness of temporal and spatial relationships that are artistically expressed in literature' (1981: 84). I am not dealing with literature as a text but with society as a text. The same criteria apply. The social text is an ongoing conceptual creation that is functionally operative within the confinement of a specific, that is to say chronotopic, spatiotemporal frame. This establishes spatial and temporal indicators within which a cognitive logic and the individual generic expression of this logic can exist. An overtone that I am using from Bakhtin's analysis is the limiting, even deterministic, nature of the chronotope. Despite the totalitarian implications of the word, I respect its meaning and consider it vital to an understanding of the dialogical interaction of individual and group reality.

Individual reality can be compared with the Bakhtinian 'genres,' based as they are around specificity, 'with specific points of view, specific approaches, forms of thinking, nuances and accents characteristic of the given genre' (1981: 289). Bakhtin uses genre to refer to linguistic specificity, but I use it to refer to the individual (or a collection of like-minded individuals) as a single sensual and conceptual expression, existent in the specificity of current time and immediate space.

The long-term logic of group reality must begin within the sensual experiences of the individual, as all experiences begin within Peircean Firstness. Bakhtin points out that 'the generic forms, at first productive, were then reinforced by tradition; in their subsequent development they continued stubbornly to exist' (1985: 85). Exactly as Peirce said, habits rise from 'the passage of Variety into Uniformity' (6: 97). Within the society, I translate this to suggest that the chronotopic logic of a group reality begins within the generic experiences of the individual and gradually becomes heritage to a group, and therefore establishes limits to the cognitive future of that group. Dialogic contact 'of even the most simple and everyday variety, would introduce its own rule-generating force, its own order, its inevitable ties to human life and to the time specific to that life. Events would end up being interwoven with these rules, and to a greater or lesser extent would find themselves participating in this order, subject to its ties' (Bakhtin 1981: 100). The chronotopic logic is a product of individuals, and I emphasize that the social logic must always be answerable to its origins, to the sensual-conceptual realities of its individuals. This is an ongoing accountability; if the continual dialogue between these two realities is in any way harmed, we are left with a degenerate logic that is absolute and alienated rather than reflexive.

It is emphasized that the three-point dialogical action of the action of textuality is not linear but an instantaneous interaction of two temporal realities, the past/future of the group reality and the immediacy of the individual reality. In other terms, atemporal and aspatial generative energy becomes locked into a long-term temporal group or communal logical order, be it the DNA or other atomic order; it is given individual expression that is also particle existence by a further interaction that fuses current temporality to the past/future group logical order. It is this *implicatio / explicatio* unfolding interaction that permits both phases of time, the past/future and the immediate, to exist. The immediate experience cannot exist without the cognitive logic with which to express it; the past/future logic cannot exist except within the experiences of the immediate individual. Together, meaning, which is to say, sensuo-conceptual reality, is created.

Literature and the Social Text

If we can define the temporal structure of a society, we can then understand the nature of its conceptual reality. There are many variations of the two basic forms of understanding time, dialogic and linear. These can be explored within the literature of a society.

Adventure Time

Bakhtin speaks of early Greek literature, (see diagram 4) whose 'adventure-time lacks any natural, everyday cyclicity,' such that 'no matter where one goes in the world of the Greek romance, with all its countries and cities, its buildings and works of art, there are absolutely no indications of historical time, no identifying traces of the era,' for 'all of the action in a Greek romance, all the events and adventures that fill it, constitute time-sequences that are neither historical, quotidian, biographical, nor even biological and maturational. actions lie outside these sequences, beyond the reach of that force, inherent in these sequences, that generates rules and defines the measure of a man. In this kind of time, nothing changes: the world remains as it was, the biographical life of the heroes does not change, their feelings do not change, people do not even age. This empty time leaves no traces anywhere, no indications of its passing' (1981: 91).

What we have here is a literature whose time frame lacks contact with the daily reality of individual life. There is no semiosis of the individual in his current sensual and conceptual temporality. The story line in this literature is 'characterized by ... the *reversibility* of moments in a temporal sequence' (1981: 100). Such a description of time refers only to the past/future temporal structure of group reality. This is a literature based only within the temporal reality of the group; there is no contact with the current time of individual reality. There is therefore no possibility of dialogue; conceptual reality here can only be a mimetic copy of the past. This adventure time is, like Newtonian time, absolute in its measurements and abstracted from the individual's relativity of perception. Therefore, 'it goes without saying that in this type of time, an individual can be nothing other than completely passive, completely unchanging' (105). However, unlike Newtonian time, there is no sense of cumulation and progress. Within the Greek social text, as expressed in its literature, the individual is bound within the past, to continue it into the future. This form is also the conceptual base of a variety of modern ethnocentric and self-absorbed groups, from ethnic to feminist, who regard their 'individual' reality as a direct iconic expression of the innate consciousness of the closed collective.

I have also said that group reality lacks space in itself, because space can only be experienced as a particular sensual and conceptual reality. This is only possible within the existentiality of current time, which is expressed by

Diagram 4: (Group Reality Only)

```
┌─────────────────────────────────────────────────────────┐
│  ................................................. Individual reality (current time)  │
│  _____ Group reality (past/future time)  │
└─────────────────────────────────────────────────────────┘
```

individual reality. Since the literature of 'adventure time' is non-dialogical and is alienated from individual reality, then its logic lacks spatial particularity and 'can virtually occur in any geographical space or historical time' (Clark and Holquist 1984: 282). It is important to note that Bakhtin is referring to material that is in print; that is, these tales may very well and in all likelihood did stem from oral literature. In this case, the Greek 'adventure time' literature may lack contact with daily reality because it, and the society that was using it, had removed itself from its original individual reality, which was found only within oral interaction. This written literature might well belong to a not yet developed class that was removing itself from its past dialogic infrastructure and developing a new individual reality, that would belong to the reader, the writer, and not the oral teller of tales.[5]

Oral Folk-Tale

In contrast, the oral folk-tale, as examined by Albert Lord (diagram 3), is dialogic in that 'a song is the story about a given hero, but its expressed forms are multiple, and each of these expressed forms or tellings of the story is itself a separate song, in its own right, authentic and valid as a song unto itself.' The oral folk-tale is built upon a stable 'skeleton of narrative' (1971: 100, 99) that is unchanging, but the particular expression, the actual song that details that narrative theme, depends upon the audience. What we see here is that the group reality, that logic, is the thematic structure, the key points, of the tale. There is a double individual reality: it exists as both the audience and the singer of tales. Each time and place that it is told, the tale is similar in that it retains its basic themes (within the GR logic) that both the singer and the audience share, and yet it is different, for the song must express the daily sensuality, the conceptual reality within which both audience and singer are currently existing. A dialogical interaction is one that heavily involves both speaker and listener, writer and reader, and above all it must involve both temporal realities. The singer and audience are both keepers of the group reality and must supply the understanding of these temporal themes to the current song. Both are bringing in the current individual realities within which the collective is expressed. The song is at once the tradition and an individual action, and 'syngynge tyll us that the dey cummyng is.' This is a dialogic interaction and is expressed in such folk-tales, as well as the novel of Bakhtinian analysis, which is an 'orchestration' of the social and the individual, 'artistically organized' (Bakhtin 1981: 262).

Adventure: Everyday, Romance, Spy

Bakhtin's 'Greek adventure time of everyday life'[6] seems to suggest that the two realities, with their two temporal natures, are combined. Both the long-term logic of group reality and the immediacy of individual reality are present in this form of literature. But they are not combined in a dialogical frame, as in the oral folk-tale, but in a linear manner. They deal with specific events and individuals, each locked into what Braudel has called a 'nouvelle sonnante,' a matter of a moment (1980: 27). Life is then a matter of the linear movement, step by step, of these individuals and events. What happens here is that the two realities, group and individual, collapse their distinct identities into one level of reality (diagram 5). This means that the past/future temporal natures of group reality, which have no spatial existence of their own, are in this degenerate collapsed form each given material existential natures. Each time phase exists as an isolate spatiotemporal world unto itself. However, this is not a measured and guaranteed Newtonian linearity; the movement of individuals from time block to time block is uncertain, violent, and fraught with difficulties.

Diagram 5: Collapsed Realities

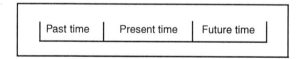

This is a basic format of all romantic literature, where the movement from handsome prince in the past to current ugly monster to handsome prince in the future are all violent actions, carried out via the intermediary actions of various devils, witches, or princesses. This form is not dialogical, because both realities, with their two different temporal natures of past/future and present, actually exist in space. The hero moves from past to current to future spatiotemporal site in a linear fashion. How is this done? Where is the impetus for this movement from world to world? The dialogical structure sets up a binary frame that demands interactive movement in order for each level to exist. Without this structure and without the guarantee of Newtonian sequence, how does one get from temporal site 'past' to temporal site 'now'? The answer – and we must remember that this is a material and a social as well as a literary answer – is the usage of intermediary forces and agents. This literature exists in a society where both the collective and the individual are powerless, and therefore strong use is made of saints, witches, devils, angels – and presidents, generals, lobbyists, or consumer goods, anyone or anything that is deemed to have access to that most basic energy of all, the atemporal and aspatial power called generative energy.

However, in all forms of romantic literature, where the temporal frame is one-leveled rather than dialogic, these agents are ritualistic or part of the tale. They are predictable rather than being, as in the Bakhtinian carnival, ambivalent, transgressional, and unpredictable. Such romantic literature, like the official feasts of the Middle Ages, did 'not lead the people out of the existing world order,' but it sanctioned 'the existing pattern of things and reinforced it ... the official feast asserted all that was stable, unchanging, perennial: the existing hierarchy, the existing religious, political and moral values, norms and prohibitions ... This is why the tone of the official feast was monolithically serious and why the element of laughter was alien to it' (Bakhtin 1984b: 9). Literature of this sort, the romantic novels, spy novels, mysteries, films, and television shows with these themes, are very serious. They show that things happen, that change is possible only by non-human means; they clearly explain that we individuals who are living in this unileveled social structure have no power at all to make anything happen.

Bakhtin's action of carnival accesses generative energy[7] and 'was the true feast of time, the feast of becoming, change and renewal ... It was hostile to all that was immortalized and completed' (1984b: 10). In that sense, carnival, which I understand as a non-normative action done by an individual in the sensual immediacy of current time, is against the spatiotemporal finiteness of the dialogical frame of reality. It is an action that bypasses the spatiotemporal frame to access generative energy. As I have said, reality as we know it is finite because, in order to experience it both sensually and conceptually, it is necessary to create spatial and temporal boundaries. To move beyond these boundaries, to access different worlds, requires access to energy that can be used to create these new worlds with their different energy content, their different cognitive frameworks. A carnival literature can be understood as imbued with this sense of energy, power, and change. It would be a vital part of a dialogic society, because a socio-conceptual frame, particularly when dialogic and therefore finite, will entropically decay. New energy to be used within that dialogical structure will be necessary. Because it is so individual, sensual, and immediate, art in whatever form, literary or other, is one of the key means, but I stress not the only means, of accessing new energy and, importantly, locking it into the group logic. In this sense, carnival actions, whether in art or physics, because they involve the element of surprise and invention, are not an expression of the aesthetics of the civilized mind but are rather a necessary means of being a dialogic society.

There are other forms of literature defined by their spatiotemporal frame. Newtonian literature (diagram 1) would be found in biography, history,[8] and positivistic science. As Bakhtin notes about the Plutarch biographical type, 'character itself does not grow, does not change, it is merely filled in: at the beginning it is incomplete, imperfectly disclosed, fragmentary; it becomes full and well rounded only at the end' (1981: 141). The Eastern-Aboriginal frame (diagram 2) is expressed within the epic, the religious tract, and the anthropological monograph, which are all understood as 'the transferral of a represented world into the past, ... the epic has been from the beginning a poem about the past, and the authorial position ... is the environment of a man speaking about a past that is to him inaccessible, the reverent point of view of a descendent' (13). Although the individuals in the epic, religious experience, and anthropological monograph are existent now, in current time, they are only representations of 'an utterly different and inaccessible time-and-value plane, separated by epic distance.' To portray an event that includes interaction with both realities and both time frames is 'to step out of the world of epic into the world of the novel' (14).

Surrealism, Deconstruction

Then there is the spatiotemporal frame that exists only within individual reality and lacks any contact with a group reality (diagram 6). This infrastructure permits an experience of only Peircean Firstness, sensation without understanding. It can only be sensual, for it lacks the logical means to move from the sensual to the conceptual; can only be immediate, for it lacks a past/future logic. Such a literature is surrealistic, fleeting, and amorphous, and is found among deconstructionist texts and films that insist on the instability of endless interpretations. It is found in the monographs of discursive anthropology that focus only on subjective experience and insist on a perception of the society as an open text, a 'manuscript' that is 'foreign, faded, full of ellipses, incoherencies, suspicious emendations, and tendentious commentaries ... written not in conventionalized graphs of sound but in

Diagram 6: Individual Reality Only

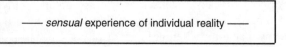

transient examples of shaped behavior' (Geertz 1973: 10). And, 'what matters for ethnography is the claim that all human groups write ... they repeatedly "textualize" meanings' (Clifford 1986: 117).

Conclusion

In contrast, dialogical literature and the dialogical society is the 'weaving of historical and socio-public events together with the personal and even deeply private side of life' (Bakhtin 1981: 247). Between these two realities, the individual and the group, there is a constant dialogue, a necessary dialogue in that this binary structure is not simply conceptually binary (as in the Saussurian, Barthes, Lévi-Strauss frames) – a frame existent only on one level – but is organically binary. By this I mean that each reality has a different temporal and spatial identity. Individual reality exists in current time, and therefore in space. To move from sensual immediacy to conceptual awareness, it must interact with group reality. Group reality is a logic existent in past/future time, and, lacking current time, does not exist in itself in space. For group reality to exist in its conceptuality, it must interact with the immediate spatial reality of the individual. Together, reality as an accountable conceptual experience of our own sensual identity is possible. It is this accountability – a word I stress, accountability – where each reality must answer to the other for veracity and for completeness, that provides the power of the dialogical structure of society.

Diagram 1: Newtonian Time

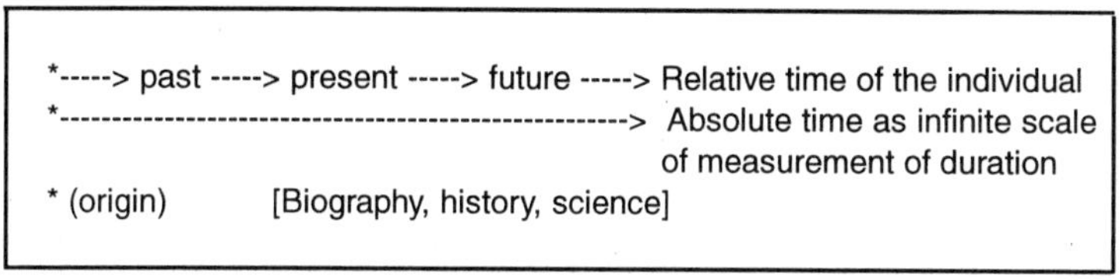

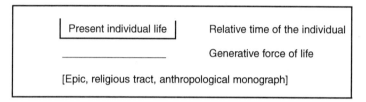

```
*-----> past -----> present -----> future -----> Relative time of the individual
*-------------------------------------------------> Absolute time as infinite scale
                                                    of measurement of duration
* (origin)         [Biography, history, science]
```

Diagram 2: Eastern-Aboriginal Time

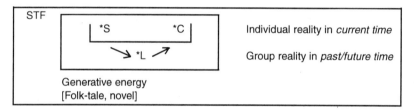

| Present individual life | Relative time of the individual |

Generative force of life

[Epic, religious tract, anthropological monograph]

Diagram 3A: Dialogical Time

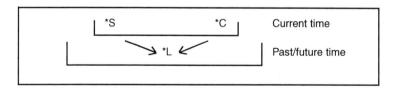

STF

*S   *C   Individual reality in *current time*

↘ *L ↗   Group reality in *past/future time*

Generative energy
[Folk-tale, novel]

S: Sensual (Firstness)
C: Conceptual (Secondness)
L: Logical (Thirdness)
STF: Spatiotemporal frame of reality

Diagram 3B: Motion of Conceptualization in Dialogical Time

*S   *C   Current time

↘ *L ↙   Past/future time

Diagram 4: Group Reality Only

```
┌──────────────────────────────────────────────────────┐
│  ...................................Individual reality (current time) │
│  _____Group reality (past/future time)    │
│                                                        │
│  [Adventure-time]                                      │
└──────────────────────────────────────────────────────┘
```

Diagram 5: Collapsed Realities

```
┌──────────────────────────────────────────────────┐
│   │ Past time │ Present time │ Future time │      │
│                                                    │
│   [Adventure: everyday, romance, spy]              │
└──────────────────────────────────────────────────┘
```

Diagram 6: Individual Reality Only

```
┌──────────────────────────────────────────────────┐
│   ----sensual experience of individual reality----  │
│                                                    │
│   [Surrealism, deconstruction]                     │
└──────────────────────────────────────────────────┘
```

5

The Pattern of Cognition

I reject the Word. The perfect Form of Plato, the sealed Sign of Saussure, the static Object of Bacon and Descartes. In these analyses, the Word exists as truth, complete within and of itself, separate from intellectual or sensual contacts, aloof and necessarily untouched and untampered by the motions of interaction. The Word as an autocracy grows despotic. Differences in actualities of the Word are untenable. Differences in perception or understanding of the Word are understood as culpabilities of the agential reading.

In contrast, the cognition that I have been discussing exists only within action. It lives or rather, becomes a spatiotemporal life, within a dialogical interaction, a sharing of energies between realities. Therefore, there can be no intact, pre-dialogical or adialogical, word-in-itself. Meaning is an action, a motion of shared energy that organizes and transforms action into 'units of cognition' or spatiotemporal experiences of meaning.

A key requirement for any species, both biological and social, is the perpetuity of the purity and distinctness of that species, 'pure' in that it perpetuates only itself and not a new species, 'distinct' in that it is separate from another species. Such a system maintains the global biological requirement of biological diversity. These variations in both the physical and biological strata of the natural world prevent decay into a universal static entropy. I see no reason to think that the social world is any different in its need for the vitality of diverse species and social group variation. Group reality, as I have pointed out, is the means by which a social group maintains its longevity as a pure and distinct entity. Individual reality provides that social group with its current-time existential ability to express its long-term habits, and also provides a means to differ from these habits sufficiently to permit more immediate adaptation and variation.

My analysis of cognition requires a zone of mediation as a means for the organization/transformation of energy from potential to actual meaning, from IRS to IRC. I locate mediation within the past/future spatiotemporal node of group reality, that cognitive action that in all species but humans is genetic and in humans is social. Mediation is an action of organization between the other two nodes, sensual and conceptual, of individual reality. This triadic and dialogical node structure, made up of these two different existential natures (the individual and the group), means that cognition cannot be analysed as simple reception or transmission, which are direct forces between two nodes rather than mediated and transformed actions. Simple reception/transmission of images are actions of 'communication' and take place only within the existentiality of individual reality. They package and move data from one spatial zone to another; there is no sharing of energy, no transformation by reorganization, and therefore they have nothing to do with cognition. These two terms – communication and cognition – should not be confused.

Mediation as a creative force between sensual experience and cognition has been well examined within medieval semiotics. Aristotle's concept of the soul sets up a zone of habit similar to Peirce's use of Thirdness. For Aristotle there is no direct connection between the IRS and the IRC, object and sign, or to use his terms, matter and form.[1] His term for this site of the action of knowledge, this zone between the sensual and the conceptual, is the soul. It is not an independent entity (as in the Platonic or Cartesian duality of mind and matter) but is rather a part of a whole, a whole that exists in action. It is 'that by which we live or sense or think, it would be the formula or the form but not the matter of the subject' (ibid, B, 414a: 13). This formula, as with the Thirdness of the group reality, does not exist on its own; 'those who think that the soul does not exist without a body or is not a body of any sort have the right belief' (ibid, 414a: 20). And, 'the soul is the cause and the principle of a living body' (ibid, 415b: 9) in the sense of its having the power of intentionality. The concepts of a long-term zone of habit acting as a mediator between the sensual and conceptual states of the individual, and importantly, acting within motion, were held by Aristotle, Boethius, Aquinas, and others of the Scholastic era, and missing or rejected in the Baconian/ Cartesian dualist era.[2]

The Syntactic Pattern

Mediation as an agency for the transformation of sensual energy to conceptual form can be analysed as a pattern within which that energy is confined, refined, and transformed into a finite entity, a unit of meaning. As such a pattern, it functions not only as a logic of organization, but also a horizon, a limit on the existence and nature of potential meaning. This idea of the existence of horizons of cognitive actuality, of limits to what can be thought, has been discussed in chapters 1, 2, and 3 within my analyses of group reality. As I have mentioned, it is not a new concept and exists not merely in the fields of semiosis but also in the social sciences. Braudel defines 'la longue durée' as 'a history capable of traversing even greater distances, a history to be measured in centuries this time: the history of the long, even of the very long time span, of the longue durée ... in differentiation from the immediate "event"' (1980: 27). And certainly the conceptual structures of living exist as 'an organization, a coherent and fairly fixed set of relationships between realities and social masses ... Some structures, because of their long life, become stable elements for an infinite number of generations: they get in the way of history, hinder its flow, and in hindering it shape it ... As hindrances they stand as limits ("envelopes," in the mathematical sense) beyond which man and his experiences cannot go' (31). Lévi-Strauss calls his 'level of order' 'the conceptual scheme by the operation of which matter and form, neither with any independent existence, are realized as structures, that is as entities which are both empirical and intelligible' (1966: 130). Chomsky calls his generative rules an 'intricate system of rules by which patterns are formed, modified and elaborated' (1964: 58). The patterns formed via this deep level of rules of 'competence' assign a structural description that specifies the linguistic or conscious elements. Foucault variously calls this level the 'pure experience of order' (1973b: xxi), codes, modes of being, episteme, archive, and power. The archive is that which 'does not have the weight of tradition, and it does not constitute the library of all libraries, outside time and place' (1972: 130). In other words, it is not stored historical consciousness; it is 'anterior to words, perceptions and gestures' (1973b: xxi); it does not consist of symbolic units; it is rather 'a group of rules that characterize discursive practice but these rules are not imposed from the outside on the elements that they relate together; they are caught up in the very things that they connect' (1972: 127). Bourdieu's 'habitus' is the 'principles of the generation and structuring of practices and representations' (1977: 72). Baudrillard speaks of the 'code,' and says that 'in the exchange of products, it is not only economic values, but the code, this fundamental code that circulates and is reproduced' (1975: 54). Kuhn has suggested that we can only know the environment by means of a 'paradigm' that has a 'status prior to that of shared rules and assumptions' (1970: 49). Ernest Gellner has called such a structure the 'norms of cognition,' and he writes that Descartes observed that 'if the first button be wrongly done up, then so will all the others be; and the first button is concerned with how we know, how we authenticate truth claims, and not what we know' (1974: 28). Many others, such as Freud, Greimas, Habermas, Heidegger, Gadamer, have talked of a conceptual horizon that orders and indeed defines how we understand ourselves and our environment. These various descriptions are not completely similar, and indeed, some may even be critiqued as extant conceptual structures rathe than logics for the formation of cognitive actions. But one thing they share is an awareness that certain factors of cognition that are not immediately perceivable play an important role for us as social beings.

The syntactic logic of a society is a method of organizing and limiting cognition. It exists as a logic, a pattern for the organization of free or potential energy that can transform it into the bound energy of cognitive units. The logic, therefore, is only a pattern of organization and not an actuality. As Aristotle pointed out with reference to the soul, it cannot be considered existential in current temporality, for it has no current spatiotemporal definition, no current spatiotemporal nature. It is therefore not an actual system of behaviour or systemic structure, such as those of Durkheim or Lévi-Strauss. Nor is it a social unit such as Dawkins' 'meme,' a 'unit of cultural transmission, or a unit of imitation ... examples of memes are tunes, ideas, catchphrases, clothes fashions, ways of making pots or of building arches' (1978: 206). The memes are reproduced when others pick up the original idea and imitate it, using a genre or code system. Such Platonic-style IRC units of original purity, where 'differences in the ways that people represent the theory are then, by definition, not part of the meme' (210), belong only within the current reality of the level of individual reality and can be compared to the external form, as explained in chapter 1. The GR logic is a pattern of organization and not the resultant conceptual forms. As with the Aristotelian soul, it is a 'formula of that which has the potentiality of being such and such a thing' (*De Anima*, B, 414a: 28). Bohm with his implicate order describes it well as 'a general relationship (or law) expressing a force of necessity which binds together a certain set of the elements of the implicate order in such a way that they contribute to a common explicate end (different from that to which another set of inter-penetrating and intermingling elements will contribute)' (1980: 195). The GR logic is a group-based pattern of cognition, within which the conscious selection, ordering, imagizing, and comprehension of sensual reality can take place. It sets up and defines the interactional behaviour of each intra-unit and of the whole group with the non-group. It is a long-term pattern, and as such 'hereditary' by means of social transference. A logical pattern can be maintained and usually is, for centuries, but it can also be changed, a topic to be discussed in

chapter 6. The fact that it can be changed, and usually within one generation, is a vital factor in the adaptive capacity of human beings. As a pattern,
it is separate from the sensuo-conceptual reality of individual reality, but as a
necessary part of that reality, as the key to the existence of consciousness, it
cannot be abstracted and considered to exist – except in analytic terms. It is
not universal (as compared to Chomsky's 'competence') but varies with a
society. A logic can be held and used by one person (the person who per-
ceives the world differently from his fellows, the 'mad' scientist), but as a
pattern it exists only within an action, an interaction within the self and/or
with others.

Biology and Logic

A society or group can be understood as a single organism, a complete,
distinct, and living entity. By the term 'living' I mean that the social group
can be understood as a socially organized *biological* system. A biological system is 'characterized by exergonic metabolism, growth and replication, all
organized in a closed causal process' (Maturana 1970: 5). Again, Maturana
writes that 'for every living system, its niche is represented in its organization
as a domain of its possible interactions, and this domain constitutes its entire
cognitive reality' (ibid). Fleischaker writes that, in biological systems, 'in the
model of operation closure, it is that stable pattern of response or repeated
behaviour of the whole system in interaction with other systems, or with its
niche, that defines the nature of any particular living system' (1984: 47). And
Varela and Johnson write of the nervous system that it should be considered
'not as an input-output information processing device, as is the current understanding in neurophysiology, but rather as a closed unit of perception
and action to maintain internally generated reference levels' (1976: 28). A
society can also be characterized as an organically closed system, functioning by defined and closed 'patterns of response' that form and reform the
operative life of the constantly renewable human beings living within that
structure. A society is an organization of variable 'heteroglossic'[3] units of
energy, all interacting with one another, changing and transforming one
another. This interaction operates within a defined, organized, and confined
logic. In biological systems the logic or pattern is maintained by the genetic
code and permits a long-term maintenance of that particular species. In social systems, the logic is developed and stored socially within the long-term
sociocultural interactions and habits of the group. The difference between
the biological and social logic is that the latter, being social and learned, can
be changed without the complete biological and physical change of the species. Such a method provides a greater range of adaptability over a much

shorter time span than the biological method, which may take many generations to accomplish an adaptational and possibly species change. As
Aquinas says of the 'will,' which I consider to have some similarities to a
syntactic pattern in the sense of its contraints, 'although the will wills the last
end by a certain necessary inclination, it is nevertheless in no way to be
granted that it is forced to will it' (*De ver.* q. 22a. 5); that is, it can be changed.

I am quite openly saying that a society, like a biological organism, operates within a restrictive logical code. I may therefore be understood to com-
mit two heresies. One is my insistence on combining rather than separating
nature and culture. The assumption that these two forms of life, the natural
and the social, are separate is simply that – an assumption and not a basic
truth. All forms of life, by which I mean that which has a spatiotemporal
reality, operate within a pattern of organization, a logic specific to their
physical, biological, or social nature; this logic orders both their internal and
external existentialities. Societies are as organic as natural life; they consist
of spatiotemporally finite 'units' (individuals) interacting within defined
and stable patterns of behaviour that maintain a long-term, continuously
regenerating 'way of existence.' Societies develop, grow, and die. The
key difference, as I have said, is that the 'codes' of the social organism
are socially, rather than biologically or physically developed and maintained. The other heresy is the suggestion that societies are closed organisms; there is no such thing as a 'universal society' because the biomic realities of geographic ecological differences are part of a society's organic
nature. Marx's dream of a global community is more myth than potential
reality. I maintain that many comparisons can be made between biological
and social life, comparisons that are natural and not simply metaphoric
similarities.

GR Logic as a Sentence of Organization

The logic of group reality is not an ideal image, nor the accumulated history,
the systems and institutions, the rules and behavioural norms that act as the
storage centres and model-formers of society, such as language, family, education, economic, religious, and cultural systems. Rather, it is a long-term
socially developed pattern of organization within which all these systems
function; it is a pattern by means of which open energy is transformed to
closed energy, and so potential meaning becomes actual meaning. The GR
organization moves free energy or the potentiality-to-mean (or 'be organically existent') into actual organic (meaningful) existence.

All humans have an innate requirement to differentiate their environment into units or finite entities and a relation or interaction between these finite units. Lacan clearly pointed this out in his discussion of the movement from the mirror stage to the symbolic stage. If we remind ourselves of the Peircean insistence that cognition is an action, then we must see the logic of cognition as something that activates and permits action to exist. Therefore, the logical pattern should be a pattern of an action, a pattern of an interaction. This is why, when I describe GR logic, I use the term 'syntax,' understood as an 'arrangment and interrelationship of words.' The logic of group reality is never of a single unit, but is a pattern that permits single units to be interactive with other units, and it sets up this interaction in a definite pattern.

The Pattern of Organization

If we consider consciousness on the level of individual reality, we may see that it consists of three vital elements: an actor, an acted-upon/with, and an action. Cognition is not simply 'cat' but 'this-is-cat' or 'cat-eats-food.' The interaction of these three elements is not haphazard and free but set into a pattern that has a powerful role in our cognition. It is this pattern, operative at the GR nodal point, that organizes and transforms energy from the IRS and moves it into the IRC nodal site of specific consciousness.

This pattern can possibly be more clearly understood if we visualize it in the form of a sentence, as if it had a subject, a verb, and an object, operative within a definite pattern. It must be emphasized that the logic is not, in its own reality, this sentence. It is an *action of organization* of the GR nodal point; it is not a thing-in-itself. The use of the sentence is simply an aid to understanding its organizational nature.

The syntax has three divisions of subject, verb, and object. We could also refer to them as agent, relation, and entity to lessen the influence of the term 'sentence,' but for the sake of simplicity I shall use the former terms. As a complete action, the subject, verb, and object function within a specific pattern. The syntactic logic can be understood as a pattern of restrictive potentiality . It permits sensation to be a 'verb' as opposed to an 'subject' or 'object'; to be a subject as opposed to an object; it permits the subject and object to act together or separate from each other. These potentials are not open but are absolutely fixed within a finite, limited pattern. That is, a society will operate within one dominant syntactic logic, not within multiple patterns. If it did that, it would not be able to function as a coherent group and should not then be considered a society but a collection of quite possibly asocial individuals.

The following is a particular pattern that the three parts might take:

Subject:	Verb:	Object.

An example of this pattern is expressed in the phrase, man/grows/wheat. This is one pattern of interaction, which I term a type B logic. Using the same semantic terms, I can change the cognitive pattern to man-wheat/grow. This is a type A logic. The same terms, but a different pattern of interaction between them and a different semantic conception of relationships. In the first pattern, it is quite clear that it is man who is actively causing wheat to grow, along with other agents within his active control, such as earth, fertilizer, seed, water. In the other pattern, man and wheat are together involved in an action of growing. Man is growing as wheat is growing as man is growing. This is not the metaphor of Daphne and her tree, which obliterated the one to permit the other, but that of man and woman moulded by Zeus as separate, so that 'love for one another has been implanted in the human race,' and by the 'sweetness of their coupling' they would propagate the race and enable its survival. Neither is specifically causal of the other but both are instead intertwined within their existentiality. Neither is the 'object' of the other. In fact, as will be discussed further, in the type A syntactic pattern there is no object.

The pattern of interaction of subject, verb, and object within the sentence can vary, and so too does the nature of the individual reality that emerges. Consciousness of the environment, therefore, is a selective and not a simple arbitrary or reactive process. The actualization, the making conscious of the environment by such a cognitive structure, is done at the expense of other possible structures and therefore other possible cognitions. Limitations on comprehension of the world are a precondition for consciousness of that world. Each method of articulation or consciousness of the environment is of such a different logic that the experience of living in each cannot be compared, reality to reality, and must be viewed as completely alien. There are numerous examples, such as the scholastic and the Lutheran clash of worldviews in sixteenth-century Europe, the Western and Eastern precapitalist perspectives, the colonial and indigenous peoples' total alienation from each other's ideology. Such differences are not simply those within the everyday individual experience of different foods, family, economic and political systems but refer to deeper and less accessible, less translatable frames of thought.

Type A Logic and Type B Logic

These patterns are the existential basis for the group's comprehension of the environment. The importance of this logical pattern to meaning cannot be underestimated. Barthes has said that 'the future task of semiology is far less to establish lexicons of objects than to rediscover the articulations which men impose on reality' (1967: 57). I suggest that there are only two, which I term type A and type B. This can at first glance be superficially compared with other basic 'binarisms' in social thought, such as, following the same order as types A and B, Durkheim's savagism and civilized, Lévi-Strauss's bricolage and scientific,[4] Rousseau's natural and civilized, Vico's poetic and logical, and even right- and left-brain comprehension. However, I emphasize that my analysis of the GR logics is quite different from and can in no way be reduced to the above binarisms. It is not simply that no value terms (savage, civilized) are applied to them, but that the GR logic has no historic foundation. Type A logic is found within a tribal hunting and gathering society, European feudalism, *and also* modern late-industrial society. Further, the two logics are not oppositional in the manner of all the above binarisms. The logic refers only to the pattern by which the energy of a society is organized – with energy understood as population, resources (both material and conceptual), and technology. Either logic may organize a small or a large amount of energy. That is, both are viable within large or small populations, simple or complex technology. There is no hint here of progressive or evolutionary movement between these syntactic logics. The difference between them is only in the conceptual understanding of what is known as reality and the relations that individuals have with each other and their environment.

The most stable pattern is type A. This logic permits a society to establish its cognitive and technological reality and maintain it with little change over many centuries. Type B appears only within what I have previously defined as collapsed realities, when the two levels, individual and group reality, merge into one level – a 'degenerate' form of cognitive reality that collapses the dialogue with social habit. This permits a long-term phase of several generations of bypassing the horizons of stability and thereby accessing the randomness and potential for variation of generative energy. This type B logic emerges from and into type A; it cannot exist on its own for long periods of time. It is short-term but extremely powerful, for it provides almost constant access to generative energy and, as will be discussed, provides more of the population with the right to access and use the potential changes of generative energy. We now turn to a more exact description of these two logical patterns.

The nodal point of the GR level organizes energy from the IRS, the sensual node. It does this via two different patterns of organization. The particular or semantic IRC experiences of individual reality differ according to whether the mediation pattern of group reality is type A or type B.

Type A Syntax

The type A pattern is:

Subject/Object	Verb

The type A pattern puts *both* the subject and the object in the subject part of the sentence. There is no independent object. This permits an understanding that the subject and object are consciously differentiated from each other but are operative together. For example, 'man/wheat | grow.' Both man and wheat are active subjects in growth. When the man harvests the wheat he will, dependent on whether it is an early indigenous or late industrial society, thank the formative earth spirit or the basic nutritive value of the wheat for assisting him in his own life span.

Their relations are an act of discourse between them, a vital interaction of self-existence. Barthes wrote that the modern writer is 'born simultaneously with the text' (1977: 145). The writer and the text emerge in their respective self-consciousness together. Eco writes of an 'open' work of music, in contrast to a 'closed' work, that a performer (agent) of an open work does some of the actual 'organizing and structuring of the musical discourse. He collaborates with the composer in making the composition' (1979: 56). Readerly analysis makes, in varying degrees, somewhat similar points (Fish, De Man, Iser). Iser's implied reader exists via 'predispositions laid down, not by an empirical outside reality, but by the text itself' (1978: 34). As Foucault writes of discursive acts, 'they are caught up in the very things that they connect; and if they are not modified with the least of them, they modify them' (1972: 127).

This actualization or emergence into consciousness of the subject and object in the same action is a key to the unique nature of this cognitive frame. The logical sentence does not include an object that is effectively separated from the subject. In type A, the object exists *within* the interactional exchange with the subject, not as a separate functional entity. It is not only the object that is affected by the verb; both the subject and object are alike affected. Consider the sentence 'The man cuts down the tree.' Both type A and type B people, on the individual-reality level, physically differentiate the tree from the man. But to the type A mentality, the cognitive pattern is 'man/tree | cuts down.' Therefore the individual who is cognizant in this pattern has the conception (IRC) that the verbal action of cutting affects *both groups*, the tree and the human being. On the other hand, the type B cognitive pattern would order the same words as 'man/cuts down/ tree.' The subject is not also an object of the verbal act. The individual functioning within this cognitive logic considers that the action of cutting affects only the tree. Type A logic not produce a separate object existential in its own right. It is 'poetry without the poem, production without the product' (Barthes 1974: 45). The Mbuti pygmies, when on the hunt, pass through the smoke of a fire because 'the smoke invoke[s] the spirit of the forest, and by passing through it the hunters [seek] to fill themselves with that spirit, not so much to make the hunt successful as to minimize the sacrilege of killing' (Turnbull 1983: 41). Neither the hunter nor the hunted can be abstracted from the action; both are subjects and objects within the same action; both are hunters and both are equally the hunted.

Semantic Forms of the IRC Node

I have been discussing the means of organization of the GR node and have explained that it organizes energy within two syntactic patterns, A and B. The IRC node further refines this energy coming from the syntactic pattern to produce distinct semantic or individually existent signs. The IRC node of Peircean Secondness permits the individual consciousness a specific cognitive interaction, understood as Peirce's interpretant, Saussure's signified. However, as a formal means of organizing energy within the triadic interaction, this node operates within what I term a semantic frame of organization, which Peirce termed the 'Final Interpretant' to distinguish it from the 'Immediate Interpretant.' The Immediate Interpretant 'is the interpretant as it is revealed in the right understanding of the Sign itself, and is ordinarily called the *meaning* of the sign; while in the second place we have to take note of the Dynamical Interpretant which is the actual effect which the Sign, as a Sign, really determines. Finally, there is what I provisionally term the Final Interpretant, which refers to the manner in which the Sign tends to represent itself to be related to its Object' (4: 536). Peirce classified these forms by which the sign represents itself into sixty-six classes, outlined in his Division of Signs.[5]

I shall now discuss the IRC, not in its nature as an Immediate or Dynamical Interpretant, as individual consciousness of the result of the triadic interaction, but in its nature as the code system, the 'manner of representation' of this interaction. I term this system of the final interpretant, the system of semantic signs.

The semantic signs of the IRC node are also organized within a binary frame, but this binarism is quite different from the GR syntactic binarism. Syntactic binarism is the presence/absence of a particular logical pattern. The GR syntactic nodal point organizes energy into only one of two types, the presence of either an A or B logic. Only one syntactic type can be dominant in a society, though there may be smaller groups within the society operating by the other logic. Semantic binarism, on the other hand, refers to the organization of the coded expressions of the IRC node along a closed ordinal scale having two poles. As a scale of terms, rather than a presence/absence form of existence, it permits a variety of expressions both within a particular society and even between societies. Therefore, you may have a society operating within type B syntax, but its IRC code system, the everyday semantic expressions of this logic, may vary over two hundred years without there being a change in logic. Fifteenth-century Europe and eighteenth-century Europe, seemingly quite different on the semantic (historic) level, nevertheless functioned within the same type B logic. As another example, two societies may both operate within type A logic, but their semantic IRC expressions of that logic may vary (to a limited extent). I mentioned previously that a sixteenth-century Aboriginal society and our late industrial society both function within a type A logic. A less dramatic example is the Chinese Shang dynasty and the Dobe !Kung, both examples of a type A syntactic logic. The actual IRC code terms may differ but the logic is the same.

The horizons or binary poles of the ordinal scale and the variations of normative semantic expressions between these poles are all socially defined and limited. However, because the scale is ordinal rather than simple presence/absence, a certain variety of the normative code of semantic expressions is possible within different societies. This semantic binarism of the IRC node is very different from the signified/signifier binary frame of Saussure. His terms refer to what I have defined as the IRS and IRC nodes, whereas my semantic binarism refers to a polarized scale of expression found within only the IRC node. As a further reminder, I have already rejected the Saussurian dyadic frame and insisted on a triadic interaction of all three nodes, the IRS, GR, and IRC.

The three terms of the syntactic pattern are subject, verb and object. How are they expressed, as semantic forms, or codes, within the IRC node? The subject of the syntax is semantically expressed within the IRC node as an owner and/or worker; the object functions as an original and/or a copy; and the verb is an action of either storage or history. These poles (owner/worker; original/copy; and storage/history) are not oppositional but merely horizons or limitations of socially valid behaviour. I reject the oppositional binarism of Barthes and Lévi-Strauss, where 'the dialectic of superstructures ... consists in setting up constitutive units (which, for this purpose, have to be defined unequivocally, that is by contrasting them in pairs)' (Lévi-Strauss 1966: 131); for example, 'high and low, right and left, peace and war' (217). I agree with the binaristic horizon but not with the sense of opposition.[6] The normative expressions of these semantic terms are different for each syntax. But before discussing their differences, I shall outline the semantic meanings.

Owner/Worker

An owner is understood to be someone who has the social right to define and create knowledge. This person can be a scientist, a government official, a god. An owner can receive this power in various ways depending on the society: by biological heredity (intelligence, physique); social heredity (class, caste, clan); social systems (education); fate. The worker does not have this right to define and create knowledge. A worker can own an object, such as a house, and yet not have the social right to define its particular existence as an object (that would be up to the owners of the building code). A worker receives this lack of power in similar fashion: biological heredity (intellect, other genetic weaknesses such as physical/mental disability); social heredity (low class/caste/clan); social systems (education); fate. Essentially, I am saying that in every society there are some members (human or otherwise) who are understood to have the social rights to define and control activity, and there are some members who do not have this right.

Original/Copy

The object is also coded along a binary scale of original and copy. The original is the generative or 'true' form of an object; it exists as the formula, whether biological or mechanical, to produce particular versions of itself. The original can be an actual object that is defined as the first; or it can be, not the object, but the method of creation, such as a technique of manufacture or a chemical formula. An original can be a concept (god, ideal) and it can be forbidden to make existential versions or copies. The original exists on a long-term basis; it is stored within the society and therefore functions within the storage activities of the verb. The copy is a particular version of

an original. It is linked to an original.[7] The original can be the genetic structure of the chicken, the patent of the car, the method of production. But
there is an original that validates the historical existential copy. The copy
does not have the ability or social right to materially produce or socially
validate itself. The copy exists within the verbal action of history; it has a
particular historic moment of entering and leaving conscious existence. So,
the original can be a chemical formula of water and copies can be ice, mist,
snow, water, steam, or the word 'water.' The original can be 'energy harmful
to human beings' and copies can be the devil, AIDS, totalitarianism, or the
local strip joint.

The semantic codes of the IRC node provide a means by which a society
can articulate itself within both stable and variable forms of behaviour. The
original may provide stability over the generations, but the copy with its
minute variations permits and even encourages change. What society can
exist if it has lost its powers of adaptation? Why did Zeus choose Io over
Hera? Why did he choose a copy of Hera rather than the original form? Was
it simply a rejection of Hera's notorious temper or was it that Io 'was a copy
endeavoring to imitate a statue. But Zeus chose the copy; he wanted that
minimal difference which is enough to overturn order and generate the
new, generate meaning. And he wanted it because it was a difference, and
her because she was a copy' (Calasso 1993: 24). We shall explore later why
the textual society must permit, must require the variances of heteroglossia.

Storage/History

The verbal actions function within two forms, storage and history. Storage
'abstracts' the subject and object from time. Whatever is in storage is unaf-
fected by time in any of its forms; time affects only those things involved in
the action of history. Storage 'transforms documents into monuments'
(Foucault 1972: 7). Storage permits stasis, stability, duration of a society over
time; it stores social norms and values such that they can be repeated. History involves things in time, it permits entropy, it permits inventiveness. It is
here that unique existential forms exist in the brief particularity of their
Secondness.

Semantic Reality of Type A Syntax

The type A syntactic pattern permits a specific semantic consciousness.
First, because of the syntactic pattern, the owner and original perform the
verbal action together. Therefore, they are identical as powers; they both

express the power to make life and I only differentiate these terms in this syntax because of their placement in the logical pattern. The owner is subject; the original is object. However, in a type A syntax, there is no object as we understand the term, (object OF) and these two forms of existential life exist in a merged interaction. The same lack of differentiation is valid for the worker and copy. They exist within the social text on an equal basis in their supposed impoverishment; both lack any powers of definition or origination. Second, the subject and object, those two units that act together, are socially defined via the IRC nodal organization in both an abstract and a particular version (see figure below). If I use a particular example, 'man/opera| sing,' then I come up with a semantic form, functional within the type A syntax of:

owner/original|

storage/history

worker/copy |

This simply means that the abstract power (not power*s*) of composer/music termed owner/original are involved via a particular man (worker) and a particular work of music (copy) in a current expression (history) of the long-term social activity of artistic expression (storage). Let me further explain these terms and their social roles in type A logic.

Owner/Original

The abstract form as ultimate owner/original is the power of life, seemingly akin to generative energy; however, these two must not be confused in any way. The owner/original is a specific form of the powers of stasis (origin and authority) within a human society. Because this power as owner/original is considered to exist within the spatiotemporal horizons of a society, then it is more socially defined, bound, limited, and potentially exhaustible than generative energy. To show its presence within the textual reality of a society, it is given a name or image. It may be conceived of as a god, an angel, energy, absolute consciousness, the sun, a hero (whether Apollo or Elvis Presley), the power of the president (sometimes confused with the actual person), the power of a magical token, a type of car, a type of perfume. Grube says of the Greek gods that 'any power, any force we see at work in the world, which is not born with us and will continue after we are gone could thus be called a god, and most of them were' (1980: 150). Lévi-Strauss says that in 'mythical history ... the original ancestors were of a nature different from contemporary men: they were creators and these are imitators' (1966: 236). These abstract owners and originals are direct representatives of generative energy and function as intermediaries between ordinary humans and the great forces of generative energy. People living in this type of society, with the almost constant presence of these intermediaries to generative energy, have social rituals that acknowledge and access this energy more often than a type B logic, which permits no abstract powers within the social frame and views any attempts at contact as asocial witchcraft. Shamanism, ecstatic rituals, trance states, fortune-telling, religious festivals of access to abstract power, religious evangelism, are all a regular part of type A social norms. The abstract owners and originals in both form and action are understood to walk freely among the living. The gods of the Greeks were in frequent touch with ordinary human beings, whether in anger, pity, or amorous pursuit. The Dobe !Kung *gangwasi,* who are the spirits of the recently dead, remain in close touch with the living because 'they miss their people on earth' (Lee 1984: 109). The real owner/original in type A logic can therefore never be an existent human being or even a particular being of any kind. Among the Mbuti, the ultimate owner and origin of life is the surrounding forest (Turnbull 1983). With the Australian Mardudjara Aborigines, it is the power of the Dreamtime, a phase of the world long before human beings (Tonkinson 1978). Even Zeus, with all his meddling in the lives of ordinary human beings, was never meant to be observed in the magnificence of his reality, as Semele learned when she demanded too much from the coils of his embrace. Following the ordinal path of variation, the abstract power can be, like the Greek gods, frequently fallible or instead totally complete in knowledge and beyond the weaknesses of the particular. We can see here its quite direct links with generative energy. The Brahmanic life-spirit is 'the source of all power' (Zimmer 1956: 147). As described in a cabbalistic text of the medieval Hebrews, it is 'the Aged of the Aged, the Unknown of the Unknown,' and 'has a form and yet has no form' (Haidra zuta, Zohar, iii, 288a). The abstract Christian spirit, the basis of humanity, is 'not conscious of anything' (Eckhart 1941: 147); that is, it is not trapped within the particularities of spatiotemporal reality. 'The divine intellect knows things, no matter how diverse they be, by one act of knowing, even if they have different truths considered in themselves' (Aquinas, *De ver.* q.1a.5). So closely tied to generative energy that its nature is outside the horizons of definition, it can thus quite arbitrarily provide the particular experiences of *both* good and evil. 'And it shall come to pass, that as the Lord rejoiced over you to do you good, and to multiply you; so the Lord will rejoice over you to destroy you, and to bring you to nought' (Deuteronomy 28: 63). Ugatame is the Creator among the Kapauku Papuans of West New Guinea, and 'evil as well as good have been equally created and determined by Ugatame' (Pospisil 1963: 84). The buboes of the bubonic plague were 'the marks of God, God's tokens' (Braudel 1981: 83). However, 'in 1635 the inhabitants of Reims formed a solemn procession to thank God for having delivered their city from this scourge' (Foucault 1973: 4). Note the causal tie of both the origin and the demise of this disease with the abstract power. It was well understood how the gods of the Homeric tales forced human beings to distasteful actions, for 'indeed the bridle bit of Zeus forcefully compelled him to do such things';[8] we know how often the gods interfered with the life of Odysseus with both good and bad results. In a similar fashion tribal groups relate specific events and situations to spirit intervention. Illness that does not heal in a natural way is frequently understood to be caused by malevolent spirits, and shamans must then be called in to drive those spirits away.[9] Whatever the semantic image, this power of ownership and origin provides the group with its moral authority and its abilities to remain stable within the actualities of life.

Worker/Copy

I term the particular versions of this abstract force the worker and the copy. These terms are selected to suggest their *dependent* natures and the sense that they lack the power to conspicuously effect change in their society. Both the worker and copy have a spatiotemporal and therefore finite life; they are subject to birth and death. The only difference between them is semantic, a distinction between the one and the other in their physical existentiality and the role they play in the syntactic logic. There is no difference in their social existentiality. Both are to varying degrees without the social power of defining, ordering, and managing the environment. Both lack the power of origin, of creation of themselves or anything else. Invention as an action performed by the human individual is shunned within type A social logic because creation is the prerogative of the abstract, not the particular.[10] In this cognitive logic, in opposition to the Christian and Cartesian split between man and nature, both human and nature's beings are similar and equal. A human being is a particular temporal being and as such is a finite version of the abstract and eternal lifeforce. Similarly, the deer, the pig, the bird are other finite versions of this same abstract life force. To kill it – and it can only be for food – one must acknowledge its gift to you of its particular experience of the life force. There can be little sense of long-term private ownership, and 'the idea of exclusive ownership of land is an absurdity to the

Batek. They say: "only the Batek hala [superhuman beings] can own the land" ' (Endicott, in Ingold 1988, II: 113).

In a type A society, almost all human beings, fragile, finite, and temporal, are functional at the worker end of the semantic pole. They do not have the social power and right to define, own, and ultimately control their lives. They might easily be differentiated into status groups, including age grades, gender, clan, or caste; these different social levels might at first glance seem to indicate a certain measure of control over their lives. But no matter the social roles and the varying levels of prestige, these individuals are without that ultimate power of the owners to control the forces of life. The human being in this society can only go so far and no farther. To do more would be to confront the gods. Therefore in this society human beings are merely current expressions of the overarching life-power of the owner/original; they are 'us two-leggeds sharing in it with the four-leggeds and the wings of the air and all green things; for these are children of one mother and their father is one Spirit' (Neihardt 1961: 1). As Lee has pointed out in his study of primitive communism and capitalism, respectively type A and type B logic, in the communal society 'the common people have not yet been separated from the means of production, have not yet been divorced from their land' (in Ingold 1988, I: 263). All members in this society are equal in their human weakness and therefore 'forbidding (anyone) to ask for alms ... is evil, vicious and in conformity with a principle of Luther which has been condemned' (quoted in Davis 1979: 17). In 1531 the magistrates were warned by theologians at the Sorbonne that they 'must not prohibit public begging and alms-giving in the streets; any attempt to appropriate ecclesiastical revenues for poor relief would be the part not of good Catholics, but of impious heretics, Waldensians, Wycliffites or Lutherans' (ibid). I should point out that the stridency of these comments on what was an accepted social practice stems from the fact that, during this period between the fourteenth and sixteenth centuries, syntactic logic changed, from the feudal type A of the Middle Ages to the scientific (and highly individualistic) type B logic of the Renaissance. Certainly, hunting and gathering sustenance systems operate on the principle that all food gathered and hunted is shared with all, regardless of participation in the actual collection. 'Each !Kung is not an island unto himself or herself; each is part of a collective' (Lee 1984: 55). And 'it has been said that there are no [Ainu] who die of starvation but if any do the wealthy and poor perish together after the rich have exhausted their resources in supporting the poor (Watarashima notebook [1808], cited in Shinichiro 1960)' (Lee, in Ingold: 1988, I: 252). In the type A perspective the images of the poor, the mad, the ill are simple reminders of two facts of reality. The first is the reality of semantic binarism,[11] that human experience naturally exists in both good and bad forms and has its origin in factors beyond the scope of the individual. The transient and fallible powers of the ordinary human cannot rid the world of such unwanted elements. Second, the conceptual reality of a type A syntax requires that both forms of the subject actually exist as accessible forces within the society; therefore both the abstract owner with all the power and the particular worker who lacks power are to be found within the daily experience of social reality. When one image of the owner loses its power in social consciousness such that it is moved from the abstract to the particular, from being unmanageable by ordinary humans to manageable (for example, tuberculosis, the plague, the Soviet Union), then a new image (such as AIDS, pollution, the Middle East) will appear to play its formidable role of reminding human beings of the necessity of humility. This lack of a proprietory power over life experiences contributes to the sense of stasis, the commitment to stability of social norms, that is found within such a society. The younger generation does not have the authority to change the eternal rules, and 'the group that takes over must don the same spiritual clothes as the old one. ... the contract between human beings and the Ancestral past is maintained as one set of people replace another in a continuing relationship' (Morphy, in Ingold 1988, II: 270).

With this understanding, a type A society has only two classes. The upper or owner class is abstract, which means that, whether the membership is composed of gods, god-kings, heroes or multinational corporations, these agents exist beyond the laws that define and the standards that confine that society. Everyone else in society exists as spatiotemporally finite and subject to the limitations of rules and regulations. Small populations, most frequently hunting and gathering sustenance systems, reach their decisions by consensus, and the owners are completely abstract conceptually. Once the population reaches a critical number (in the thousands) there may well be physiological leaders, but they too are of the worker class. They are leaders without ultimate authority and are accountable, for 'the government of the kingdom must be so arranged that opportunity to tyrannize it is removed' (Aquinas, *On Kingship*, I, chap. 5; in Aquinas 1960: 239). 'Anthropologists have come to be sceptical that "chiefs" are really chiefs, especially in Melanesia; in the months to follow, I was to learn that the Kwaio had chiefs only on Tuesdays' (Keesing 1983: 3). Among the Kapauku Papuans, a headman keeps his position by the constant display of generosity and assistance. This requirement, common among many such societies, prevents self-aggrandizement. If a headman stops this constant largesse and concern for others in the tribe, he loses the esteem of the people and therefore his social role as headman. The powers of the abstract that enforce the rules of duration do not belong to human beings. Images that seem to explain or foretell both past and future events may well appear in the dreams of a single person; however, it is understood that they do not originate in that person,[12] who is simply an intermediary to the abstract powers. Since all members of the human population are workers, there is no middle class, no set of individuals who can, like the slippery gods, sometimes play the role of owners and sometimes hide as workers. In a society with a large population (over one hundred thousand), the owner is presented as a physical object but with abstract powers; he is a god-king, as in the large irrigation societies of dynastic Egypt, the Inca, the Mayan states, and the Aztecs; or a multinational corporation, as in our own society. This existentiality of the abstract in a physical presence provides that state with hereditary material evidence of the contact with generative energy, with material evidence of the right to define and order the variable populations of this society and so provide stability and order.

Origin

Because the owner/original is abstract, there is no particular human being responsible for the development of that society, and equally, no particular single original from which current versions biologically or historically descend, evolve, or are copied industrially. This cognitive perspective does not operate within a Darwinian scheme of gradual evolution, nor within any scheme that defines biological or conceptual entities as derivatory and related to previous species. As Albert Lord says in his analysis of non-written composition, 'each of these expressed forms or tellings of the story [could be] itself a separate song, in its own right, authentic and valid as a song unto itself.' But 'no oral poet has the concept of a single version ... which must be written down to be kept' (1971: 100, 152). Lévi-Strauss says of totemic myths, another form of oral song, that 'the poverty of totemic myths is therefore due to the fact that the function of each is only to establish a difference as a difference: they are the constitutive units of a system. The question of significance does not arise at the level of each myth taken in isolation but at that of the system of which they form the elements' (1966: 231). There is no concept of a unit that is temporally first in material spatiotemporal existence and therefore causal of all 'copies' that appear thereafter. There is no concept of linear development from a particular spatiotemporally first original nor from a unique spatiotemporal creator/owner. All material versions *at any time* express the basic atemporal abstract force. 'Stories never live alone: they are the branches of a family that we have to trace back, and forward' (Calasso 1993: 10). 'To be an "individual" in Aboriginal society is to be part of a unity that is trans-human and trans-temporal.' And 'the realm of the Dreaming and other concepts of Great Time or Mythological Time are significant primarily as legitimating and allowing the establishment of rituals and other fundamental practices of the society *outside* normal historical time and the process of ordinary human agency' (Samuel 1990: 101, 103). Newtonian linear time, which we understand as 'history,' has little meaning in this society and Whorf's analysis of the Hopi indifference to such time is illustrative of this.

The Verbal Action: Storage and History

This brings us to a necessary structure that is unique to this social syntax; that is, the need for an intermediary, an agential force to bridge the conceptual and physical gap between the abstract and the particular. There are two methods. One is that the verbal actions of storage and history are performed together. The atemporal, aspatial act that removes something from time and the spatiotemporal act that involves something with time are carried out within the same action.

Verbal interactions between subjects and objects can take two forms, again within the two requirements of a society, the need for duration and for variation. Storage provides stability by establishing normative standards against which current expressions are measured. It does this by abstracting images from current time and storing them by a variety of means (codes of language, law, symbols, behaviour). History is the action of a single expression, a single existential unit as measured against the standards held within storage. By these two actions, the society includes the functions of both stasis and heteroglossia, stability and change, within its semantic reality.

Type A logic establishes an interactional frame within the semantic node such that the history or the actual experience of an event/object *and* the storage or abstraction from current experience take place at the same time. There is no separation of these two actions, archival and immediate. The particular man experiences daily, immediate life; but since he exists as a version of the abstract life-power, his unique daily actions also express the more long-term and more general social experience of that abstract life-power that underlies him and his social group. The workers and the copies are thereby bonded to the abstract powers of continuity; change can be quite difficult in this society. Barthes says of the 'writerly act' that 'the writerly text is a perpetual present' (1974: 5). The text, a system of preservation, is used also as a system for immediate experience, and certainly this is the basis of Bakhtin's analysis of the modern novel (1981). The two actions, of storage (of the memory-image of the experience of an act) and history (the immediate actual experience of it), are performed together and there are no separate systems or institutions devoted to each action as opposites of each other (no surplus, no savings, no museums, no libraries, no archives). The verbal action in type A cognition is extremely important; it is not simply a communication channel for a message to pass through, in the Cartesian manner of the hollow linear tunnel of the Shannon and Weaver model (1946). The particular act of life is also an expression of archival time, of the 'motion of before and after,' and is thereby regenerating the energy content of that society. Without particular versions of itself, the abstract owner/original would 'turn to stone' and entropically decay. By the oral singer's act of singing a song (copy) he keeps the essence (original) of the song in social memory (storage) and in social existence (history) (Lord 1971). Among the Australian Aborigines, 'adult males in ritual recreate the Dreaming directly by dancing and singing the creative travels of the Dreaming beings, of whom they are the contemporary representatives' (Samuel 1990: 101). The Dobe !Kung are hunters and gatherers in the Kalahari and, 'because they do not amass a surplus of foodstuffs, the relation between local food production and consumption is an immediate one. A diagnostic feature of their subsistence economy is: food is almost always consumed within the boundaries of the local group and within forty-eight hours of its collection' (Lee 1984: 50). The Mbuti pygmies, another hunting and gathering society, are similarly against surplus. They explain this by their origin myth, telling how they once lived in the forest as gatherers (the forest is understood as the abstract owner of all life). Then one day a Mbuti 'killed an animal and to conceal the crime consumed it, turning to practical use every part that he could not eat. Since that day, say the Mbuti, all animals (including humans) have been condemned to die. Until then they were immortal, like the forest itself ... Any change that compels the Mbuti to increase their hunting activities will, as they see it, increase their mortality' (Turnbull 1983: 17–18). Because the individual in this semantic code is a worker, without the power to regenerate either himself or his environment, his contact with the owner, the abstract stability force of life, must be constant. Redfield refers to it as the 'idea of pious contract' and writes that 'the Maya villager has the idea that whatever he takes from nature by his effort is loaned to him by the gods, and that it is his obligation to express his part in the sacred contract by returning to the gods some portion of what is loaned him. The successful hunter does not eat of the meat until he has left some part of it for the supernatural protectors of the deer. The agriculturalist does not cut down more trees than he needs for space to plant; if he leaves part of the forest cleared but not planted he has taken wrongly from the guardians of the bush' (1960: 23–4). I note the word 'loaned'; there is no personal ownership of an 'object.' The medieval world, also functional within a type A logic, considered that the usurer who sold surplus goods or lent money was sinful, for as Innocent IV considered, 'the usurer sells time, which belongs only to God' (Le Goff 1988: 47).

I suggest that this non-production of surplus is not due to a primitive economic system and most certainly not to a 'primitive' mentality, but rather to the requirements of a sociocognitive pattern that requires one to be in constant interaction with the abstract powers of life by repeating the daily actions of social life that put one in touch with such generative powers. This is because the storage of the energy and power of existence, which is 'surplus' to and also generative of one's current usage, rests within the control of the abstract owners. An acceptance of the power of the abstract forces is shown by the collection and production only of what can be consumed in that day. More is not required, for that would be both an infringement on the storage power of the owner and an act of doubting its powers to provide.

The Verbal Action as Ritual

The intermediary action accesses generative energy, but it does so in a manner different from the pure action of accessing generative energy;[13] this latter action requires that one move out of spatiotemporal reality and is an infrequent and quite dangerous undertaking. The intermediary action functions within the spatiotemporal frame of the realities, it is bound to a particular society, and must happen on an ongoing and ritualistic rather than chance basis to maintain the energy viability of the society. Such actions are ritualistic for two reasons; one, because the stability of their performance ensures continuity of that society, and second, the ritual lessens the potential dangers of accessing the formidable powers of generative energy. The rituals are organized communication systems, made up of 'certain modalities arbitrarily isolated from a formal system, the function of which is to guarantee the convertibility of ideas between different levels of reality' (Lévi-Strauss 1966: 76). By the formalism of ritual one acknowledges the aconceptual power of the generative force and one's submission to its will. By the ritual, one also acknowledges the bond between stasis and heteroglossia,[14] such that the current reality is both a version of and a bond with the stored original. These bonds must be maintained; 'human action ... brings about an interruption of continuity' and the means to access stability is to maintain the ritual contacts. The rites will therefore 'periodically and momentarily ... re-establish the contiguity between production and consumption' (226), between the power of storage and the finiteness of history. The original in this cognitive pattern can take on the form of a static grid of semantic classifications of reality. The systems of classification are stored within the mind of the abstract owner(s) as the original pattern of the society; the current event as expressed in the ritual is a version of that original. 'Totemic classifications no doubt divide their groups into an original and a derivative series: the former contains zoological and botanical species in their supernatural aspect, the latter human groups in their cultural aspect, and the former is asserted to have existed before the latter, having in some sort engendered it.' The '(Australian) churinga are palpable proofs of mythical times' (1966: 232, 242); and in this type of society, change can be difficult because contact with the original is not via a linear sense (history as past event) but in the present (history as current expression). The function of rituals is to put members of a society in touch with the classificatory structure of their society and also to keep open the communication line with the stored energy of the society. Ritual must be respected and maintained.

The Intermediary Agent

The second type of interaction between the abstract and particular reality is via an actual agent of mediation between these two realities. The supreme power of a *deus otiosus* is a power beyond spatial and temporal images. How can human beings as finite material entities be in contact with that which has 'no form'? Only someone who can exist in both worlds, the absolute and the particular, can establish such a link. The Buddha, Mohammed, Siva, Jesus – these beings are conceived as human; yet they are able to communicate with both human beings and with the abstract powers of life. Abstract power keeps in contact with the particular via the intermediary, the part-human, part-god agent who can communicate with both worlds, for 'O Mohammed, God said, hadst thou not been, I would not have created the sky.' The intermediary is not necessarily a specific agent but can also be an action.

The agents or actions of this mediation are not for the trivia of everyday life; one does not approach the violence of the gods unless it is absolutely necessary. When something with more force, more energy, threatens the stability of a society, then contact with the abstract forces in their generative powers, not their stable functions, is needed. This generative type of intermediary as agent or action is created within a phase of violence. By this violence it is moved from a being existent in only one of the two worlds (generative or finite) to a being capable of interacting with both. In this sense mediation becomes even more important to this type of society than the abstract gods, the *deus otiosus*, for 'the violent death of the demi-divinity is not only a "creative" death, it is also a way of being continually present in the life of men and even in their death' (Eliade 1963: 106). A passive yet violent transformation can be seen within the transformation of the Buddha:

> He placed himself, with a firm resolve, beneath the Bo Tree, on the Immovable Spot, and straightway was approached by Kama-Mara, the God of love and death. The dangerous God appeared mounted on an elephant and carrying weapons in his thousand hands. He was surrounded by his army, which extended twelve leagues before him, twelve to the right, twelve to the left, and in the rear as far as to the confines of the world; it was nine leagues high. The protecting deities of the universe took flight, but the Future Buddha remained unmoved beneath the Tree. (Campbell 1968: 32)

By withstanding this violence the man emerged as a buddha, an intermediary. The Christian tale of the death and 'rising' of Jesus follows the same pattern of violence against the spatiotemporal reality. The intermediary, in his particular image as a man, 'remembers' his own particular death, as in the tale of Jesus who 'rose from the dead after three days' and was perceivable as a material being; 'Behold my hands and my feet, that it is I myself; handle me, and see; for a spirit hath not flesh and bones, as ye see me have' (Luke 24: 39). By the conscious experience of death as a violent *threshold* action between the abstract and the particular, a being emerges with access to both worlds.

The development of the intermediary involves, first, a separation from the current spatiotemporal world. This can be by a violent death (Jesus); by enveloping madness that, as Socrates outlines, sets a human being free from established concepts; by moving oneself pyschologically and physically into a biochemical state of heightened perception (shamans achieve trance states sometimes by the actual use of hallucinogens and sometimes without, by contact with special tokens or totems).[15] The separation can be by an act of intuition, as in the act of painting, whereby 'the artist may be able to ... unlock the valves of feeling and therefore return the onlooker to life more violently' (Bacon; in Sylvester 1975: 17). By this action the intermediary gains access to the ultimate powers and then willingly returns to the particular realities of the world to act as a mediating link between the two worlds of storage and history.

The intermediary is understood as an agent of life, for 'when the Prince of Eternity kissed the Princess of the World, her resistance was allayed ... the horses in the court stood up and shook themselves ... the fire in the kitchen brightened, flickered and cooked the dinner' (Grimm, 'Briar Rose,' no. 50). Briefly, the result of the intermediary is 'the unlocking and release again of the flow of life into the body of the world' (Campbell 1968: 40). Paraguayan tribes have a myth that describes how human beings obtained fire. Fire was in the possession of 'vulture-sorcerers.' Man pretended to be dead, and when the vulture-sorcerers approached him as carrion and lit a fire to cook him, man sprang up and took possession of the embers that became the material source of fire on earth (Lévi-Strauss 1975: 140). Shamans form 'a special category of human beings who belong neither to the physical universe nor to society but whose function it is to act as mediators between the two worlds' (261). For instance, game killed during a hunting expedition or the first garden products are unfit for consumption until the 'bari' or shaman has been given his share, which constitutes the 'mori' owned by the living to the spirits of the dead. The intermediaries may, in larger populations, be separate from the powerless workers, but they are still intermediaries and not owners (feudal monks and knights, Aboriginal warriors). In some cases, particularly in smaller populations, they may only be intermediaries during certain events (trance rituals) and may have no powers the rest of the time. Or the intermediary may assist transition states, for example, the violence of transition rites of circumcision among many tribal peoples is an example of an action that moves the individual from a status of non-power (childhood) to a status of more power (adult).

Type A logic has been the key cognitive pattern for most of humanity's existence in the world, and therefore the typology of intermediaries is extremely rich. They include gods, saints, prophets, medicine men, shamans, elders, as well as government leaders. The intermediary may be an action, such as a ritual or prayer. It may be an object, such as a lottery ticket, a private computer number providing access to data, a sacred object. A social group may be developed that has the social right/ability to perform this interaction, such as priests, sorcerers, kings, businessmen, lawyers, computer experts. A spatial site may be developed, such as a sacred tree, a courthouse; or a temporal time, such as Easter. The key feature is that these agents/actions are, unlike the rest of ordinary humans, capable of interacting with both the 'sacred and the profane.'

The type A cognitive pattern of interaction with the environment promotes these concepts:

1. The syntactic pattern does not include the production of an object; both

subject and object are equally affected by the action. Dominance over nature cannot be part of the cognitive reality of such a society. Because of this there is no capital accumulation; if such does occur at various times (harvests, war) then this is depeleted via feasts of redistribution and even destruction of the goods.

2. The individual-reality forms of this logic include a timeless abstract form as owner and original, which take a material form in the particular worker/copy. The worker/copy do not exist independently but are 'forms' of this abstract power.

All members of the social group, as equally finite versions of a more abstract power, have the same social standing. Therefore, a middle class, with its stress on individual gain and achievement, is absent. In his well-known analyses of the Dobe !Kung, Richard Lee writes, 'Say there is a Bushman who has been hunting. He must not come home and announce like a braggard, "I have killed a big one in the bush!" He must first sit down in silence until I or someone else comes up to his fire and asks, "What did you see today?" He replies quietly, "Ah, I'm no good for hunting. I saw nothing at all ... just a little tiny one"' (1984: 13). The group rather than the individual is socially privileged. Stress on the individual leads someone 'to think of himself as a chief or a big man, and he thinks of the rest of us as his servants or inferiors' (ibid).

Interaction between the two levels of existence, the abstract and the particular, is accomplished by:

3. The relations of storage and history (past/future and current time) that take place within the same action.
4. An intermediary, agent, or action that will mediate between the two levels.

The Primacy of Type A Syntax

There are several reasons to suggest that type A cognitive logic is the key logic for social groups over almost all of human history. It has the capacity for longevity, with societies using this logic easily maintaining an adaptable yet stable functionality for thousands of years. In small groups it provides cohesion by its invariable privileging of group rights over those of the individual. Such an arrangement means that potential instability from individual variations will not destabilize the group. Moreover, it permits a flexible adaptation to a variable environment by removing causality from human beings. In any small group the larger misfortunes that are beyond the technology or organizational structures of that group are considered to arise ultimately from abstract powers, abstract in the sense that such power cannot be interacted with on a basis of direct equality. It can be the Biague or spirits of the 'has-beens' among the Yuqui, the *gangwasi* or spirits of the recently dead among the Dobe !Kung, the ever-harassing police among a bikers' gang. Whatever the metaphor, the individual within the group is not at fault. The social integrity of the beliefs and behaviour of the group remains intact.

In groups with a larger population (1,000 and up) type A logic provides this same basic long-term cohesiveness plus the important generative power of social heteroglossia, which I define as the existence of smaller peripheral groups that may operate within the same logic but express it with different metaphors or even use a different logic. A large population requires more specialization and more organization simply on an organic basis; a large population has more 'energy content' and a higher energy content must be organized in a more complex manner to maintain that energy. Such a society has a variety of specialized labour, classes or different definitions of citizens, varieties of work functions, political levels, cultural expressions – but still, a cohesion of unity is maintained. The flexibility of expression provided by heteroglossia prevents entropic decay and keeps a large society adaptive. Examples of small-population type A cognitive groups are pre-contact hunting and gathering indigenous peoples; pastoral nomadic and horticultural economies; small-scale peasant groups; inner-city, neighbourhood, and extended family groups. In larger groups, it existed in the entire Indo-European and European feudal era, in the imperial agricultural civilizations of China, India, Egypt, Babylon, the Inca and Aztec, and is the dominant pattern in the modern post-industrial era.

Societies operating with this cognition may seem extremely varied at first sight, but a closer analysis of their two realities shows the above points. To move into an analysis of a system operating by a different logic is to move into the analysis also of a different semantic consciousness.

Type B Syntax

This logic is a short-term and yet extremely powerful cognitive frame, lasting, at an informed guess, only four or five generations (about 250 years) in its prime and moving through three distinct phases during its existence. I would define it as a 'carnival' logic, in that it permits the destruction of an old cognitive horizon, the release of individuals from the confinement of a no longer functional conceptual paradigm, and the input of a large amount of generative energy, to be gradually organized and bound within a new social structure. As such a phase, it cannot last for the many centuries of type A logic. Its very nature is to provide a multiple rather than singular access to generative energy. It empowers human beings rather than abstract forces to function as owners; these people access generative energy, and the amount of new energy potentially taken into the spatiotemporal frame of such a society is enormous. Energy has to be organized, and the IRC node organizes type B logic in a way that is very different from type A IRC semantics. Indeed, with the impact of the tremendous amount of energy available, the IRC imagery 'explodes' in this type of society. It is (and was) a 'renaissance,' a bursting forth of new concepts, new technology, new ideas. Obviously, the period from the thirteenth through sixteenth centuries in Europe, the era of the Renaissance, is a key example of type B syntactic logic. This high-powered access to pure energy cannot be maintained; the GR syntactic node and the IRC semantic codes cannot maintain the organizational patterns to stabilize it and the society, with its new ideas, new technology, must change to type A logic in order to be stable. If this does not happen and the society instead tries to stay within the functional requirements of type B logic (constant access to new energy, constant pressure of invention, domination over the Other, problems with the definition of owners versus workers), the society becomes so trapped within the pressure of having to organize this constant articulation of energy that it becomes totalitarian, able to deal only with spewing out multiple copies of its energy base, unable to deal with any variation, any deviation. It cannot maintain this and quickly destroys itself, as happened with the fascist systems of recent years.

The pattern of type B syntax differs from the type A pattern. It is Subject: Verb: Object. The primary point to note here is the separation of the subject from the object by the verbal action. The action becomes something done *to* the object and not also to the subject. The object functions as isolate and without ties, dependent on the actions and intentionality of the subject for both its identity and its social existence. The subject now has the power to effect change in the social environment without also being affected. This vital separation means that, whatever action the subject is involved in with the object, it is done *to* the object and not also to the subject. We can immediately see that the concept of Otherness as shared energy is no longer viable in such a society. In the early seventeenth century, in 'The Great Instauration' Bacon said it well: 'that the mind may exercise over the nature of things the authority which properly belongs to it' (1960: 7). In Bacon's era scholastic knowledge had become reified and dysfunctional in a degenerate form of its earlier glories; it had become trapped within the dyadic sign of Saussure and had slipped into the degenerate forms of cognition found within a binary code and external form.[16] Bacon explains the conceptual traps of his era in his description of Idols of the Cave, Tribe, Marketplace and Theatre, which leave members of a society bound within structures that 'so beset men's minds that truth can hardly find entrance' ('Aphorisms,' Book 1, 38; in Bacon 1960: 47). A new socioeconomic order[17] required a new knowledge, a new way of thinking about the roles of human beings within the world. Bacon, again, expressed it succinctly: 'for let a man look carefully into all that variety of books with which the arts and sciences abound, he will find everywhere endless repetitions of the same thing, varying in the method of treatment, but not new in substance' (ibid). This 'old wisdom' is of little use; it 'can talk but cannot generate.'

This split of the subject from the object is a key factor in a specific logic based on creating and using social units that do not interact in a retributive manner with the subject and that are, in their own existence, defined and limited by these powers of the subject. A cognitive logic that provided such a separation of the subject from the object gave Western Europeans in the thirteenth century their sense of themselves as dominant over the environment, which became their 'object' to own, explore, and manipulate. With this syntactic separation, the semantic organization at the IRC node also changed to give these individuals the imagery they needed to express themselves with these new powers.

Semantic Reality of Type B Syntax

In this logic, the binary forms of the IRC semantic node are completely particular. There are no abstract forms as are found within type A.

In type B syntax, both forms of the subject and object are understood as material, physical, accessible; there is no abstract ultimate source of particular life and knowledge; the gods have fled, in horror one might later say. If there still remains a commitment to the image of 'god,' then this god is removed from interference with current temporal existentiality and becomes a site of past origin, a brief nod to 'in the beginning.' This is a different syntax, a different world, and 'after that remote time when gods and men had been on familiar terms, to invite the gods to one's house became the most dangerous thing one could do, a source of wrongs and curses' (Calasso 1993: 387). Bacon wrote that, just as 'things human may not interfere with things divine,' then it is an equal mistake to fall 'into the opposite error, which they will surely do if they think that the inquisition of nature is in any part interdicted or forbidden.' And even, 'it is the glory of God to conceal a thing, but it is the glory of the King to find a thing out' (1960: 14, 15); kings, of course, become defined as human beings. Others in this transition era felt the same – that God might indeed have been the ultimate origin, but after that original creation it was up to human beings to explore. Bernard of Chartres said, 'We are dwarfs perched on the shoulders of giants. We therefore see more and farther than they, not because we have keener vision or greater height, but because we are lifted up and born aloft on their gigantic stature' (cited in Le Goff 1993: 12). The Chartrian humanism of the twelfth century declared man as the centre of life, 'for this world was created for man.' Man was a *Homo faber*, a person who worked and transformed the world. For practical purposes, there are in this world only particular human beings whose Cartesian minds are 'washed clean from opinions' and particular natural reality; neither has any taint of a conceptual heritage covering their real identity. The abstract forms found within either the gods or the dusty arguments of the scholastics are irrelevant; human beings are the ultimate namers and owners in this syntactic pattern.

The object functions as separate, isolate, and dependent on the actions of another material being for both its social meaning and its material existence. In a natural environment, birds may spread seeds, but human beings can take over this task and control both the number and location of plant growth. Water may be a necessity, but human beings may dig wells, build canals, divert rivers, and so control nature. The subject has the power of 'knowing' the object as an 'other.' However, in the semantics of this society, 'other' takes on a meaning quite different from the interactional one of a type A society. 'Other' becomes understood within a binary opposition, where 'the other' is a negative version of the valid form. 'Man was created, not a savage, a hunter, or warrior, but a horticulturalist and a raiser of grain, and a keeper of cattle – a smith, a musician – a worshipper, not of the sun, moon, and stars, but of God' (H.R. Schoolcraft 1851-7, quoted in Pearce 1988: 127). Said's *Orientalism* (1979) is another explanation of this binarism of the other. Authors (owners) writing about the Orient within a type B syntactic reality see it as 'one of the deepest and most recurring images of the Other ... the Orient has helped to define Europe (or the West) as its contrasting image, idea, personality, experience' (1–2). And 'the Oriental is irrational, depraved (fallen), childlike, "different"; thus the European is rational, virtuous, mature, "normal" ' (40). The object is 'other' to the subject. To maintain this separation, otherness as difference, as opposition, is a semantic requirement.

To some, this separation of man from the objects of the environment made him a 'wise man,' for he could finally fully explore and explain the environment and need accept no other explanation than his own. Descartes described such an attitude in the Fifth Meditation: 'as soon as I understand anything very clearly and very distinctly I cannot help but believe it to be true' (1960: 124). Consider the framework of this thought, also articulated as his First Rule, 'never to accept anything as true unless I recognized it to be certainly and evidently such' (15). It focuses on the particular perception as a valid representation of reality and on individual man as not only the perceiver but also the definer of truth. There are here no tombs of sacred knowledge, no Dreamtime, and of course, no necessary intermediaries. Bacon comments that a human being 'can do and understand so much and so much only as he has observed in fact or in thought of the course of nature' (*New Organon*, book 1: 1; in Bacon 1960: 39). And again, Descartes sees the individual and his perceptions as the ultimate Namer, the chief source of truth, in his famous 'cogito, ergo sum' or 'I think, therefore I am.' Writing within this same frame, Locke says, 'the objects of sensation, one source of ideas. The operation of our minds, the other source of them' (1975: 2). Cognition includes only the hard physical data and specific iconic thoughts. Consider in contrast the comment of Socrates, who felt that 'by observing objects with my eyes and trying to comprehend them with each of my other senses I might blind my soul altogether' (Plato). This type A statement affirms that the power of understanding cannot simply rest within the individual and his direct observations of the environment. Type B cognitive logic, with its stress on the power of the individual operative within current sensual experiences, encourages the relegation of previous knowledge to the past and will naturally be of greatest benefit in a period of technological and conceptual change, when it is most necessary to forget past knowledge and forge new methods. Within the period of actual dominance of type B logic in Europe, a brief five-hundred-year span from the fourteenth through the nineteenth centuries, we should note the number and style of inventions – inventions that didn't simply harness the power of human beings but rather the power of the environment, and then put that power into their control. The steam engine, ballistics, hydraulics, gas, electricity, chemical formulas, medical concepts – the list is endless. The ownership of the body by human beings, not by fate and intermediary agencies of priest or shaman, with Da Vinci's anatomy, Harvey's blood circulation. I doubt that human beings suddenly 'evolved' into inventive beings. Rather, the syntactic framework of the society encouraged and fostered and required such creativity. This society had the capacity to store old semantic forms, the dried whispers of the scholastics, and remove their burden from daily discourse. It insisted, demanded, that all human beings 'speak out,' that they have 'freedom of speech,' something that a member of a type A society would consider laughable. The great religious wars of this period were basically what I would call the 'wars of the namers.' Who would name the environment – human beings or the gods? It was the finite, limited, temporal powers of the human mind that won.

The Power of the Individual

The type B pattern permits the development of a mentality that locates knowledge within the sensual and conceptual environment of the particular individual rather than within the abstract group. The individual human being has the power of understanding and explaining the environment. Not the abstract original powers of the society, as in type A, where it was a god 'who divided the light from darkness ... and called the light Day, and the darkness he called Night' (Genesis 3:4). Rather, in this society, it is human beings who are the owners, who say that 'I have the ability to conceive what is generally called a thing, or a truth ... and it seems to me that I do not conceive this from anything but my own nature' (Descartes, Third Meditation, 1960: 94). Or, 'We must lead men to the particulars themselves, and their series and order; while men on their side must force themselves for a while to lay their notions by and begin to familiarize themselves with facts' (Bacon, *New Organon*, book 1, 36; in Bacon 1960: 47). The emphasis is put on the individual who is expected to explore, define, redefine, discard, discover knowledge. The inventor, defined as the creator of a physical object previously non-existent, was recognized with Inventors Acts passed in France in 1791, in the United States in 1789. The world is understood as man's 'object.' Will it work? Will this syntactic logic produce what a society requires? Will it permit human beings to live, to love, to last? As with every question dealing with human beings, the answer is 'yes' and also 'no.' Individuals never exist alone, even though they may think they do; human beings have no genetic archives locked within their bodies; they are dependent on the group archival knowledge of 'how to live.' Therefore, to dream for even one minute that, rather than being a temporal flicker of life, a being who is in specious contact with the gods from time to time, but is actually one of their kind, is to invite their anger. The gods, that ultimate source of stability, will wait, they will watch human beings play with their stolen metaphors of power, they will permit them to explore and seemingly control in an almost drunken intoxication more and more of the world, but eventually, no god will ignore such an affront. 'In the *Iliad*, all living things, even the horse Xanthus, even the river Scamander, tell us that they are not the "cause," not responsible for anything. But they don't say this in order to lay the blame on someone else.

No, that recognition is the supreme act of Homeric devotion, a stepping aside before overwhelming power. Every affirmation of an ego would be crude, here where the distinction between how much each person may do alone and how much a god allows him to do or gives to him is so subtle' (Calasso 1993: 341). A type B syntax is the most powerful means of bringing in new energy to a society, far more powerful than the intermediary methodology of the type A method; it permits a sudden burst of energy, of new life, new thoughts, but it cannot last.

Although I have used Bacon, Descartes, and Locke as examples of this cognition, it is emphasized that they were by no means causal of it. Such a direct and linear causal analysis, focused only on the subjective power of individuals, is only operative within type B cognition. Rather, they were expressing in words a deep cognitive pattern that was already in place and developing among the majority by the time of their writing. Foucault's classical experience can describe the type B syntax, where it is man's task 'to ascribe a name to things, and in that name, to name their being' (1973b: 120). The task is to name the environment and thereby function as the actual creator of its social existence. This power of the particular subject is specific to and vital to this logical frame. Bernal quotes Descartes who, in speaking of environmental units, said that men could 'employ them in the same way to all uses for which they are appropriate and thus become the masters and possessors of Nature' (1969: 447). This is a precise summary of the semantic results of living by a type B logic that splits the subject from the object and permits all semantic forms of both subject and object to be particular in form and governed by human beings as owners. Individuals act as the ultimate source and discoverer of ideas, creator of their particular form, definer of their material and functional existence. The object in its semantic form is composed of finite, knowable compounds that are easily governed by the decisions of human beings, Whether this object is the atom, the molecule, the psyche, or the geographic environment, it is named by and eventually governed by humans. In this syntactic logic, it is understood that 'the human race seeks to recover its right over nature' (Bacon 1960: 284). Exploration of 'new lands,' the 'right of discovery,' 'title to land,' the idea of the frontier – these are all functional within a semantic consciousness that defines owners and originals as material realities, with the latter controlled by the former. In contrast, we should recall the indigenous indifference to particular ownership, a perspective functional within a type A syntax, for 'groups of people, not individuals, own the land among the !Kung ... the !Kung regard the n!ore (territory) as their storehouse or larder, and if food runs out in one n!ore all people have a claim on the resources of several other n!ores' (Lee 1984: 87).

Time in Type B Logic

The nature of the semantic forms of the IRC node that appear within type B logic completely change the understanding of temporality. Time, as has been explained, is a means of organizing energy. In type A logic the power of organizing storage, the energy of the past and future stability of a society, belongs within the intentionality of an abstract force – the Greek gods, the Aboriginal Dreamtime, the quantum potentiality. The individual can only experience current reality, understood as history, and any realities of the past or the future are beyond the normal individual's power of access. The past and the future are understood only 'as a timeless model, rather than a stage in the historical process' (Singer 1959: 277). In type B logic both storage and history come under the control of physical subjects. Time becomes an actual form of physical matter and therefore all three phases or experiences of time become accessible to the individual experience. Type B time is understood as an external measurement of the unidirectional linearity of past, present, and future, what I refer to as analogical rather than digital time because all three time phases are visible to the human perception. This is the Newtonian time analysis, where 'true time' is an 'absolute truth and mathematical time, of itself and from its own nature, flows equably without relation to anything external' (Newton, *Principia* 1687; quoted in Koyre 1965: 103). Time as material content is understood as a measurement of that content, of the developmental and progressive nature of such matter. The civilized society has more 'time' in it than the savage society and is understood as more developed.

The Original and the Copy

The semantic forms of the IRC node within a type B syntax are all particular; there is no abstract version of the object, with one form, the original, being abstract and the copy being particular. In type B logic, both forms are particular. How does one differentiate between them? The original is understood within temporal linearity; it is first in space or time. The term 'original' comes to refer not to the abstract power of generation of, for example, Aristotle's formal cause, but to the first particular or conscious unit existent in current spatiotemporal reality. Originals are defined as temporally 'first' and named in a manner that emphasizes these qualities: 'patented invention,' 'original creation,' 'early form,' 'primitive society.' Copies are duplicate or lesser images of these prior existences and are named as such: 'unchanged since 1750,' 'exact reproduction of,' 'paperback version of.' Originals are the first defined, the first named, the first made, the first discovered, the first

owned. The germ, the fossil, the country, the telephone, the drug, the car –
all are specifically 'nailed down' in linear temporality. Later forms are considered diffused copies, as in the anthropological diffusionist analysis of the
spread of tools or social behaviour around the world. Or, using an evolutionary analysis, these later forms can be understood as 'evolved' from that
first step, progressive developments of an earlier less perfect form, as outlined in Morgan's well-known formula of social evolution from savage to
barbarian to civilized society.[18]

In type A logic, based on abstract energy as the origin of particular
expessions of life, the concept of something temporally first and physically
isolated in its 'original uniqueness' is illogical, and there are no social patterns or institutions based on such concepts. In type B logic, however, social
systems develop that validate temporal firstness of existentiality as the basis
for the socially truthful definition of an 'original' existence. This perception
is expressed in the search for material originals – in archaeology, palaeontol-
ogy, and history, as well as material causality in physics, chemistry, biology.
Copyright gives an individual the right to make copies of a particular creation and excludes others from so doing. Such acts were passed in Venice in
1476. Titles are unique names on books, rather than the medieval content-
summaries or the first few lines acting as the defining aspect of a manuscript.
These appeared circa 1495 and helped to establish the book as a material
entity authored by a single owner, rather than existent within the flexible
public discourse of the Greek era.[19] The Statute of Anne, in 1710, changed
the printer's rights to author's rights by its explicit recognition of the author
as the real owner. In this period, the author was the owner.[20] The author
registered his work in the stationer's register and had copyright for fourteen
years, renewable for another fourteen years. The adoption also of the principle of a limited term of protection for a published work gave social recognition to the concept that an original was a material entity, with a specific
spatiotemporal life span. The patent, which defines a particular object as a
material original created by a particular individual with a precise date of
creation, appeared in Florence in 1421, in Venice in 1471, and multiplied
rapidly over the next two centuries, to appear in England in 1624, in France
in 1791, in America in 1789. By the end of the nineteenth century a large
number of countries had established patent laws.

As expressed by the seventeenth-century Port Royal group of linguistic
philosophers, the sign as a copy or reference to its object was supposed to be
a 'duplicated representation doubled over upon itself' (Land 1974: 20). No
variation was permitted in the copy. Variations in language came to be considered the mark of the uneducated; variations in products indicated poor
manufacture. Variations in physical existence were, from the fifteenth cen-

tury, withdrawn from interaction, as Foucault (1973) has pointed out in his analysis of the houses for the insane, the blind, the physically and mentally handicapped, the poor. The essential point is that the original is a material specimen; it is, as an object, under the control of another material entity, the subject, the owner. The original of an object cannot be active in generation of itself or in knowledge of itself. Once created, it may carry its identity as 'first,' but an original is not also its own originator. It is known by and created by a subject, the owner, who is also a material being. 'Human knowledge and human power meet in one,' as Bacon pointed out.

The Owners and Workers

If the subject, semantically coded into owners and workers in the IRC node, is expressed in particular forms, then such a society is going to have to differentiate between these two types of human beings. There will be some who are owners and some who are workers. The Marxist binary frame defines those who have the power to create, to know, to control as owners and those who lack such power as workers. This establishment of human beings as both owners and workers and yet separate from each other, as God the owner was separate from man the worker, can be understood within Braverman's separation of hand and brain, or 'the separation of conception from execution' (1974: 114). It is clearly described in F.W. Taylor's classic work on the principles of scientific management, where the 'managers assume ... the burden of gathering together all of the traditional knowledge which ... has been possessed by the workmen and then of classifying, tabulating and reducing this knowledge to rules, laws and formulae ... (so that) the work of every workman is fully planned out by the management' (Taylor [1911] 1977: 36–9). The owner is given the social right to own and control knowledge; the worker is denied these rights. Both groups, in this logic, are particular, are human beings. It could easily lead to a truce, a merging and blending of the two forms of the subject, the mixing of owner and worker into one group, as Marx so fervently hoped. This cannot happen. As I explain in chapter 7 on stasis and heteroglossia, it would lead to the total collapse of the society. Here, I shall simply say that a society must have representatives of its two means of organizing energy, stasis and variation.[21] To combine these two forces would result in a catastrophic implosion, a social 'black hole.' The owners are the key means of maintaining stability; the workers are the source of variation. The continual effort to keep these two forces separate, when both are so similar in the immediate semantic form, can lead to many degenerate semantic code systems. Race, ethnicity, social status, education, profession, are all code systems that a society adds on to the basic code of 'a human being' in order to differentiate its human beings and provide semantic expressions of both stasis and variance, both owners and workers. Such requirements are not found within type A logic, because the differentiation between these two forces is simple: it is obvious that the gods are the forces of stasis. Type B logic, with its 'quick-fix' mentality, removes such unmanageable forces from 'true science' and relegates such a perspective to 'animism' and 'magic,' the definition of a 'primitive' or 'savage' mind (Maine, Morgan, Rivers, Lévi-Strauss).[22] In this syntax, the ultimate owner is a human being, whether that person has attained such rights by heredity, merit, stealth, or otherwise. The worker is equally human, equally having attained such a position by heredity, merit, stealth, or otherwise. The difficulty comes in deciding over the years which sector of the population is which. Since human beings are by their very semiosis of being, tellers of tales, then the clarity of exact definition blurs, mingles, and thus sets the foundation for the numerous harangues, battles, and wars over these vital powers of stasis and variance within a society.

The Verbal Action: Storage and History

The actions of storage and history, understood as past/future time and current time, are existentially operative within the same action in type A logic. In type B logic, they are carried out in separate actions. History operates within the measurable linear movement of time, Storage is an action that abstracts people and objects from this historical time-scale. Type B storage removes both material objects and conceptual experience from current time, so that they are conserved to remain as they were at a specific time period. This is the 'historic definition of reality' that ties an event, an object, a person, to a specific knot on this singular time-scale. Such static existentiality is not possible in type A logic, where all objects and experiences can only exist within current experience and as such are temporally finite versions of the original abstract form.

Institutions emerge to deal with the social existence and preservation of these material originals and the manufacture and marketing of the copies. Printing presses and copyrighted books gather and store the original form of socially valid thoughts; public education, bookstores, and libraries spread their copies. As Caxton said in 1481, 'Vox audita perit, littera scripta manet'; the spoken voice passes away, the written letter remains. 'In 1264 the statutes of the University of Padua declared: "without copies there would be no university"' (Le Goff 1993: 84). Print developed rapidly from the Mainz Gutenberg Press of 1450; its usage spread copies of new concepts to a broad audience, dispensing with the role of the church as both mediator and controller of the relationship between knowledge and men. 'Paris saw its first printed book in 1470, Lyon in 1473, Poitiers in 1479, Venice in 1470, Naples in 1471, Louvain in 1473 and Cracow in 1474. More than 110 European towns were known by their printing presses in 1480. Between 1480 and 1500, the process had reached Spain, spread throughout Germany and Italy,and touched the Scandinavian countries. By 1500, 236 towns in Europe had their own print shops' (Braudel 1981: 400). Libraries developed rapidly during the sixteenth century (Florence 1571, Madrid 1557, Hamburg 1529) and particularly in the seventeenth century. The thirteenth and subsequent centuries saw the rapid development of colleges and universities, with such examples as Balliol (1261), Cambridge (1209), Oxford (1167/1214), Merton (1263), Pembroke (1347), Corpus Christi (1352), All Souls (1438), and the universities of Bologna (1160), Paris (1160), Padua (1222), Naples (1224), Toulouse (1229), Sorbonne (1257), Prague (1347), Budapest (1389), Turin (1404), St Andrews (1411), Bordeaux (1441), Pisa (1345), Caen (1432), Glasgow (1451), Turin (1404), Uppsala (1477), and Aberdeen (1494).[23] It should be noted that many of these were not 'founded' at this time, but grew out of existing schools and became separate from the church order (and therefore the old ways of thought). As well, many private and national collections of books were developed in this period. That is, in the fourteenth century, systems were developing that could define knowledge in an entirely different way. Schooling became compulsory for young children in England by 1876 and removed children from the variability of local and family perspectives to a more general state perspective. These methods for the storage and dissemination of duplicate copies of new knowledge are quite alien to a type A pattern of consciousness. Albert Lord writes of the people who use what I term type B logic (us in his reference), that 'it seems to us necessary to construct an ideal text or to seek an original and we remain dissatisfied with an ever-changing phenomenon. I believe that once we know the facts of oral composition, we must cease trying to find an original of any traditional song. From one point of view, each performance is an original' (1971: 11).

The importance of the storage of these original units, clearly separate from their historical daily usage, can be seen in the development of museums from the fifteenth, sixteenth, and seventeenth centuries. Museums developed rapidly from such private collections as that of Jean, duc de Berry (died 1415); the 1570 collection of Duke Francis I of Tuscany, origin of the present Uffizi Gallery; the 1638 collection of J. Tradescant the elder; the 1735 Sloan collection of over 69,000 items, which became the basis of the present British Museum. Collections of other forms of imagizing the environment in stored static form also appeared at this time. Dictionaries were collated, such as a Latin thesaurus in 1538, a Latin-French in 1538, a Latin-German in 1568; the latter two also showed the increasing importance attached to literacy in the local language. The development of the use of the vernacular for the actual definitions and discussions of these new truths was vital. Tyndale's 1525 English translation of the New Testament, which led to his execution (though possibly for Henry VIII's political rather than moral goals), is one important example of this movement. There were others: 'in England, for example, Brandt's book appeared as *The Ship of Fools*, Van Diest's as *Everyman*, Castiglione's as *The Courtier*, and Machiavelli's comedy as *The Mandrake*. In 1503 Thomas à Kempis's *De imitatione Christis* came off London presses as *The Imitation of Christ*. Erasmus's *Institutio principis Christiani* became available as *The Education of a Christian Prince*, and Hartmann Schedel's illustrated world history was published simultaneously in Latin and German' (Manchester 1992: 102). The Royal Injunctions of Henry VIII (1536 and 1538) stressed the vernacular, and ordered 'the parsons, vicars, and other curates ... to teach or cause to be taught their children and servants, even from their infancy, their "Paternoster," the Articles of our faith (the Creed), and the Ten Commandments in their mother tongue' (First Injunction, 1536; in 1967: 79). Henry went further; 'you shall provide on this side the feast of Easter next coming, one book of the whole Bible of the largest volume, in English ... (and you shall) exhort every person to read the same' (Second Injunction, 1538; in 1967: 82). Not only was the old knowledge repudiated but, importantly, the code systems by which knowledge was expressed were further changed to lessen the viability of that former knowledge.

I suggest that these various systems developed as social mechanisms to give validity to the cognitive pattern. Imagizing vital concepts, such as the particular individual functioning as owner and creator of units of the environment, both in their original and their copy form, is done by defining generative activities such as creator, namer, inventor, owner, artist as semantically referring to human beings. Showing originals as particular units, not as abstract powers, is done by naming the site and date of the first appearance of a particular object, with the consideration that it was functionally non-existent before this appearance. The archaeological search for physical evidence and the precise temporal dating of a Neolithic mandible is very different from the Australian Mardudjara's acceptance that humans came out of the 'Dreamtime' an indefinite time ago. Defining originals on the basis of this temporal firstness and showing change from this origin as a progressive development is done by showing changes within a linear and cumulative manner, and emphasizing that such 'additions' of temporal energy are necessary to the functional 'struggle for existence' of all matter. Visibly showing the difference between storage and history is achieved by having different social systems perform each action.

The Phases of Type B Logic

Type B logic is a short-term cognitive frame. It provides an enormous burst of generative energy that enables a society to move out of the stagnant bonds within which it may have degenerated into a dysfunctional structure (as outlined in previous chapters) of collapsed realities, single realities, obeisance to external forms, dyadic interactions.

In the beginning stage, that of the first generation, the individual members of a population act with a seemingly unlimited direct access to generative energy. Type B logic diminishes or even totally removes the long-term accountable requirements and limitations of both a syntactic logic and the semantic images tied to that logic. These stable images become open to constant suspicion and testing. In any society, reality must remain open to a certain amount of variable interpretation, but in this first phase of the type B era, the old syntactic logic is no longer stable but fragile because of its very inadequacy in providing for its society. Reality becomes situated within the focus of the individual, an existentiality that is basically short-term and non-generative (of itself), and therefore by its very nature amenable to difference, change, variety.

This second node of cognition, the syntax, by its commitment and ties with a stable logic, reorganizes sensual experience to a sign or image. In type B logic, the transformation of the temporal aspects of the two realities to an external absolute scale of measurement rather than an interaction means that the past and future are not part of the dialogical aspects of current conceptualization but are rather static scales against which to compare current experience. Images are no longer created within a conceptual accountability to past/future reality; the past/future values are removed from any viability and stored separately from daily life. This removes both the past and the future from affecting or rather binding the current experience to a particular meaning. Current experience becomes experienced without dialogue and only in and for itself; what is defined as reality is stripped of its former bonds to any logic or form. Deconstruction is a powerful action; it separates the old ties between the IRS and IRC, the sensual and the conceptual parts of the sign; it permits new alliances, new signs, new understandings of the world. It is the very essence of being human, for 'the strength of the mind lies in the cleverness with which it manages to separate those particles from one another and then question them one by one' (Calasso 1993: 355). As is well known, Descartes set himself the task of questioning everything he knew, leaving only the direct IRS sensual experience dyadically tied to his own IRC conception. The fact that such a direct experience of 'reality' may be impossible is beside the point; the power of this era lies in its insistence in denying the dominant logic and thereby gradually enabling itself to develop a new definition of reality. Truth becomes understood as asocial, outside the constraints of a defunct society and accessible instead to the powers of the individual in all his variations. This phase is man confronting, not merely the gods of knowledge, but all human beings who have aligned themselves with those gods. The chastisement of Galileo, the burning of Bruno, were evidence of two things. First, the old syntactic ideology was no longer operative without dissension. Second, the old syntax had reached its socioeconomic limits and had decayed itself out of viability. Even if it fought every day for every last breath of its population, the results would have been the same. 'Even if all the angels had stayed in heaven, man with all his posterity would have been created all the same. For this world was created for man' (Honorius of Autun, 12th c; quoted in Le Goff 1993: 52). Le Goff sums up this period nicely: 'the final word of this humanism was clearly that man, who was nature, who could understand nature through reason, could also transform it through his actions' (57).

In its early stage in the first generation within the society, the semantic images are amorphous and debatable, subject to the analysis and hesitations of a great variety of human opinion. As is discussed in the next chapter, it takes at least three generations for a syntactic logic and its specific semantic forms to attain stability. In the first stages, the syntax and semantic images (the GR nodes and the IRC node) are highly volatile, unstable, permissive of the greatest variations. This phase is Bakhtin's carnival at its height, 'the birth of the new, of the greater and the better.' And 'during carnival time, life is subject only to its laws, that is the laws of its own freedom' (1984: 256, 7). All members of the society are involved; there are no specialists, no intermediaries, no shamans, for 'carnival is not a spectacle seen by the people; they live in it and everyone participates because its very idea embraces all the people' (7). This phase functions only in current time, without the restrictions of past/future imagery. The early stage of type B logic, in the height of its nature as carnival, is a 'temporary liberation from the prevailing truth and from the established order; it marked the suspension of all hierarchical rank, privileges, norms and prohibitions. Carnival was the true feast of time, the feast of becoming, change and renewal. It was hostile to all that was immortalized and completed' (10). The actions of carnival, of deconstruction of the means of storing energy (in logic and signs) and an almost constant access by individuals to generative energy, can never become a logic or a stable state. They are actions within current time, with no commitment to a past or future. If the carnival experience with its freedoms, its permissiveness, its amorphous semantic imagery, becomes the basis of a society, then I call this a situation of 'individual reality only';[24] it is a distortion and perversion of the carnival purpose and expresses its degeneracy in ongoing violence to both meaning and life; such a society destroys itself within one generation. Examples of this type, one version analysed by Durkheim under the theme of *anomie*, are discussed in chapter 6.

In its middle stage in the second generation, the logic gradually becomes stable and functional, and long-term IRC codes that validate this GR logic are created by the initiative of social officials, combined with the validation by the social means of dialogue and deliberation. This period is the era of conscious articulation (IRC) of the syntactic pattern, the phase of Descartes, Comte, Locke, and is the height of the benefits derived from this social text. In this era, the society defines itself and its interactions with all beings both natural and human; it develops the systems by which it organizes the new energy available to it, it develops the new code systems it uses to express itself. This phase is stable and prosperous. However, type B logic is inherently flawed, because it locates its generative origin within the particular, within the material reality of the humanly perceived environment, within the physical powers of individuals rather than within the mythic powers of pure unfocused energy. Although in its first phase it provides a tremendous input of generative energy by empowering individuals, if it becomes a long-term logic, then it actually gradually loses access to generative energy, to the power of myth, of illogicality, of diversity and new life. A society cannot live around human beings because they are by their very nature finite echoes of life. Even if a society calls its members heroes, defines them as generative, unless these are in contact with generative energy, they will, because they are human, entropically lose their powers. In many horticultural indigenous societies, the leaders are defined as 'big men'; this simply means that these men accumulate surplus energy in the form of food and various goods. They must distribute this surplus to all members; if they diminish this largesse, they quickly lose any respect and power in the society. All societies must ensure that their contact with the sources of life remains constant and accessible.

In the first generation, this logic establishes the individual as owner with the ultimate authority to create, define, change the cognitive reality. Eventually, in the final generation, group reality becomes a static external demagogue, operating within collapsed realities as an autocratic law.[25] But in the first generation, the deconstruction of the semantic forms and their bonds with a syntactic logic transforms the former syntax into an irrelevant code (IRC); this frees individuals from the mediation process and provides a powerful access to the free energy of generative energy. Contact with generative energy is open and accessible, rather than only during special occasions (such as trance states), and above all, it is available to all, rather than to designated intermediaries. Societies operating within this logic will see a great 'burst' of inventions of ideas and technology, both feasible and unfeasible. The question we must ask is whether this conceptual logic is a true social logic capable of stability and the continuing maintenance of a society. Is it an aberration, a result of the breakdown of the regular type A logic, a stage between the rebuilding of that logic? Is it an action of Bakhtinian carnival, of Peircean abduction, a phase of the individual by-passing the stability of group reality and accessing generative energy? I suggest that it is an actual social logic, albeit aberrant, active only for a short period and quickly degenerating into an asocial phase of collapsed realities. Accessing generative energy, the source of life, is the prerogative only of individuals, never the group. To use a biological comparison, change comes within the individual not the whole species. But type B society is an active cognitive paradigm, a way of looking at the world, a mind-set of a whole community and not a few individuals. Therefore, type B logic is capable of raising at least two to three generations within this pattern. It provides many of its members with the right to access generative energy, and thus such a logic has a powerful capacity to increase the long-term energy content of a population and is therefore a key means of social transformation. However, it should be noted that this increase of energy can only be of value if the society can also provide the capacity to organize and 'frame' this energy by both new technological and conceptual means. Such a requirement for a rapid development of new social systems and technology may also result in the development of a society with a more rigid organizational structure to deal with these new systems; this is the third phase, when type B logic moves into the phase that I have previously termed 'collapsed realities.'

The final phase of type B logic comes when the two realities collapse into one cognitive level. This collapse changes the interactive frame from the dialogical interaction of the two realities to a monological frame, where past and future become reference points within an IRC code rather than a part of a dialogical interaction. The syntax changes from being a pattern of action and becomes itself a code system, a static structure, an ideology rather than a logic for potential action; it becomes an external semantic guide rather than only a pattern for the action of transforming energy from potential to actual meanings. It becomes existent as an entity-in-itself; it is itself transformed into signs, metaphors of meaning, rather than acting as a pattern within which signs become extant.

I consider type B syntax a functional aberration, even a mutant form of type A. Type A is the normative social logic within which all societies, over all time, can be found to operate; it fulfils the requirements of a social text, the requirement for both stability and variation. It may express itself in a variety of sustenance patterns, from hunting and gathering through agricultural to industrial. Is type B logic both self-generating and self-sustaining? To use biological terms, is it a species or a mutant? I have to consider it a mutant, a powerful method that permits a population as a whole to access and use generative energy as a group and not simply as individuals, as is done within type A logic. As such, it permits the development of new technologies and new metaphors of meaning, which, after several generations or more become stable within a new social system operating within type A logic. Type B logic permits rapid change; it was this logic that permitted the Soviet Union to transform its identity from a peasant agricultural economy to an industrial economy, all in one generation, whereas the Western world, using the same logic, had done the same in an equally bloody manner over four hundred years. Can human beings remain in this logic? I think not; to pretend to be one with the gods is not possible. 'The heroes were the first to look at the earth before them as an object. And seeing it as an object, they struck out at it ... Zeus wanted to see the heroes, whom he loved, wiped off the face of the earth. They had to go, before they began to tread that earth with the same heedlessness with which the Olympians had trodden it before them' (Calasso 1993: 358). By the restrictions of their very biological nature, humans cannot constantly access generative energy; by the restrictions of their conceptual nature, their confinement to 'thinking only in signs,' humans cannot constantly access the amorphous clouds of generative energy. They must instead drink this elixir slowly, savour it, think about it, work within it. Tantalus stole this nectar from the gods and was punished for so daring; Prometheus betrayed the knowledge of the arts and was punished for so daring.

The two logical patterns outlined provide for different comprehensions of and interactions with the environment and cannot both be socially dominant at the same time. One or the other is dominant within an individual or group. The nature of these and other conceptual patterns that structure the semantic consciousness of reality are an important area for future research. Many of the social systems to whose emergence and development we have ascribed particular or individual reality–level causal explanations can be more validly explained within syntactic frames, and Braudel says it well: 'in history, the individual is all too often a mere abstraction. In the living world there are no individuals entirely sealed off by themselves; all individual enterprise is rooted in a more complex reality, an "intermeshed" reality ... we do not believe in this cult of demigods, or to put it even more simply, we are against Treitschke's proud and unilateral declaration "Men make history." No, history also makes men and fashions their destiny – anonymous history, working in the depths and most often in silence' (1980: 10). Europe's movement to Africa and America, the nurturance of democracy, of free enterprise, and so on can all quite possibly be given more accurate explanations by being considered part of a specific social text that required such social systems (not the semantic explanations) for its actual existence. Modern developments of non-literate methods of dealing with information and images, the changing nature of the family and state can be explained and understood as part of the semantic expressions of a different syntactic text and so dealt with.

Syntactic logic cannot be introduced to or removed from a society, as if it were a separate system, as can literacy or private ownership or a language style. The syntax is only a pattern by which we express and experience our sensual reality as conceptually meaningful. Therefore, the syntax is not separately causal of semantic signs but part of the production process of all conscious thought. Our thinking takes place on the immediate level of individual reality, that level of knowable, conscious reality, the level where we observe, define, remember, and interact. All of these actions fall within the existential reality of the individual. But no individual can, on his own, become a cognitive person. Such is only possible within the stability of a social text. That does not mean simply that a person becomes knowledgeable by obtaining *data* from other people. It means rather that our particular perceptions of the world become meaningful within a logical frame of behaviour. This logical pattern is only existent within interaction and communication. Voloshinov, a member of the Bakhtin circle, writes that 'no utterance in general can be attributed to the speaker exclusively; it is the product of the interaction of the interlocuters, and broadly speaking, the product of the whole complex social situation in which it has occurred' (1976: 118). Meaning comes about within the interaction of multiple variations of organization of energy. The textual society exists within such variations of organization; to lessen these levels, to access energy more directly, is productive but unstable. We shall now turn to examine the organization of these levels of energy and the requirement for both stability and change.

6

Textual Change

A society is an organic living system. From a thermodynamic point of view, it is an open system in that it is interactive with the environment; it both takes in and gives back energy in a variety of forms. From an organic point of view, this system is closed, in that the cognitive nature by which it organizes and transforms this energy is stable and finite and the amount of energy a particular structure can deal with is equally stable and finite. As in any organic system, both stability and diversity must exist within its spatiotemporal frame,and they do so in the dialogical interactions between the group-reality (GR) level of the syntactic logic and the individual-reality (IR) level of everyday experience.

The nature of change is completely different on these two levels. Change on the IR level deals with particular existentially discrete (whether material or conceptual) units and actions. These changes can be fleeting and temporary, such as colouring one's hair or using a word in an idiosyncratic way. Or they can be gradual and accumulative variations, such as in the development of an individual's consciousness of the environment, much as children change in their understanding of the world around them as they grow or as a professional learns of different approaches to a problem. In the first instance, fleeting change, water may change from a snow crystal to a liquid drop; in the second, gradual change, a plant can develop from a seed to a flower. Semantic change is considered a normal fact of existence and is socially acceptable; and 'each form had its own perfect sharpness, so long as it retained that form, but everybody knew that a moment later it might become something else' (Calasso 1993: 11). To permit cognition, Secondness, or that 'perfect sharpness' of form, that sense of alien differentiation from an other, is necessary , but this intactness does not remain. If it did, it would lock energy in and would subject it to what Bakhtin refers to as 'canonization,' something 'distanced from contemporary consciousness.' Logically, the syntactic pattern, whether genetic or social, remains the same despite the surface variations. The surface semantic instabilities are functional within a long-range syntactic order through which the system acts as a whole.

Let us look at an example of semantic change that has not been definitive of any change in syntactic pattern. In America in the 1840s, cigarette smoking was a sign of poverty or lower-class status. In the 1860s cigarette smoking extended beyond the poor to also define someone of a 'shallow heart and depravity.' However, by the 1920s cigarette smoking came to be part of the image of the young American male, individual and strong and completely different from the depraved businessman with his cigar. The 1940s offered images of soldiers smoking between the battles and of Humphrey Bogart, who 'spoke' with his cigarette – images that portrayed a man who has finally reached the age of both acceptance and commitment. By the 1960s, this same image included women (recall the Virginia Slims statement of 'You've come a long way, baby'). In the current era, smoking has once more become associated with poverty and lower-class status, defined not merely in economic but also intellectual and moral terms.[1] These images are all functional within the semantic binary code of the IRC. However, any change to the syntactic logic involves a complete change in the pattern of this basic code. It is not gradual but immediate and complete. It either *is* one pattern or it *is not.* Therefore, change on the level of GR logic is complete, sudden, and catastrophic to the sensual and conceptual signs of the IR level. Change on the level of the IR is ongoing and frequent. Syntactic change is rare and may occur only once in a millenium.

The Balance of the Two Levels

The IR level of everyday life develops and changes IRC (individual reality conceptual) images and their meanings on an ongoing basis within the limitations of the STF or conceptual horizons and the GR syntactic logic of that society. A homeostatic balance between the two levels exists so that a specific IR level semantic system will work in balance within a specific GR syntactic logic; the 'centripetal' and 'centrifugal,' the Bakhtinian centralizing and decentralizing forces, are in a balanced interaction. One can then speak of two types of social change: *variable* or *heteroglossic*, which affects the IR semantic level and is variational; and *logical*, which affects the GR syntactic level and is revolutionary or catastrophic. Variable, everyday change keeps the same logic. Logical change is a complete change of both the syntactic pattern and ultimately of the meanings that exist within this logic. It occurs only when the dialogical balance between the two levels is destroyed.

All spatiotemporally framed (STF) systems are made up of finite amounts of energy, constantly being renewed and changed. As systems actively engaged in the transformation of energy, they must have an ability to change their energy content (within strict syntactic limits) and the semantic expressions of that energy (again, within strict limits). This adaptive power gives them the ability to react to current realities both within and outside their spatiotemporal horizons. However, societies perceive and react in different ways to the need to deal with energy requirements, depending on whether their GR syntax is a type A or B.

Generic or Semantic Code Changes

Type A logic accepts variations in everyday life by considering all IRC or sign experiences as variable versions of a more indeterminate and undefined original. Type B logic accepts primarily iconic signs, which are mimetic and not deviations from a 'pure' original. A type A society can permit greater flexibility and adaptability in daily life without considering life to have 'changed' than can a type B logic society, because it sees many IR level differences not as 'changes' but as 'variations.' Indigenous peoples saw no problem associating themselves with both the Christian and their tribal religions; the new metaphors were simply absorbed along with the old. However, Lenin, operating in the second stage of a type B syntax, attempting to change his society from a type A peasant agriculture to an industrial economy, said, 'Wherever there is small business and freedom of trade, capitalism appears' (quoted in Braudel 1984: 631). That is, in a type B society, change is obvious and frequent and, in this case, potentially uncontrollable. Bakhtin writes that 'each generation at each social level has as a matter of fact its own language, its own vocabulary, its own particular accentual system that, in their turn, vary depending on social level ... and other stratifying factors.' And also, 'at any given moment, languages of various epochs and periods of socio-ideological life cohabit with one another ... at any given moment of its historical existence, language is heteroglot from top to bottom: it represents the co-existence of socio-ideological contradictions between the present and past' (1981: 290, 291). In a dialogical society, with dialogue understood here in the traditional Bakhtinian sense of a dialogue of multiple meanings rather than my usage of dialogue as interaction and exchange of energy between different organizational nodes, these variations are all part of the semantic level (where language as an IRC code system exists) and, if kept in balance, do not affect the syntactic level.

However, a type A society has much greater difficulty effecting deeper and more enduring changes to social beliefs or behaviour. First, because of its basic polyphonic nature, it tends to ignore or absorb variations, and second, it assigns the power to effect such changes to special intermediary agents within the group, such as prophets and heroes. These agents alone have access to generative energy to move completely new (not variations of) beliefs and behaviour into the society. Indeed, this is so privileged a role that an 'average person' is not expected to come up with anything different and would not be taken seriously if he did. He could very easily become a 'non-person' and be banished from the group. The type A infrastructure permits a long-term stability of its GR logic because it limits access to 'differences' to only a few people in the group. Such societies change their basic GR logic only with great difficulty and only when the dialogic balance between the two levels has become so degenerate due to overpopulation, disease, economic imbalance, or other factors that change is the last resort. This was the case in Europe of the thirteenth and fourteenth centuries, a period of epidemic diseases that quickly wiped out normative standards. Another forced change can be by the implosion of an external agency, for example, the way colonization forced its way among indigenous peoples.

The linear temporality of the collapsed realities of type B logic permits existential entities (IRCs) on the IR level of current time that are independent of the GR logic's temporal identity of past/future. Therefore, entities on the IR level can be immediately understood as new because any variation is perceived as something different from the past. In this society, change is constant and expected.

The Agent of Change

In both syntactic types, the individual is the source of new ideas, but in type A logic this individual is socially defined as 'special,' while in type B logic everyone can and is expected to be an entrepreneur. Descartes clarified this concept by regarding man as unique in his possession of a soul; the special prerogative of the soul was to originate, a view rejected by Aquinas, who considered that the special function of man's intellect was to 'understand,' for God 'has given us the light of reason, through which we know principles' (*De ver.* q. 11, a. 1). The historic period of the dominance of type B logic in western Europe was therefore a sociopolitical era of individual freedom to create, explore, and change, and a key period (lasting only five hundred years rather than thousands) for the development of an enormous amount of new technology, enabling human beings to access far more energy, on a geometric rather than arithmetic scale, than in any period of their existence. This explosion of energy, all controlled (or so they thought) by human beings, spread over the entire globe in a space of only two hundred years. This period of a 'frontier' mentality, of a *grundnorm* of new ideas and forms of behaviour, permitted Europe to deal with its overpopulation by the two co-agencies of intensive exploration of land and mind, based within the actions of colonialism and industrialism.

The inventor is a person who sees the world differently. He is frequently first classified as a madman, a non-namer. It is part of our historical consciousness that Socrates was required to drink hemlock for his different perceptions, that Galileo had to recant and deny his cognition, that the views of Copernicus were condemned, that Bruno died at the stake. The society did not permit the thoughts and the man who created them to exist within the group. As Koestler notes, there is a social archetype of the 'mad professor' who 'practices black instead of white magic for the sake of his own aggrandisement and power' and who as 'either a sadist or obsessed with power – looms large in popular fiction' (1970: 258). Like the witch, this person's evil nature is understood to be based within his own individual self; his desires, his inventiveness, is focused for his own sake.

The important factor, however, is that the group must require that invention, that perception, or the perceiver will be labelled, not as a creative agent, but as an evil threat. We, in our obsession with names, will wrangle over whether the discovery was by Darwin or Wallace, whether the inventor was Gutenberg, Waldfogel, or Koster. The real issue is that something was created, defined, and used. As Braudel points out, 'the steam engine ... was invented a long time before it launched the industrial revolution – or should one say before being launched by it?' (1981: 335). At the time of its first perception, the steam engine was not needed in any real socioeconomic sense. When a need for more energy and a different organization of energy caused the society as a whole to require such a system, then its inventor and the invention became socially valid. Inventors should be viewed as catalysts for change but not solely causal of change. This is another factor that suggests that neither inventions nor indeed any particular single factors cause historical or social change. Such linear determinism is too simple and ignores the deep dialogical organic actions of the textual society. Rather, these new perceptions become socially valid when the organic system requires them.

Perhaps it is correct to emphasize here again the concept that society is not a sum of individuals or systems but an organic structure. A new perception appears via an individual who is perceived in either a separate or intermediary role. This individual is still part of the organic structure of the group. If this new image is socially functional, then it is understood within the society to have a valid meaning that can be made available for broader usage. If it is not accepted as part of the group discourse, then it may not disappear but does not spread further into the society. It remains a short-term unit tied directly to its creator, who may be seen as a 'weird person.' There are a myriad of examples of such forgotten and hidden inventions. The inventor, however, has this vital role of introducing new concepts; he can readily be understood as an initiator of 'discursive practices,' someone who produces 'not only [his] own work, but the possibility and the rules of formation of other texts' (Foucault 1977: 131).

The Act of Creation

What is the act of creation and the nature of the creator? Koestler describes the action well, quoting Sir Lawrence Bragg: the 'essence of science lies not in discovering facts, but in discovering new ways of thinking about them' (1970: 235). The agent of change must have a 'scepticism towards the conventional answers, the refusal to take anything for granted, the freshness of vision of the unblinkered mind' (459). Such a perspective allows 'thought to play outside of the ordered table of resemblances' (Deleuze; in Foucault 1977: 23). The creator, whether artist or scientist, permits his understanding to be fragile, and 'the poet has a new thought; he has a whole new experience to unfold ... for the experience of a new age requires a new confession, and the world seems always waiting for its poet' (Emerson; in Maritain 1955: 110). Every new concept has been made by 'the invention of a hypothesis which, though verifiable, often had little foundation to start with' (T.H. Huxley; in Koestler 1970: 234). This new concept frequently comes as a sudden insight, a 'flip' of consciousness or what Koestler defines as the 'Eureka' action. Popper notes that 'the initial state, the act of conceiving or inventing a theory, seems to me neither to call for logical analysis nor to be susceptible to it' (1972: 20). For Bakhtin, this stage would fall within the carnival and laughter actions, which 'clarified man's consciousness and gave him a new outlook on life' (1984b: 91). But the gathering of concepts and exploration of knowledge that takes place before this moment of insight can last for many years. Thus Charles Peirce, in his examination of the creation of new ideas, which he terms 'abduction,' can say that it 'consists in studying facts and devising a theory to explain them' (5: 145), and then 'the abductive suggestion comes to us like a flash. It is an act of insight, although of extremely fallible insight' (5: 181). It tries what '*il lume naturale* ... can do. It is really an appeal to instinct' (1: 630).

This action of discovery is made by an individual removing himself from the ongoing dialogical interaction with the GR logic that binds his experience of the sensual (IRS) and both permits and limits its ultimate conceptualization (IRC). Essentially, this means that access to the potential energy of the GE (generative energy) is possible when the conceptual path of the individual moves via Individual Sensual 1 → generative energy → Individual Sensual 2, rather than the normative route of IRS → GR → IRC. Individual Sensual 2 has more energy than Individual Sensual 1 and requires a different logical organization in order to be conceptualized into an IRC sign. The individual in discovery does not separate himself from the trauma of the unknown, which is one of the care-giving roles of a society, but joins with it in a carnivalesque sensual and aconceptual union. Here, the outlines by Koestler and Bakhtin of the creative power of laughter in 'deconstructing' normative meanings, and the various analyses of the importance of play in the discovery of new, adaptive forms of behaviour, suggest that some action is required to separate the individual from the normative horizons of meaning. This action will be explored more fully in the next chapter, but we can consider here that the society and the individual must be somehow pushed to a 'critical threshold' that will move the agent outside the strictures of the STF (spatiotemporal frame) to access new energy to be moved into the conceptual frame.

Change as Revolution

We are aware of the power of syntactic logic in forming human conception, the most necessary durability and even sluggishness of its force, and can understand that it takes a great effort to change a group's comprehension and usage of the environment. If a society cannot encode a sensual perception for conceptual use within the group, then it not only denies the existence of that perception, it renders the agent who uses that concept speechless (outside of his own verbalization). If you do not acknowledge the perception of the environment by giving it a name or semantic sign (IRC), whether verbal or visual, then, once past the immediate physical perception (IRS), that unit no longer exists. You cannot talk about it, you cannot discuss it, you cannot even think about it. The syntactic logic organizes the sensual data in such a way that that GR node is also involved by extension in the semantic organization of the IRC nodal point. If you cannot think of a human being as separate from the environment, then you cannot conceive of the concept of ownership of that environment.

What about a perception that already has a sign that for some reason is no longer socially functional? Is it really that easy to change the belief that a disease is caused by an uncontrollable evil spirit and accept that it is caused by a physically existent and possibly controllable germ? Changing the meanings that a group holds changes its consciousness of itself and the environment. This can only be a destructive action, even if the change in the long-term is beneficial. People involved in such changes are often seen as tragic figures. A revolutionary is 'a doomed man.' He has no personal interests, no dealings, feelings, attachments or property, and often not even a name. A revolutionary, and by such I mean not only a political but also an intellectual revolutionary, destroys the old way of thinking. He is not also empowered to create a new mentality. The revolutionary is not also an inventor. What the revolutionary does is destroy the old system of cognition, the basic GR logical pattern, so that the new one, which is *already* existent within the IR existential level of everyday life, can emerge as part of the dialogical frame. A society that is on the verge of changing its cognitive content exists in an unbalanced state of energy. Its GR logic can no longer deal with (conceptually organize) the mass of energy available within its STF. It has existed for a number of years within a certain conceptual logic, with understandable generic code systems of signs and a balanced interaction as such a group. For a variety of reasons, these signs become unable to express the current existential sensual reality of the group. The IRC meanings must therefore be changed and new ones created. The only way to do this on any long-term basis is to destroy the GR logic that is part of the 'triadic nodal-string' that leads to IRC comprehension. It is not enough to 'deconstruct' semantic signs, to separate the Saussurian signifiers from their signifieds. This is equivalent to killing one hundred mosquitoes and ignoring the swamp that is breeding new ones. Meaning is created only within the dialogical interaction between the IR and the GR level. To create new meanings (IRCs), the society must replace the syntactic logic. The role of the revolutionary is not to separate the semantic signs from their old meanings (deconstruction), but to remove the power of the GR logic from the society so that a new syntactic pattern, already existent in the IR level (within a small abberant group or number of groups), can become dominant in the society and so permit new meanings to be conceptualized in the dialogical act.

Colonization as Revolution

Colonization is not generally considered a revolutionary action. It should be, although there are important differences. The revolutionary act is a rather neat and linear, if violent, change. There is first the old cognitive system; then second, via the revolutionary agent(s), a revolution that destroys the old cognitive frameworks. Then there is a new leader (the hero), who permits a different GR logic to exist and thereby a state of freedom for the invention of new signs. The point to note is that the new syntactic pattern and the new generic encoding systems were *already* existent in the society's territory and had unbalanced the old dialogical stasis. They were marginal to the official system but they were spatially and temporally located within that society. The American Revolution expressed an understanding, based on the primacy of the self-governing individual, that already existed within the territory. Such an understanding was not only possible within the enormous spatial and conceptual openness of that territory, but was also required if the incoming group wished to access the resources of those lands. The belief in the individual, which had been the basis of the Reformation and Renaissance in Europe in the fifteenth and sixteenth centuries, had decayed there by the eighteenth century. The American Revolution extended for another two hundred years the existence in the Western world of this type B syntax with its individualistic mentality.

Colonization does not operate in this manner. The old way of thinking exists, but there is no revolutionary action that destroys it and permits the other marginal system to emerge as the dominant group cognition. Rather, a new and completely external group cognition totally foreign to the society is moved into the society's territory and established as dominant. 'From very large tracts we have, it appears, succeeded in eradicating them; and though from some parts their ejection has not been so apparently violent as from others, it has been equally complete, through our taking of their hunting grounds, whereby we have despoiled them of the means of existence' (*British Parliamentary Papers*, 1837; cited in Bodley 1990: 26). And 'the political autonomy, economic habits, religious practices, and sexual customs of organized native groups, in so far as they threaten European control or offend Western notions of morality, must be abandoned' (Reed 1943; cited in Bodley 1990: 95). There are thus two cognitive systems side by side within the same geographic space. It becomes a species fight, for the two groups should really be seen as two different organic entities. What frequently happens is that the old mentality does not die out but moves to an extremely restricted usage. It may be restricted geographically to the poor sections of the cities, to the uninhabitable and unprofitable lands of the far regions. The people who use this cognition may be restricted in all their actions to a lower class. They may be confined to reservations. Their traditional cognitive system may be segregated to a linear time period; they are called 'backward,' 'uncivilized.' 'People must learn to be scientific and progressive in outlook instead of living by ancestral laws and long-tried rules of thumb' (Jones 1965; cited in Bodley 1990: 103). The indigenous peoples operated within their traditional cognition before attending the Western-style school. The educational system that they are obliged to accept functions within a different logic. The many problems that these people have with the educational systems have nothing to do with capability or even with the fact that they are changing from a native language to English; the problems arise from changes to deep cognitive patterns. Such changes cannot be accomplished easily or without great trauma – and certainly not within one generation.

Changing the methods of cognition within a colonized group is not the same as offering a logic that people may choose, much as they may select items in a market-place. To move into a society and change, for example, the valid namer of truth from the 'spirit of life' to the 'intelligent individual man' is an action not simply on the level of words and their meanings, but involves the cognitive structure within which that reality exists. This same action moves the site of the storage of truth from god to individual memory and books. Learning about the environment is no longer guided by discursive interaction with the learned people in one's society, but from indirect and private reading of the knowledge stored in books and meant to be memorized by all, no matter their intellect or usage of this knowledge – an action that horrified Plato. Because all systems of everyday life are rooted in the syntactic logic, then if one generic system in daily life is changed, all systems must be changed. If you enforce a change in, for example, an economic genre (from a no-growth sustenance economy to a surplus cash-based economy), then all social systems must change, including the political, legal, family, and religious genres. Such changes are disastrous to the society because the old logic that is expressed by all generic systems – it is carried by the adult generation – is destroyed if it is no longer used. To destroy the syntactic logic of a society renders its people incapable of articulation, thought, and self-awareness. The destruction by warfare and disease of both the adult and new generation of indigenous peoples in colonized areas essentially meant that the physiological means of preserving the old cognitive logic was destroyed. The further destruction of the coding systems of the IRC nodal point as expressed within their linguistic, kinship, religious, political, and economic generic codes assisted the destruction of the syntactic logic by depriving it of the semantic means to articulate itself. This permitted a new syntactic logic and new semantic codes, those of the Europeans, to move into those spatial areas of the world and spread their generic methods of behaviour.

The Stages of Colonization

Once a threshold level of dialogical interaction of a logic and its generic codes is reached, the logic can be considered stable. Reaching this stage can well take another generation. You cannot simply introduce one method of defining the environment, which is only operative within a particular GR syntax, and expect it to become existent only in its surface nature. The two social realities, group and individual, must interact dialogically. This change takes time – time measured in terms of generations, not of years. This has been the mistake of 'developers' in all parts of the world – of introducing methods of living on the immediate level and totally ignoring that these methods are not 'rootless' but are tied to a deeper level, a deeper conceptual logic. Literacy, bottle feeding, working for wages, purchasing goods, elected governments, and other life practices are none of them valid within themselves. They operate within a deeper conceptual logic. To introduce them 'from the outside,' which really means from a foreign syntactic frame, is to introduce only the action and not the meaning of that action. To develop a society that has both levels of cognition operating as a dialogical text takes at least two to three generations. The ignoring of the fact of the two realities has been the tragedy, not only of colonization, but also of current Third World 'development' actions.

The first stage in colonization is the separation of the group reality syntactic pattern from the individual reality level of everyday expressions. This is done by a colonizing force that destroys the agents of expression of the dialogical actions (the indigenous population) and also forbids them to carry on their former way of life (redefinition of norms of religion, education, economy, politics). 'The native tribes must withdraw from the lands on which they have pastured their cattle and so let the White man pasture his cattle on these self-same lands ... For a people, as for an individual, an existence appears to be justified in the degree that it is useful in the progress of general development' (Rohrback, leader of the German Settlement Commission of South-West Africa, 1907; cited in Wellington 1967; cited in Bodley 1990: 53). The colonizers see their actions as 'simply intended to utilize the vast undeveloped territory now held by the Aborigines in the island' (Formosan government 1911; cited in Bodley 1990: 56). The second stage is educating, forcibly or otherwise, the new generation in the semantic realities of the colonizers' cognitive pattern. This alienates that generation from the guidance and teaching of their normative group logic and from their historic identity. 'As religion plays a part in every Naga ceremony and as that religion is not Christianity, every ceremony must go' (Elwin 1959; cited in Bodley 1990: 107). It completes the loss of a deep cognitive level. In this phase, semiosis has lost its triadic nature; it has lost the essential stabilizing force of Thirdness, of a syntactic pattern rooted in a sense of a past/future social identity. Consciousness in this period is only semantic, superficial, inexplicable, operative within all the degenerate forms of individual reality, of external form, of semantic discourse. The third stage for the colonized is the experience of working and existing within only a surface reality that is not grounded in any deep logic within the group. This is the era of despair and suicides, of a people without a syntax and therefore with neither past nor future; this is Durkheim's *anomie*. It is the direct result of colonization and 'development' and can be found among not only indigenous peoples, but any social group torn from a syntactic base (inner city, urban poor, homeless). The fourth stage is the development of a new logic within and by the colonized group. With the development of a new syntactic logic, the indigenous people gain the cognitive strength to start to define and redefine their group identity, to own their history, to exist as a conscious, knowing group. However, the transition from the colonial destruction of the original logic to the development of a new logic takes at least three generations. During that period the people lose much of their heritage and ideology and are thereby forced to create new semantic codes adapted to the current reality of a new syntax.

Three Generations

'Legitimacy is the only force that guarantees the continuance of a government; but for a government to become legitimate, it must already have lasted a long time' (Calasso 1994: 53). Syntactic stability is a basic requirement of cognition and therefore a requirement of a textual society. A syntactic logic must exist for at least three generations in order to be conceptually and not simply existentially existent; that is, to be operative as a logical agent in the triadic function of transforming sensual experience to conceptualization. A human generation should be understood as fifty years, by which I mean the years of accountability, when an individual has established in his own identity the conceptual frame of movement from Firstness via Thirdness to Secondness, such that it governs both his actions and his thoughts. Using this measurement, at least 150 years or three generations of actual experience are required for a social text to gain the stability to be not simply expressed in the individual sensual reality, but conceptually understood and analysed. If we consider the introduction of a new group reality, then the first generation to experience it sensually (Firstness) nevertheless developed in an older text and understand it conceptually (Secondness) based around its old logic (Thirdness). Those of this generation, even though currently living in the new social text, still understand their experiences within the old logic and educate their young, the second generation, in that reality. They conceptually deny or misunderstand the experiences of the new text. The second generation experiences the new social text but lacks the logic to analyse it. This is the generation that actually deconstructs or destroys the old logic. This is a difficult period, for such people are living within a social text with no analytic means to understand it; they have no conceptual access to the logic of a stable group reality. It is the third generation that experiences the new text in its full existentiality; is aware of the inability of the old to classify, analyse, and clarify; is therefore 'free' of the constraints of the old logic and able to formulate the analytic structures of a new conceptual reality. Therefore, a conceptual paradigm or syntactic pattern may have changed and been expressed technologically and socially in year one, but more than one hundred years must pass before it is conceptually functional within the society.

The Nature of Social Change

Group reality syntactic change occurs *before* the conscious experience and expression of it on the IR everyday level. The catastrophic period of syntactic change is an era of either revolutionary or colonizing actions. This phase, a form of Bakhtinian carnival contact with generative energy, destroys the old GR logic. It does not establish a new GR logic, but by destroying the old, it permits a new logic to emerge. This new logic already existed within minority groups in the larger social group – in the case of a revolution – or is introduced from outside – in the case of colonization. Biologist Stephen Jay Gould analyses biological species change, stating that 'splitting takes place rapidly in small populations ... a new species can arise when a small segment of the ancestral population is isolated at the periphery of the ancestral range. Large stable central populations exert a strong homogenizing influence ... small, peripherally isolated groups are cut off from their ancestral stock' (1990: 152). That is, species change, which I compare with syntactic social change, emerges within a small population (the poetic-inventors) that splits itself from the hegemonic domination of the normative semiosis of the society. If the old species is degenerate, this new one rapidly infiltrates itself within the spatiotemporal area of the old society. The next phase is the gradual development of the dialogical structure, that interaction of the two levels, the IR and the GR, and the establishment of the three nodes of articulation – the IRS, GR, and IRC – as a relatively stable structure of semiosis in that society. This establishment of the dialogical infrastructure can be understood as moving through three stages.

The first stage, after the change in GR logic, is a period when the everyday expressions of this new cognitive pattern are expressed, but without a clear consciousness of what is being expressed. Everyday life is still filled with the semantic imagery of the previous cognitive pattern; new images are experienced within the old generic code systems and may easily be misunderstood. It is here that we see the furore over new theories. In the Reformation era a political and social struggle tool place between the medieval church and the state government. It was not a fight between individuals or even a battle for political power and control. Rather, these were wars over a 'way of thinking.' Which is, after all, the basis of power. Was knowledge to be based within the group or within the individual? The medieval church based knowledge within the group; the individual played a submissive role. The new humanism based knowledge within the individual; all its verbal harangues against the scholastics were geared to empower the individual to greater freedom to decipher, use, own the environment. Abelard said: 'it was not my custom to have recourse to tradition to teach, but rather to the resources of my mind' (in Le Goff 1993: 37). The difference between this form of change and the change enforced by colonialism is that in this society, it is caused by internal rather than external forces. This is an important difference. Internal social change is a result of imbalance within the society; external social change unbalances a previously balanced society.

Using concepts of dynamics, we can consider a society that is in a state of weak stasis, that is reaching a critical threshold in its ability to organize energy via its three nodal points. As Gould points out, 'change occurs in large leaps following a slow accumulation of stresses that a system resists until it reaches the breaking point' (1990: 153). European society of the fourteenth century was certainly at that point, having tried and failed to deal with overpopulation by means of various famines, plagues, and wars. The last – and it is a last resort – was syntactic change. This alone would permit a new way of thinking and so permit a new technology that for a few hundred years could ease the problems of that population. I must emphasize that syntactic change is a last resort. It can only be catastrophic, because not only must a syntactic logic be changed; the people who carry that logic within themselves and their behaviour must be destroyed. As I have explained, the syntax, the GR, does not exist on its own; it is carried within the semiotic interactions of its people. Therefore, changing this syntax is not a mere matter of substituting one semantic code for another, as the developers so ignorantly assume, but destroying at the very least one generation of people. It happened over many hundred years in Europe, over one generation in the Soviet Union and China, over one generation in Europe in the two world wars, one generation in Vietnam. Gould again states it clearly in quoting Derek V. Ager: 'the history of any one part of the earth, like the life of a soldier, consists of long periods of boredom and short periods of terror' (154).

The second stage, after the syntactic change, is the period of semantic definition and redefinition. It is an awareness that what is currently conceptually valid within the society is distinct and knowable and also different from the previous metaphors of meaning. The society can differentiate itself from its former ways of belief and behaviour and develop the generic semantic codes in their full strength. Bakhtin's outline of the poet as differentiated from the novelist is relevant. 'The world of poetry, no matter how many contradictions and insoluble conflicts the poet develops within it, is always illumined by one unitary and indisputable discourse ... In poetry, even discourse about doubts must be cast in a discourse that cannot be doubted ... The poet is not able to oppose his own poetic consciousness ... he is completely within it and therefore cannot turn it into an object to be perceived, reflected upon or related to.' The novelist, on the other hand, 'the writer of prose ... attempts to talk about even his own world in an alien language, he often measures his own world by alien linguistic standards' (1981: 286, 287). The novelist reflects on, comments on, observes the multiple variations of his syntactic order. The novelist stands outside his discourse because he has the power of a syntactic logic within his conception; he has the power of a past/future perception to what he says. The poet lives without the consciousness of a syntax, without the extended horizons of a past/future stability. The revolutionary is an agent of the syntactic change, the poet is an agent of the second stage of semantic articulation, and the novelist is the agent of the third stage of analysis.

We can see these expressions in the current struggles of the Islamic world both for and against the 'novel,' against self-examination. Or, looking back again at the sixteenth century, we can see this in the establishment of the new (Protestant) church with its stress on individual interaction with truth, in the ratification of the market economy and its support for individual entrepreneurs, trade, banking, new wealth. We can see it in the development then of social systems that assisted the individual in his personal exploration of the material environment and emphasized his control over it – the development of printed books, universities, libraries, museums, and banks, trade centres, and factories, and of a political system based on state laws and democratic elections. I am not suggesting that any of these systems of living are 'right' or 'wrong'; they are operative within a particular conceptual logic and are 'right' only within that logic.

When the dialogical infrastructure of the two levels of thinking, the GR logic and the IR generic codes, is well established, then the third stage can begin. This is the period when a society analyses 'why' it is, and tries to examine and explain itself. This is the period of greatest philosophic, social, and artistic exploration. It is also a period when, in examining what it is, the group also becomes aware of what it is not. This is the basis of dialogue, the awareness of 'otherness.' In this situation, 'they both illuminate the world and are themselves illuminated by it' (Bakhtin 1981: 45). Every syntactic era has this phase and it is its height of power. It was the finest expression of the scholastics; it was the later era of Descartes, Kant, Locke, Hegel, and others. Without such continuous self-examination, a society falls into the trap of authoritative discourses, the degenerate forms of discourse that preclude dialogue and the potentiality of adaptive change. The conceptual infrastructure of a society is almost fully operative by the time its members begin to explore, explain, and critically examine their textual metaphors. That is, these philosophers, historicans, novelists, do not cause a period; its logic is fully operative by the time they began to explain it.

Change in the Syntactic Pattern

GR logic is only a pattern of interaction. It cannot be analysed directly but only through the observation of the objects and actions of the IR in everyday life. These logical patterns are total structures and therefore cannot be 'evolved into' or 'developed from.' They either are or are not. But *within* the everyday experience of that pattern, there are developmental stages, when the dialogical interaction of the IR level, with its syntactic pattern, is either balanced or unbalanced. I repeat that the syntax is only a pattern of interaction and does not contain within itself any developmental stages. Further, there is no determinable path of future development. There is no inherent need for a cognitive pattern to change. Finally, neither the IR level nor the GR logic exists alone; they are operative together in a constant dialogue. Textual reality is a *historical* expression of an *ahistorical* pattern of thinking. A logic or pattern of cognition cannot exist on its own. It only provides the conceptual framework within which particular sensual experience is conceptualized.

The concept of long-term cognitive structures that change is not new. Anaximander suggested that 'innumerable world-orders arise and perish again into that from which they came.' They are 'dissolved and born again according to the age which each is capable of attaining' (Aetius I. 3. 3; in Robinson 1968: 39). Anaximenes said that 'there are innumerable world-orders, but they do not overlap' (Diogenes Laertius IX, 19; in Robinson: 54). The Mexican world cycle has 'nine hells'; Yeats describes twenty-eight phases of world cycles. Braudel's 'longues durées' last for many centuries; Bakhtin's 'chronotopes' are long phases of conceptual reality. These phases of group longevity are finite. They last for a certain number, usually many hundreds, of years, and then must completely change.

Eliade comments that 'the Egyptians, the Mesopotamians, the Jews and other peoples of the ancient Near East felt the need to renew the world periodically.' And 'the beginning was organically connected with an end that preceded it, that this end was of the same nature as the "Chaos" preceding Creation and that hence the end was indispensable for every new beginning' (1963: 50, 48). This sense of a periodic change of worlds or social texts is not confined to Eastern mythology, Greek mythology, Islamic, Far Eastern, and Judaeo-Christian apocalypses, but is found in all mythologies. Whether the metaphors used are mythic, political, or religious, the image of a traumatic change of cognitive framework is the key concept.

There are theorists who explain social systems as changing in an evolutionary and developmental manner, in a series of stages, with each stage developing from and/or incorporating the earlier. The exact nature of these stages may differ according to the theorist, but such various social analysts as Comte, Turgot, Condorcet, Saint-Simon, Schopenhauer, J.S. Mill, Spencer, Morgan, Hegel, Darwin, and Marx outlined theories of the progressive development of man. Other theorists, such as Piaget and Freud, used a developmental or evolutionary model as the basis for their theories of individual maturation. All these concepts, however, are confined to the semantic level. The thought that there is a deeper level of consciousness that also changes is not part of their analyses. Further, these theories are all temporally linear; they understand time as developmental. The point is that change to the syntactic logic of the group reality is *not* linear, developmental, or progressive. It has neither history nor future; it is a change of a cognitive framework and complete within itself.

The causal factor of change to the syntactic logic is therefore a matter of debate. Some research insists on a distinct IR level causal agent, a kind of 'messenger particle.' For example, actions of violence in society are examined as directly related to violent images on television and other media systems. The one is seen as mimetically causal of the other. But could it not be that both the media images and the street reality concurrently express a deep social violence? This deep violence is not simply against people but is expressive of a current imbalance between the semantic and syntactic levels. This is also where we find the imagery of the revolutionary or inventor as a causal hero. Again, I point out that their actions would be totally ignored if the society were not already in a dysfunctional state and ready to be reorganized. If human beings had not already been in such a sorry state, filled with troubles such that they had 'eyes to look, but looked in vain, and ears to hear, but did not hear,' then the organizing peace of the gifts of Prometheus of language, mathematics, and all the skills of social living would have been ignored. The organic text, whether it be social, chemical, or biological, must be at a transitional state of disequilibrium, such that the old logic will actually break down and a new one emerge. We are currently in the early phase of a new group reality logic that is quite different from the one that has lasted for the five hundred years of the capital-industrial period. In these early stages, the everyday level is operating via the images and beliefs of the previous logic, a phase that stressed individual causality. Until generic code systems are developed by our poets that can fully express the new logic, this violence will continue, breaking down old semantic metaphors and codes and establishing a new set of social relationships. The semantic level of change is always behind that of the syntax.

Two Steps: Catastrophe and Self-Organization

A change in syntactic logic is not 'caused' by a specific causal agent (whether material or social), but is the result of an imbalance of the dialogical interaction between the two realities, group and individual. This type of change follows the catastrophic theories outlined by René Thom in *Stabilité Structurelle et Morphogenèse*, 1972. The change from logic to logic is not a developmental act but a transformation, a catastrophic change, with many of the implications that these words imply: sudden changes in behaviour and reversals of belief; extreme violence, both social and physical (disease and famine are as much a part of this phase as are aggression and war); inexplicable reasons for the changes (which are afterwards explained by means of various everyday factors). Change in logic, since it involves the whole logic as a pattern, cannot be gradual.

Eliade writes of mythic analysis of change that 'for something genuinely new to begin, the vestiges and ruins of the old cycle must be completely destroyed. In other words, to obtain an absolute beginning, the end of a World must be total.' And 'the myths of the End of the World have certainly played an important role in the history of mankind. They have shown that the origin is moveable. For, after a certain moment, the origin is no longer found only in a mythical past but also in a fabulous future. That is, these "Worlds of Consciousness" are finite' (1963: 51, 52). Prigogine says that 'successive regimes of ordered (oscillatory) situations follow regimes of chaotic behaviour' (quoted in Briggs and Peat 1989: 137). Importantly, there is no direction, no intentionality other than an increased complexity of organization. As the quantum physicists have pointed out, you cannot predict or determine the future.

GR logic, as a complete cognitive sentence, sustains all everyday behaviour. This includes physical existence, with such factors as population size and density, sustenance, housing, health and disease, as well as the social metaphors to sustain the material nature of the society. When these everyday operations are balanced within the logical pattern, the group functions well. When, however, IRS experiences on the everyday level cannot be conceptualized by GR logic into socially viable IRC units, then the dialogical relationship between the two levels begins to break down and may eventually reach a threshold level of imbalance that will collapse the structure. When famine as an IRS action moves into a society and cannot be justified within the IRC, then the syntactic stability of that society weakens. Actions on the everyday level alone do not cause a collapse in the tie between the two levels. A single revolutionary cannot bring down a society. It is when the dialogical interaction between the two levels has become so weak, so incapable of reorganizing and stabilizing the energy transformations of the IR level, that such a collapse can occur and a new ground logic may appear. What must happen is that a state, which in chemistry is called 'far-from-equilibrium,' must occur; this is a 'threshold' state of dis-equilibrium, and within this phase the old organizational pattern collapses. A new one appears, but from within the spatiotemporal form; that is, a new syntactic order 'self-organizes' from within the society. 'Prigogine and his colleagues see self-organizing structures emerging everywhere: in biology, in vortices, in the growth of cities and political movements, in the evolution of stars' (Briggs and Peat 1989: 138). Fluctuations in thought and behaviour are ongoing in a society. Looking at these in a chemical sense, 'there are always small convection currents appearing as fluctuations from the average state, but below a certain critical value of the temperature gradient, these fluctuations are damped and disappear' (Prigogine 1980: 89). But there is a crisis point, and ' above this critical value, certain fluctuations are amplified and give rise to a macroscopic current.' A new molecular order appears and stabilizes itself, that is, 'a giant fluctuation stabilized by the exchange of energy with the outside world. This is the order characterized by the occurrence of what are referred to as "dissipative structures"' (90). Above a threshold point, variations from the norm suddenly magnify in number and effect, a 'giant fluctuation' in molecular order appears, and a 'new molecular order' comes into a stable existence. Stability is possible in systems capable of maintaining their identity within a continual openness to the flux and flow of their environment. Once a 'far-from-equilibrium' phase appears, then a dissipative structure forms, a phase of imbalance. Stasis is destroyed, for 'once a dissipative structure is formed, the homogeneity of time, as well as space, may be destroyed' (104).

These dual actions of catastrophic disequilibrium and dissipation followed by a subsequent self-organization can be understood as a two-step process. The first step is the chaotic destruction of the old syntax; the second step forms a new order; importantly, this new order already exists, hidden, within the organism. This concept of an existent yet hidden order has nothing to do with determinism, nothing to do with any primal intentionality. Rather, when a textual organism, by which I mean an organic entity that is both spatiotemporally self-sufficient (defined and distinctly 'other') and also open to the dual actions of taking in energy while producing entropy (waste), when such an organism changes its energy content such that it loses its ability to retain and transform that energy, then it must reorganize its holding/transforming patterns. This new pattern comes from within itself (except in colonization) and, like Mandelbrot's iterable fractals of order that repeat their logic infinitely, the new syntactic order quickly, indeed instantly, moves into dialogical place. It moves within an 'awareness of self-similarity,' where, via a process of iteration, the same pattern is repeated in various complexities throughout the whole mass. In our semantic experience, a syntactic change may seem, although catastrophic, to be slow; however, in a larger sense, the spread of a conceptual order through a massive population within one generation is essentially instantaneous.

A syntactic pattern can potentially be infinite in its spatiotemporal spread. A type A pattern can be functional within a small hunting and gathering society or within our current global society. What limits the iterable spread of that pattern, and therefore establishes horizons of existentiality for a society, is the capacity of the semantic level's systems of organizing the expression (conception) of energy. A simple example occurs in the natural environment. If there are two semantic level (IRS: sensual energy) factors missing from a certain geographic area, such as water and a freezing temperature, then the pattern (syntax) of organization of energy that is a snowflake (IRC: conceptual energy) does not become existential over that whole geographic space; it happens only where there is both water and a particular temperature. However, the iterability of the pattern that is transformed into a snowflake has in itself no limits; it is infinite and could exist if the semantic level factors also existed.

Interactional Breakdown

The semantic level functions within a particular syntax. Does the group have the naming power to define new sensual experiences or redefine old ones (a heliocentric world rather than a geocentric one), or does it refuse to accept the validity of physical proof? Does it, if operating by an encoding system based on abstract sources, have the power to repel signs offered by encoding systems based on empirical proof? Does it have the ability to remove and store concepts that are no longer operative in current discourse? Does it have the ability to remove/silence people in current discourse who espouse a belief that uses a different cognitive framework? Can it teach its generic metaphors to all its people, or if a massive influx of immigration occurs and negates its teaching ability, will these people also bring in new concepts that deny the group's current reality? Does it have the power to use its new concepts in meaningful discourse, or do new concepts remain among a small set of researchers? For example, is an antibiotic unrecognized as a valid method because disease is generally considered to arise from a spiritual force and not from physical causes? If the group's cognitive structure becomes unbalanced, such that its semantic systems cannot handle either the decay of its old metaphors or the introduction of new ones, then this unbalanced state may reach a critical threshold point, where the catastrophic 'flip' to a new logic may occur. This new logic permits a different organization of semantic reality, a different conception of reality. This cognitive change is entirely natural, despite its aura of catastrophe and destruction. Following biological tenets, the change of a single pattern – the syntax – is far more plausible than the change of the semantic complexities of an organisim. As D'Arcy Thompson said, 'we cannot transform an invertebrate into a vertebrate, nor a coelenterate into a worm, by any simple and legitimate deformation ... Nature proceeds from one type to another ... To seek for stepping stones across the gaps between is to seek in vain, forever' (quoted in Gould 1990: 160). That is, transportation by horse does not gradually transform into transportation by car. The change that permits each is focused within a much more basic (to the organism) organization – the syntax. Again, Gould writes, 'no one would ever think of transforming a starfish into a mouse, but the embryos of some echinoderms and protoverte-brates are nearly identical' (ibid). Therefore, change at a less complex form of organization, the syntactic node, is the key to basic, rather than variable, social change.

Before the fifteenth-century Reformation, there were a number of large-scale wars and epidemics, which destroyed both the material basis for the reality of the medieval beliefs and the everyday ways of life that expressed these beliefs. This period of social and physical destruction and catastrophe was an expression of a conceptual breakdown and a change to a new way of thinking. The two world wars of the twentieth century were a similar catastrophic expression of a change in conceptual logic. Every deep conceptual change is accompanied by an inevitable destruction of the everyday semantic level, its people and its material and conceptual reality.

What happens on the semantic level is not empirically causal of another event on that level, except in the simplest mechanical terms. Certainly, thirst is eased by water and turning the light switch will lead to light. However, syntactic change cannot be linked directly to an IR level incident. The invention of the printing press did not lead to a switch in the pattern of thinking; the removal of God as prime naming power within the culture by Luther, Copernicus, Kepler, Galileo, and Darwin, and the substitution of material forces and agents in such a role, did not cause such a deep logical change. Rather, the mental structure within which all these actions were expressed was *already* in place and thus permitted the particular semantic expressions of these metaphors and the group acceptance and usage of them.

The two levels of cognition are not existent 'in themselves' but as actions within a dialogical interaction. When this relationship breaks down, then the resultant release of 'free energy' can be enormous. In this sense, I am obviously comparing the social system to the nuclear structure. The break in the dynamic interaction of the two levels, the syntactic and the semantic, destroys the bond of the dialogical infrastructure of the two levels and releases a great amount of chaotic or deviant energy that destroys the functioning pattern of the logic and the social systems that maintain it on the semantic level; 'things no longer have a fixed weight. They fluctuate – immense, vaporous, poisonous bodies. They do not rest in themselves. Nothing stands firm' (Calasso 1994: 28). This permits, indeed necessitates, the appearance of a new syntactic pattern that will trap and organize that energy.

Textual change refers not merely to semantic level but also to syntactic level transformations. A society thus lives within an eternal conflict in its nature as a text, of being both 'centripetal and centrifugal,' necessarily stable and necessarily open to change. It is a 'hard life' and yet this dilemma, to be considered in the next chapter, is the basic power of textuality.

7

Two Bodies / Two Powers: Stasis and Heteroglossia in the Textual Society

Dialogical Text

Society is a dialogical text. It is a continuous interaction and amalgamation of what we may call forces or systems of energy that are differently organized from each other. A key function of the text is its establishment of common, which thereby means social, definitions of reality. By such common definitions both human beings and society become real, with reality understood as a 'thing in itself with independent qualities that exist in an historical (that is, a spatial and temporal) sense.' However, contrary to the discursive deconstructionist and phenomenological emphasis on the nature of reality as semantic discourse, society and human beings are not simply semantic but are rather semantic versions of physical matter.

I intentionally use the word *version* rather than expression. By this I mean that physical matter exists, not in the Baconian sense of being objective in itself, but as spatiotemporal expressions of energy that are experienced but not necessarily known within our particular human organic nature. There is a difference between 'the real' and 'the experienced,' and the two are not necessarily identical.[1] These versions of reality are all dependent for their existence on confinement within a conceptual frame that establishes their spatial and temporal boundaries. This follows the Copenhagen understanding of quantum reality, where 'reality only makes sense within the context of a prescribed measurement or observation.' With this stress on the need for an action of observation (and therefore an observer), we also note, in the words of Bohr, that there are 'fundamental limitations, met with in atomic physics, of the objective existence of phenomena independent of their means of observation' (Davies 1990b: 122). So, too, we have the Peircean insistence that 'reality is independent, not necessarily of thought in general, but only of what you or I or any finite number of men may think about it' (5: 408). Lotman's semiosphere and Bakhtin's chronotope are similarly textual worlds that are created by human beings. Reality is only experienced (not known) through the semiosis of signs.

Essentially, this means that observation or, more accurately, interaction establishes frames of existence whereby physical matter 'collapses' from an indeterminate state into a specific spatiotemporal entity. In essence then, the physical matter of reality exists as a multitude of probabilities (Aristotelian prime matter, Aquinas' potencies) that become existential upon the intentional or unintentional establishment of a finite interactional frame that permits intra-energy dialogue.

Socio-organic Text

Society is a socio-organic text because it is a creation of beings whose nature is both organic and social. The textual society is made up of energy. There are two sources of energy within the textual society: one is the physiological organic forms of human, animal, plant, and physical matter within its boundaries; the other is the conceptual organization of this material energy by the human mind. A society therefore, is 'socially organized organic and conceptual energy.' A biological organism with a small energy content has a less complex organizational structure than one with a high energy content; the latter requires complex organization to maintain its energy stability. In a similar manner, societies cannot be compared as equivalent simply because they all contain the organic entities of human, animal, plant, and other material beings. Societies as socio-organic texts contain different amounts of energy and are therefore differently organized.

The principle being developed here is that physical reality exists in multiple versions; these differences are not simply semantic or conceptual but are different spatiotemporal versions of physical matter or energy. The textual society is one such physical reality; it has been transformed by cognitive actions into an existential 'thing-in-itself' with a spatiotemporal base; it has history or temporality and it exists in a particular place. With the addition of these two essential infrastructures (time and space), the textual society exists not merely as a concept but as an actual version of physical matter. This text, being made up of such a large mass of potential energy, exists over a long period of time. Its spatiotemporal existence or Secondness lasts for several hundred years or more. Not simply its Thirdness, which is syntactic habit, but its actual spatiotemporal existence (Secondness), its consciousness of itself as a social text, a 'distinct society,' lasts for a long period of time.

Used Text

A society is a text because it is used. By this I mean an 'organic living usage'; the metaphors or individual energy units in that society, whether they be physical or conceptual entities, are not consumed intact. The textual society and its metaphors are chewed over, interpreted, reinterpreted; bits are diverted, rejected; new ones are created by beings who experience these textual metaphors in a variety of ways. This is the basis of the Bakhtinian dialogic act, where the novel, that supreme example of dialogue, is 'defined as a diversity of social speech types (sometimes even diversity of languages) and a diversity of individual voices, artistically organized' (1981: 262). We should not overlook the importance of 'artistically organized'; this implies an 'orchestration' of order, a sense of profitable interaction, an organized circulation of mutual, interlocking agendas. As a text, a society is an ongoing and active socio-organic experience.

Closed Text

Finally, a society is a text because it is closed, in the sense that it is a finite amount of spatiotemporal material and cognitive energy that is socially organized by systems particular to that energy content. A society contains a specific amount of energy; it functions within that energy content and the particular methods required to maintain the stability of that energy. Two social systems can contain very different amounts and organized types of energy and therefore require a different overall organizational structure. To ignore this difference is the mistake we make when we define societies as 'developing' and assume that if the people of X society simply grow their crops by using machines rather than by hand, produce a surplus rather than sustenance, and govern themselves by a state rather than communal system, then they will be 'developed.' The nature of available organic energy within that geographic area, and above all the conceptual systems that organize the energy content in each social text, are completely different. Technology cannot be transposed from one society or even one geographic area to another because technology exists within a particular textual organization. Living in the Arctic versus living in the Mediterranean versus living in the Kalahari desert versus living in the Brazilian rainforest must result in different social texts. It is a reality that most plants cannot be grown in the Arctic and therefore human beings cannot live there within any type of agricultural social structure. An agricultural system that depends on European rainfall has a specific organic and conceptual logic that cannot be set up in the thin soil of a rainforest, where a swidden typology of agriculture can function; a pastoral nomadic system cannot function in a semi-desert, while a hunting and gathering organization can establish a long-term social text in that same area. Each of the variety of sustenance systems extracts a different amount of organic energy from the material environment, and therefore conceptually organizes itself within a different logic; they are a different social species, just as animal and plant species are different biological species.

Two Bodies: Two Powers

As previously discussed, two levels of social organization are required to maintain this energy. There is the long-term syntactic logic of group reality, which is the key organizational frame ordering a particular society, and there are the more short-term regional semantic or particular generic code systems of the individual reality level. A society requires stability (stasis) to maintain the integrity of its identity and prevent entropic loss of its two forms of energy, the material and the conceptual. It also requires the ability to vary (heteroglossia) both its metaphors and its organizational logics to maintain an adaptive vitality. Heteroglossia or actions of variability confront, question, and thereby promote change in both the syntactic and the semantic codes, to permit the creation of new genres or semantic codes and the less frequent creation of new syntactic logics. Referring to biological organisms, Laborit writes that they are 'a complex system of reactions, mutual adjustments programmed in the structure in such a way that this information structure is preserved,' and specifically comments on the multiple levels of organization. There is a need for 'a constant evasion of the second law of thermodynamics' (1977: 40, 27) by the acceptance and transformation of new energy to provide the stability of self-preservation. Human beings are universally similar in organic needs; however, they live in different environmental biomes; the textual society, by its ability to socially vary the organization of this matter, develops societies that must be examined as different species.

The textual society is made up of two forces that are different, confrontational, and yet constantly interactive with each other. Metaphors of these two forces are found in every society that has ever existed, whether they be presented as gods/devils, love/hate, health/illness, life/death. One may arbitrarily define such different intentionalities as good and evil. The cognitive act, which is always experienced within the individual, is triadic, but the textual society is binary and made up of two bodies. As Bakhtin notes, speaking of language, 'the centripetal forces of the life of language, embodied in a "unitary language," operate in the midst of heteroglossia.' The social text is made up of two forces, the centripetal or centralizing force of stasis and the centrifugal forces of deviation and heteroglossia. They are fundamentally in opposition; however, they exist only within an awareness of and interactions with, each other. They function together, so 'the processes of centralization and decentralization, of unification and disunificiation, intersect in the utterance ... Every utterance participates in the "unitary language" (in its centripetal forces and tendencies) and at the same time partakes of social and historical heteroglossia (the centrifugal, stratifying forces)' (1981: 271, 272). The metaphoric acknowledgment of these opposing forces is an awareness of a basic conflict of goals within reality. These metaphors, which are always violent, with their sense of both change and renewal, acknowledge a binaristic identity as essential; they make no attempt to unify those opposing forces into one, knowing full well that such an act would lead only to monologue and death, as Orpheus, wishing to look and so unite with his wife, Eurydice, so quickly learned.

These oppositional forces must not be understood as something semantic added by the intellect. Such binarism would refer only to a value, and I am instead suggesting that these two forces are actually existent in themselves within the wholeness of the textual society. Their differences are not, however, innate, a state that would need no maintenance as such, but are instead developed by the society. Human beings devise and nurture ever constant metaphors of these two realities, carefully maintain and renew their bodies, and so permit an endless, insistent confrontation. To hesitate even for a moment, to slip into the stasis of unification can only be compared to the effect of Pan on Argos, who lost his life as he lost his vigilance. This essential gap of their differentiation can be compared to the 'bar' that Lacan insisted upon between the Saussurian signifier/signified, such that they can never unite; there will always be both an overwhelming desire for and yet an incessant sliding away or rather a fleeing of the one from the other. In a particular society, we may court with great diligence one or the other force of stasis or heteroglossia; we may define quite clearly in our minds their nature as good or evil and the social desirability of either force. But there is no such finality of existences in the textual marriage, for like the gods, these forces will only laugh at our attempts at semiosis, our conviction that our words can ever have any stability. They know better, and what was good surreptitiously befriends, slips toward and dissolves into evil; what was evil emerges and walks along with the good. In language, 'no living word relates to its object in a singular way: between the word and its object, between the word and the speaking subject, there exists an elastic environment of other, alien words ... and this is an environment that is often difficult to penetrate' (Bakhtin 1981: 276).

The Social Body: Stasis

The human being as a socio-organic species is highly adaptable to a great variety of geographic areas and means of sustenance. Other species adapt themselves to only a limited number of environments and sustenance styles. For example, deer are found only in specific parts of the world and are foragers, not hunters; particular animals eat foods found only in one terrain; birds have quite limited breeding areas. Unlike these, the human species can adapt to a hunting and gathering or an agricultural or an industrial sustenance system. The human species can adapt to any environment, whether it be an ice or sun desert, a rainforest, or a grassland. The price of this adaptability is the loss of an inherent or genetic infrastructure of stasis. The means of providing continuity in behaviour, which also means continuity of the species, is not genetic but social. The human species must provide some means of stability of behaviour over a number of generations, and this is done by the development of the long-term syntactic logic, the social body. This social body is the force of stasis, a stability of organization. It is our conceptual habits; we and all our echoes have created it together. It is Peircean Thirdness, Bakhtin's genres and chronotopes, Lacan's symbolic, Lotman's semiosphere, Kristeva's chora/genotext.

When we speak of a society, we primarily think of a stable long-term system capable of renewing its identity over the multiplicity of generations of individuals. The human as a component of society has a short-term existence, and people, as Bakhtin has pointed out, 'are incomplete, they also die and are revived and renewed' (1984b: 12). As organic cell components of the social text, human beings learn to exist as social cells within that particular text. Spatiotemporally static organizations of reality are an absolute requirement for human existence because they provide continuity beyond the immediate. Peirce refers to this stasis as 'synechism,' 'which insists upon the idea of continuity as of prime importance' (6: 169). The idea of repetition of patterns is similar to the idea behind Mandelbrot's fractals, where each part in the infinite series is an iteration of the whole; this permits a continuity of type in both space and time. Peirce says that 'no collection of points placed upon a truly continuous line can fill the line so as to leave no room for others' (6: 170). All participants, no matter how few or how many, must be able to function within the stability of the patterns of the textual society. Such a stability is expressed both as a logic and in codes, at the GR and IRC nodal points. The syntactic force, like Bakhtin's chronotope 'serve[s] to unify and centralize the verbal-ideological world' (1981: 270) of the individual, or rather, to centralize and thereby limit the immense potential for variation that is inherent in the physical human being. Bakhtin's chronotope is a long-term pattern for the ongoing generation of the metaphors or codes of relevant genres, for 'it is precisely the chronotope that defines genre and generic distinctions' (1981: 85), with 'genre' understood as a code of IRC behaviour, a specific, limited, and learned way of creating and using social metaphors.

A society that loses such organization moves into random disorganized behaviour; its members are unable to function to exploit the environment for the satisfaction of biological and psychological needs. The society collapses as a system of organization; the population disintegrates both pyschologically and physically.

The social body is therefore fragile; a society dies when its ability to conceptualize its habits breaks down. This happens when human beings, who are the mediaries of such conceptualization, no longer articulate social images. Why does this happen? Superficially, we may say that it is because the interaction of the two bodies has for some reason become harmful to the perpetuation of the lone articulator of both bodies, the individual. More deeply, it may be a sign of the perpetual battle between the two bodies, the society and the individual; it may be a sign of their battle for power over each other. The social body may seek to become monologically dominant; the individual will be reduced to mimesis. Such actions are not functioning as a voice (of the social body), but as an echo; the social body, seemingly in supreme power, becomes reduced to hearing only its echoes; these too will entropically disappear and the text will fall silent.

Therefore, society, as made up of finite biological and physical matter, is in an eternal conflict because it requires both stability and also instability. A society lives within 'the discrepancy between the discontinuous and the continuous, between rational numbers and real numbers – and the realization that continuous and discontinous must remain linked' (Calasso 1994: 215). The interaction of the two forces of stasis and heteroglossia, the centripetal and the centrifugal force, is a textual requirement.

The Individual Body: Heteroglossia

The validity of the syntax must stand above the variable use and interpretations of individuals because its function is to provide for iteration, the repetition of behaviour and the continuity of the group as species. Stability as a habitual pattern for the development and usage of social metaphors is vital, but as I mentioned previously, it is not the only requirement of the textual society. The other requirement is for precisely the opposite – instability. With only the stasis of the syntactic logic in existence, a society will entropically decay. It will turn the potentiality of meaning into an 'authoritative discourse' that 'permits no play with the context framing it, no play with its borders, no gradual and flexible transitions ... it enters our verbal consciousness as a compact and indivisible mass ... it is indissolubly fused with its authority ... and it stands and falls together with that authority' (Bakhtin 1981: 343). This is where 'canonization,' the development of the single voice of authority, sets in. Peirce's analysis of the various methods of 'fixing belief' are relevant. Tenacity, the individual method, is a refusal to open an IRC sign to dialogue and results in the transformation of a 'belief into a truth.' Another method is the group use of authority, the enforcement of a rejection of dialogical semantic interactions, where 'let an institution be created which shall have for its object to keep correct doctrines before the attention of the people, to reiterate them perpetually, and to teach them to the young; having at the same time power to prevent contrary doctrines from being taught, advocated, or expressed' (Peirce 5: 379). This method of political correctness 'has, from the earliest times, been one of the chief means of upholding correct theological and political doctrines' (5: 380). Without new energy, entropy of both form and structure will set in; if you listen too much to the 'sweet dew upon his tongue' then you will be so mesmerized by the sound that thought will cease. Actions that are iconic repetitions provide stability for a period of time, after which the society inevitably collapses. Any society whose cognitive structures, the nodal points of the two realities, have become closed to new energy, cannot sustain itself; this is why fascist and totalitarian states cannot endure beyond one generation. Even 'in the most priest-ridden states some individuals will be found who are raised above that condition. These men possess a wider sort of social feeling; they see that men in other countries and in other ages have held to very different doctrines from those which they themselves have been brought up to believe; and they cannot help seeing that it is the mere accident of their having been taught as they have ... that has caused them to believe as they do and not far differently. Nor can their candour resist the reflection that there is no reason to rate their own views at a higher value than those of other nations' (5: 381). A new society can be born, using the same species, from the destruction of the old. This is the unbelievable strength of human beings, that they can 'change their species,' their syntactic and semantic codes, and yet remain the same biological species. They can do this only because their 'codes' are in a social rather than genetic form.

The textual society within its stasis must have a means by which it can deviate from the force of stasis. The climate may change, the flora and fauna may absent themselves, a disease may deplete the population, a new food source may be found, another group may make contact, a different tool may be developed. Deviation, as the acceptance of abnormality within the society, is the only means of bringing more energy into a society. A society that simply brings in the same amount of energy to replace normal entropic loss needs no change of organizational logics and remains the same. Deviation permits adaptation and has therefore permitted 'history' in all its conceptual and technological forms to exist. The ongoing interactional dialogue between the syntactic and semantic levels of energy both confine and stabilize genre expressions and, as well, introduce new energy or variation from individual deviations into the syntactic logic.

Change in the textual society is achieved via the individual reality level, via the short-term and therefore more unstable nature of the individual. Individuals are indeed carriers of stability by their commitment to the expression of the ideologies of the syntax within the various semantic codes. A code of any type permits only the reproduction of an entity, but not its variation. It is individuals who are susceptible to doubt, who deny, who destroy, who, as carriers of stability, also die in both body and mind and therefore permit the birth of unsocialized beings who permit existences that deviate from stasis. 'The Modern is born when the eyes observing the world discern in it "this chaos, this monstrous confusion" but are not unduly alarmed. On the contrary, they are thrilled by the prospect of inventing some strategic move within that chaos' (Calasso 1994: 40).

As I have outlined in previous chapters, there are two types of social adaptative actions. One is expressed by varying the semantic or regional codes. These local, short-term codes are highly specific to a local need and can adapt to new needs within a few years. These changes affect only local individual behaviour and maintain the integrity of the long-term and more general logic. A society can maintain its syntactic logic of a hunting and gathering economy, but can have variations in type, permitting the introduction of different means of access to water holes (such as a mechanically dug well), different means of carrying gathered food (such as the use of a machine-made bag). These changes, unless and until[2] they reach a threshold point of energy balance, do not harm the syntactic pattern. The catastrophic action, as discussed in the previous chapter, permits a change in the syntactic pattern.

The key means of finding new energy to provide the power of variable adaptation is heteroglossic deviation in all its forms, from laughter to criticism, from carnival to rebellion. 'The men of the Middle Ages participated in two lives: the official and the carnival life. Two aspects of the world, the serious and the laughing aspect, coexisted in their consciousness' (Bakhtin 1984: 96). The key word is 'coexistence,' a coexistence of 'the pious and the grotesque' forces of stability and deviance. The textual society exists within a dialogue between stasis and heteroglossia, between conformity/stability and the transience of deviation. Such dialogue is the basis of human history because it permits both continuity and adaptation, the essence of the historical presence of human life on this planet. The explicit rejection of interaction with the inexplicable, the uncontrollable, the rejection of pain or death, any emotional trauma, any instability, as without value (as is found within our current society), is equally atextual. These experiences were celebrated by Rabelais, de Sade, and Bakhtin as necessary and vital to knowledge. They are also absolutely necessary for the existence of the textual society.

Conflict between the Two Bodies

The stasis of the social body is by its very nature oppositional to the short-term fluctuations of the human body. What, after all, is the human body but some 'dust of the ground'? However, as our myths acknowledge, this dust is the very essence of the mother life. Destroy one individual and another just like it appears, just as the earth regenerates itself after every rain. Therefore, human physical bodies (not their conceptuality) predate the physicality of the society. As such, human bodies predate their own existence as realities, because to be 'real' is to be conceptual, which requires sociality, something achieved only by contact with the social body. That human beings are in articulatory touch with both polarities – the pre-conscious mystic beginnings and the group oblivion – is why they, not the social body, are the real power in the social text. The individual alone has the power of beginning again, of birth, of invention – for remember, it is the individual whose body is made of dust, of the mother. And the individual also, once conscious, is the only means for the social body to articulate its own identity.

Therefore is it unreasonable to suppose that the society, with its larger body, its longer time span, and yet its lesser powers, would not be jealous, would not try to confine and restrict the enormity of the powers of the individual? This is the *first conflict*, the despair of the social body over its own weakness and the rage at the individual that engenders and articulates this awareness.

The human body exists as a physiologically separate form, temporally finite and spatially distinct from other physiological entities. Reality is experienced by the body, as with Adam and Eve 'after the fall,' as a physical and conceptual awareness of finiteness, both spatial and temporal. The individual body becomes conscious of this essential isolation of itself only by mediation with the social body in its stasis nature of Thirdness. Here is the *second conflict* between these two powers. The individual only becomes conscious via an interaction with the social body, but such interaction does not engender satisfaction at the powers of the individual but instead leads to despair, to a rage of realization that these powers are brief and transitory.

> Because I know I shall not know
> Because I know that time is always time
> And place is always and only place
> And what is actual is actual only for one time
> And only for one place.   (T.S. Eliot, 'Ash Wednesday,' 1930)

These two forces, stasis and heteroglossia, the social body and the individual body, have thereby set themselves up for eternal conflict.

The Truce of Good and Evil

Homer speaks of binaristic conflict:

> Tantalos ... standing in lake water that came up to his chin, and thirsty
> as he was, he tried to drink, but could capture nothing;
> for every time the old man , trying to drink, stooped over,
> the water would drain away and disappear, and the black earth
> showed at his feet, and the divinity dried it away.

And, of course,

> Sisyphos ... he would try to push the stone upward
> to the crest of the hill, but when it was on the point of going
> over the top, the force of gravity turned it backward,
> and the pitiless stone rolled back down to the level.
> (*Odyssey*, XI, 583-8; 593-8)

Here, the movement towards something caused its retreat; the desire for the lessening of the other's existence (water) caused its withdrawal, or in the case of the stone, caused its renewal. Similarly, when the society realizes its weakness and tries to strengthen its own nature, it causes the decay of the individual, but this leads eventually to its own death as a society. So, too, the individual tries to strengthen its own nature at the expense of the stasis of the society. In literary terms, it attempts to 'deconstruct' the social body. In so doing, the individual body loses Thirdness, which is its ability to live as a rational being and may thereby degenerate into an apocalypse of madness. Both confrontations lead to oblivion. Therefore, the only way for both to live is by a truce, a treaty signed, albeit unwillingly, by both bodies. It was Hesiod who said that 'one much stronger than you holds you now, and you will go wherever I take you, even though you are a singer. And I shall make a meal of you if I wish, or set you free. A man who wants to fight against one stronger is a fool.' And so we human beings, who are all singers of tales, must become reconciled to the duplicity of our bodies, and make a truce. Lacan spoke of these two forces in their nature as powers and 'the primordial law is therefore that which in regulating marriage ties superimposes the kingdom of culture on that of a nature abandoned to the law of mating' (1977: 66). Let us explore the truce between these two bodies within a gnostic and then a Lacanian perspective.

The Necessary Truce of Gnosticism

The responsibility for such action rests with the individual body, which is not only the sole agent of intentionality but also of conceptualization and articulation. An action that puts responsibility on each individual to settle these contrasting agendas is contrary to the European political and religious heritage, which sets up a hierarchy of selected officials who alone have the authority to articulate the stable textual truths of the social body and sees the individual as simply mimetic of these codes. Among gnostics, however, each individual must do this accessing and articulation alone; otherwise, they will be 'unknowingly empty, not knowing who they are, like dumb animals' (*Second Treatise of the Great Seth*, in Pagels 1989: 102).[3] The gnostics 'assert that what distinguishes the false from the true church is not its relationship to the clergy, but the level of understanding of its members, and the quality of their relationship with each other ... [they] discriminate for themselves between what is true and false' (*Apocalypse of Peter*, 106). The true individual body finds truth within himself, for '(t)here is a light within a man of light, and it lights up the whole world' (*Gospel of Thomas*, 120). Above all it is acknowledged that 'God created humanity; [but now human beings] create God. That is the way it is in the world – human beings make gods, and worship their creation. It would be appropriate for the gods to worship human beings' (*Gospel of Philip*, 122). Substitute the word *society* for *god*, and we have the infrastructure I am discussing. It is not a mystical frame whereby the individual seeks the primal source in his own isolation, it is not a search for the mystic Platonic form or the Derridean Writing, but is rather a frame of two different physical realities, two bodies, the individual and the social, that are yet conceptualized within only one of those bodies.

The gnostics did not seek the answer to the basic questions of life in universal non-material truths accessible only by the individual, as per the Eastern mystics, but in the reality of *the social body*. Such access required individual thought and analysis: 'the mind is the guide but reason is the teacher' (Silvanus, 127). Reason rests on the analytic frame developed within Thirdness, within the social stasis, the social body. However, only the individual can access Thirdness, by the cognitive action of moving from Firstness, via Thirdness to knowledge or Secondness. 'Open the door for yourself that you may know what is. ... Whatever you will open for yourself, you will open' (ibid). To know truth, one must conceptualize the social ideology: 'there is light within a man of light, and it lights up the whole world. If he does not shine, he is darkness' (*Gospel of Thomas,* 120). We have here a very pragmatic perspective.

The Kingdom of God or truth 'is inside of you and it is outside of you. When you come to know yourselves, then you will be known , and you will realize that you are the sons of the living Father' (*Gospel of Thomas,* 128). And 'for this (one) needed the rider, which is reason ... before everything else ... know yourself' (Silvanus, 127). The point is, this contact with truth, which I define as stasis, is not mystical and gained via unconsciousness but actually via reason, which is the sole prerogative of the individual. If you lack contact with stasis, you have 'no root.' So that 'ignorance, not sin, is what involves a person in suffering' (*Gospel of Thomas,* 124). Lacking this, you behave according to your individual whims – and this is evil, because you lack the self-knowledge, the insight that sees that your physical self is speaking for two separate and conflicting bodies. Self-knowledge is not historical in the sense of remembering past individual experience, but is knowledge of this basic organizational structure of human existence. As with other physical matter, one must understand its basic organization. 'If one does not (understand) how the fire came to be, he will burn in it, because he does not know his root. If one does not first understand the water, he does not know anything ... If one does not understand how the wind that blows came to be, he will run with it. If one does not understand how the body that he wears came to be, he will perish with it ... Whoever does not understand how he came will not understand how he will go' (*Dialogue of the Saviour,* 126). And how does one's body come to be? By dialogical combination with but not assimilation into another body – a body that is older, broader, more stable, than one's own. And yet, oneself alone, the weaker, is its only voice, its only means of expression and self-analysis. The social body, the stronger, the more long-lasting, lives within the physical body of the individual. As when Zeus took Dionysus from Semele's womb and sewed it into his thigh, so human beings take the body, the metaphorical content, the rules of the society and sew it into their own body.

The knowledge invested in the social body cannot be accessed via another being such as Christ, a bishop, or other external intermediary. That would suggest that truth is both stable and external to the individual, who then functions only as a passive and unaccountable recipient. Such passivity is indeed a common frame of communication theory[4] and is a political model in state societies where the source of hegemonic communication of social beliefs is external to the individual. The Christian church as an important component of a state society has a similar frame, where truth comes from an external source and 'one must obey the priests who are in the Church' (Irenaeus, bishop of Lyons c. 180: Pagels 45).

We are, however, not talking about political and social domination, but about the awareness of the actual nature of the laws that dominate us because they are a part of our body. The gnostic sees any acceptance of a frame of external truth and authority as blinding and therefore the source of evil. 'Before gaining gnosis, the candidate worshipped the demiurge, mistaking him for the true God: now, through the sacrament of redemption, the candidate indicates that he has been released from the demiurge's power. In this ritual he addresses the demiurge, declaring his independence, serving notice that he no longer belongs to the demiurge's sphere of authority and judgment, but to what transcends it.' What transcends it? The knowledge that you as a physical human being are actually two bodies. 'I am a son from the Father – the Father who is preexistent ... I derive being from Him who is preexistent, and I come again to my one place whence I came forth' (Irenaeus: 37). The Father is the social body and a social creation. Such knowledge can only come from seeing the Father within oneself. In the same vein, Bakhtin refers to the 'canonization' of the text, where what began as differences becomes crystallized into norms, as heteroglossia becomes stabilized within the text, and may 'serve to orchestrate authorial intentions' (1981: 418), with authorial intentions understood as the reality of the social body.

The fact that you as an individual are a result also of a second body, the social body, being internalized within you is a truth that must be at some time realized and accepted. It can only be realized by you alone, as an individual, who makes contact with that other body within. 'For gnostics, exploring the psyche became explicitly what it is for many people today implictly – a religious quest' (Pagels 1989: 123). Any organization or external systems of stasis are actually a hindrance to their progress because they dominate the conceptualizations of the individual body. Using Lacanian terms, such an awareness is similar to the transition from the mirror to the symbolic stage, where the two bodies (self and other) recognize their otherness. To be an adult, you must then accept this 'alien' body within you, understand it as a social and not biological creation, and understand that you are responsible for its needs, that you articulate its concerns and that you alone have the power to change it. That may be why indigenous people have ceremonies surrounding the transition from child to adult: they realize what innocence is being lost and what responsibilities are being taken on.

Communication between these two bodies is not innate or even easy. To be 'human' in the only sense of the word, which means to be free to think, means that these bodies have to be at some time dialogical. What alienates man as mere physical dust from the powerful rules of the gods? For the Christians and Jews, it is sin or asocial behaviour. This seems reasonable; if you are asocial, you are clearly not in touch with the social norms. But for these ideologies, the means to get in touch with the social body is by passive acceptance of its words, which come from an external source. Is this freedom? Whereas, for gnostics, the suffering of sin is the result of ignorance; the ignorance to which they refer is the basic self-awareness that the physical being became human by becoming two bodies – the individual and the social – and that both come into being within the one physical form and are in constant dialogical battle. With Aquinas, it must be pointed out that 'ignorance follows from sin, which is a lack of knowledge of things which ought to be known' (*De ver.* q. 18, a. 7). However, this ignorance is not of the social body, as it is with the gnostics, but of the Divine, that 'perfect union with God.' The potentiality of such atemporal, aspatial contacts are denied by the acceptance of a gnostic, a quantum textual reality.

Such knowledge is vital, for 'lacking this (knowledge) a person experiences the sense of being driven by impulses he does not understand' (Pagels 1989: 124). And again, 'ignorance ... brought about anguish and terror. And the anguish grew solid like a fog, so that no one was able to see' (*Gospel of Truth*, 125). To see what? The answer – to see how dust had been transformed into a human being by the creation of and coupling with another being, namely the social body – the dust of the Mother and the rules of the Father, the basic metaphors found in so many societies all over the world. 'Most people live, then, in oblivion – or, in contemporary terms, in unconsciousness. Remaining unaware of their own selves, they have "no root." It is such beings who are slaves, who are mindless and therefore dominated, governed by others, and therefore the gnostics can readily say that 'self-ignorance is also a form of self-destruction.' How is one to seek self-knowledge? 'Many gnostics share with psychotherapy a second major premise: both agree – against orthodox Christianity – that the psyche bears within itself the potential for liberation or destruction' (Pagels 125, 126). Here is the awareness that the Father of Rules lies within oneself and is therefore, as shown in both the Bakhtinian carnival and the Freudian analysis, a product of the mind. It is therefore necessary – indeed we are obliged as human beings – to challenge and change the social body. Change but not destroy; the two bodies must remain. For us to return to Eden, to a life without such duality, would mean our death as human beings. Admittedly, to remain here with this duality can also lead to death, for the social body will always attempt to blind us, to overwhelm us with its voices and confine us to speaking only its metaphors. It is a constant conflict. How do we deal with this?

Prometheus described human beings as follows: 'In the beginning they had eyes to look, but looked in vain, and ears to hear, but did not hear, but like the shapes of dreams they wandered in confusion the whole of their long life.' Note how this state of oblivion is considered paradise in the Christian Eden and a state of confusion in the Greek and gnostic ideology. How did Prometheus save humans? 'I discovered for them numbers, a lofty kind of wisdom, and letters and their combination, an art that fosters memory of all things' (Aeschylus, *Prometheus Bound*; quoted in Morford and Lenardon 1977: 51). When human beings learned those symbols that serve as the semantic means to author, remember, and then communicate the metaphors of the social text , they acquired all the keys to construct and build the social body and thereby establish its identity, and also the means to think about, talk about, analyse its nature. Before, they were silent. By this means, by language, they are saved and become 'human.'

However, they are saved only if they become aware that they, as masters of language, are themselves the authors, readers, interpreters, and also characters within this social body. They create the textual society. If they forget this, if they renounce their authorship, they become slaves of the text they have written and become trapped in its metaphors. So it is human beings with their stories, who write and rewrite, who tell these varied tales to themselves and to others, as well as to the stable and enduring gods, who keep both bodies of the textual society dialogical and free.

Therefore, what we have here is a new diagram of interrelations, an elliptic form: at the very edge is the amorphous dust of physical reality, the generative force, often symbolized as the Mother. The individual body, as a spatiotemporal biological *and* social entity, takes up a finite space within that dust. In the centre of the individual body is the group reality, that social body of symbolic rules and regulations that is in many ideologies symbolized as the Father. As with Zeus, this being exists within us. However, we have not and must not absorb it as 'us' or we will lose our ability to conceptualize. It must remain other. We know that there is a difference but can never locate the exact boundaries between I and other, between the individual and the social body. We, the individual, surround the social body, the symbolic, because we are its creators, its articulators. As such, we and our other are social creations of reality; we are a text that exists within the energy horizons of our biological nature.

The Truce in Lacanian Desire

As conceptual beings we are mediating two different forms of energy, the Mother and the Father, the generative and the ordered. In Lacan's terms, the real and the symbolic, Other with a capital O; in Kristeva's terms, the chora/genotext/semiotic and the symbolic/phenotext. To unite with either the Mother or Father will result in the disappearance of the ability to exist as an individual, a being who is both author and reader of the text. Such a bond would be, according to Freud, incestuous, though I think the term is misused and am considering both ties as incestuous. The incest taboo is not simply a rejection of a bond with the Mother but a rejection also of a bond with the Father. Therefore, the subject, passing through the Lacanian Imaginary phase, must achieve a sense of separation from the Mother, from the Other as having a more basic reality than our own body. By submitting to the symbolism of the Father, the normative rules that permit us to express ourselves in our separate consciousness, we then exist as separate beings. However, there must be a second separation, equally important, when the subject, who is by now a conceptual being (symbolic), consciously separates from the Father-as-demiurge and acknowledges that the symbols and rules as used in one's individual reality are neither universal nor valid mirrors of reality; they are actually creations of human beings. This awareness is the act of gnostic knowledge to which I have been referring.

Both bodies, the individual and the social, are vital to each other; both long for each other within the Lacanian concept of an endless and necessarily unfulfilled Desire for the Other, where 'man's desire finds its meaning in the desire of the other, not so much because the other holds the key to the object desired, as because the first object of desire is to be recognized by the other' (Lacan 1977: 58). The nature of our 'being alive' is based around these numerous meetings with Desire. We exist only because of the 'unfinalized' nature of our intentionality and must accept that 'the carnival sense of the world also knows no period, and is, in fact, hostile to any sort of conclusive conclusion: all endings are merely new beginnings; carnival images are reborn again and again.' And, too, 'the world is open and free, everything is still in the future and will always be in the future' (Bakhtin 1984a: 165, 166). It was Prometheus who planted in men 'false hopes' so that they would reject finality. It is at these nodes of contact, which I have earlier discussed as 'nodes of articulation,' that the endless debates go on between the two bodies and decisions are made as to whose view, for the moment, to accept. One can compare these sites also with Lacan's nodes, the 'point-de-capiton' and 'objets-petit-a nodes,' which are found wherever there is a passageway on the body linking the interior to the exterior (Lacan 1977). These nodes of 'being symbolic' are 'anchoring points' where actions of textuality can exist. Here the subject joins with the symbolic (language) in an action of textuality, which is an 'event of meaning,' a phrase that acknowledges the Peircean insistence on the sign as an action and the Bakhtinian insistence on dialogical action. The node is defined also by Lacan as 'phallocentric,' a term that has nothing to do with phallus or patriarchial overtones, but with the reality of both the genetic distinctions and resultant combination of the phallus/clitoris. That is, the phallocentric act is an awareness of and a rejection of differentiation. As such, it is the moment of emergence from the imaginary into the symbolic, from the unconscious bond with the Mother, and into the union with the symbolism of the Father, whereby one becomes a self, a conceptual being. The phallocentric act, as an action of textuality, is the node of contact between differences. Such an event is a moment of intense joy, of 'jouissance,' 'its frenzy mocking the abyss of the infinite, the secret collusion with which it envelops the pleasure of knowing and of dominating with jouissance ... eternally stretching forth towards the "desire for something else"' (1977: 166–7). Meaning is grasped within that contextual bond – and is then instantly lost. The phallocentric union is followed by separation and both despair and desire for a new union. The moment when these two bodies contact meets 'only partially the function that produces them' (315). There is no such thing as full and complete meaning; it is forever elusive, constantly deferring and slipping away.

Our human reality is an acceptance that the social text is not a copy of physical reality and can never be. If we were to take this to a next step and actually kill the Father, the social body (cf. deconstructionism), and so acknowledge that the symbolisms of the Father indeed prevent us from access to a 'real meaning' because we are only allowed by the Father to conceptualize in symbols, this would not mean that we would finally have full access to reality. The Lacanian insistence on the *line* between the symbol and the meaning is there for a reason; we would disappear as conceptual beings without it. Thirdness, the social body, is the line, and we require its intervening mediation for our stability.

Therefore, we have this constant fight between two forces, the Mother and the Father, the biological and the social. These take place within the individual body, which is an existential combination of biological and social forces. The biological is expressed as a desire to bond with the Mother, the basic life force of regeneration. But then there is a separation from the Mother, when in Lacanian terms, in the mirror stage or early life one recognizes the actual physical and conceptual isolation of the individual self. The expression of this individuality can only be done in symbols. Therefore, the next stage is symbolic, where self-identity is expressed in the stasis codes of the Father. The symbolic codes of the society are spatiotemporal 'traps' that transform the unconscious (unsymbolized) mass of biological energy and enable us to set up our life as a distinct text. These interactions between the individual body and the social body permit both bodies to exist. Such interactions must be dialogical or interactive and never, from either side, monological. They are not necessarily consensual interactions but can be, as with the battles between the gods, violent conflicts. The subject must constantly confront the necessary solipsism of the Father and remind him that reality is not a mirror of the symbols of the Father but a force far beyond human authorship. Here, of course, is the idea behind the Bakhtinian carnival, an action that serves to remind us that our logocentric ideology is not truth but is only what we individuals have permitted to be set up as truth. We must remind the Father, who stands in stasis, that the text we use must be permitted to change; the reality of what we mean is always 'deferred and distanced' from our semantic expressions. We must also keep the Mother, as generative energy and the source of heteroglossic variation, in dialogue with the Father. That is, in both cases we cannot permit ourselves to become dominated by an Other. To do so would mean that we would live 'in ignorance,' and whoever lives in such a manner is a 'creature of oblivion' (*Gospel of Truth*, in Pagels 125).

Truth exists only within one's own dialogue with the social body, which body is internal to the individual and operational as Thirdness, one's own socialization. It is this awareness of the actual existence of these two bodies and their interrelationships that permits the individual's own transformation from life lived as simply a physical form to life as a social being.

The Binary Social Text

Textual binarism is an oppositional existence of real forms, each of which has a separate spatiotemporal existentiality. They each exist in themselves and not only 'for' each other. Judgment of good and bad is a social value added to their basic existences, but has nothing whatsoever to do with their reality. Therefore the hypothesis I am putting forward rejects analyses of binarism that see opposition or difference as unhealthy, where the good arises only when the society is 'rid' of this 'evil force'; or, as in Hegel and Marx, where the specific moves into/out of the universal (with the opposition between universal/specific rather than two specifics). Rather, as in the gnostic thesis, both forces are understood as an ongoing necessity to the existential text. I am reminded here also of Bakhtin's comments on language, where 'a unitary language is not something given (*dan*) but is always in essence posited (*zadan*) – and at every moment of its linguistic life it is opposed to the realities of heteroglossia. But at the same time it makes its real presence felt as a force for overcoming this heteroglossia, imposing specific limits to it, guaranteeing a certain maximum of mutual understanding and crystalizing into a real, although still relative, unit' (1981: 270). Peirce has a similar theme. His concept of Thirdness as habit or conformity (1: 345–7; 5: 369) exists in conflict with the forces of constant variation; this is his '*agape* evolution,' where stability and uniformity are necessarily open to the endless differentiation and variability of the world, such that there is always 'in nature some agency by which the complexity and diversity of things can be increased' (6: 58). Such ongoing interaction between stasis and variance is not a result of simple chance (known as 'tychism' and comparable with Darwinian chance: see 6: 293–5), but an actual part of the process of life. The actions of *agape* (which can be compared with the interactions between the individual and social body) are understood as 'love (that) cannot have a contrary, but must embrace what is most opposed to it' (6: 304). Good and evil as the two basic binary forces both exist within themselves as physical forces and in interaction with each other. They are transformed into various versions of this oppositional energy within the spatiotemporal frame of social interaction, which is the dialogic process. A question now arises – can one distinguish between them? Yes. Is it necessary to distinguish? Yes. Can the textual society exist without their binary presence? No. Good and evil are both physically and conceptually different from each other, and both are necessary for the social text.

We may consider the two forms of sociophysical reality as two bodies within the social text – the individual body and the social body. What are they and how can they be differentiated? Their different natures should not be located within a frame of privilege, as expressed by the concept of the 'social government of the human body,' whether by hegemonic or openly authoritative discourse. This was an early anthropological and sociological paradigm that assumed that the human body was in itself purely and only physical. As distinctly asocial it was considered degenerate and had be governed or restrained in order to be human. We are reminded here of the theories of such early evolutionary and legal anthropologists as Morgan, Spencer, and Maine, with their comparison of the asocial, promiscuous, purely sensual 'savage' and the governed, controlled 'civilized' life. In this sense, 'the body represents a regulatory problem in the development of human civilizations' and therefore 'the training or cultivation of bodies by disciplines is a principal feature of culture as learned behavior' (Turner 1992: 15). Such a perspective has been analysed by Peirce as 'anancasm,' where changes in a society are only brought about by some idea of foredained (and therefore authoritarian) perfection. Here, following the Newtonian emphasis on mechanistic control over matter, development is understood as increasing law and order over the material world, which includes both the individual body and the external environment.

To view the individual body as an object of a social or group agenda has also led to the political views of the domination of the individual by the hierarchical agenda of the group or more usually, class (Marxist analysis). This can lead to the reactionary, exclusionary frame of 'individual freedom versus the conformist agenda of the group.' The Lockean/Hobbes outline of the social contract follows this reaction in its functionalist view of the group as simply a result of individuals having agreed to shared rules and regulations. This is an attempt to disempower the social body. In the textual society, however, both bodies, the individual and the social, have actualities of freedom and power and fully interact with each other.

My hypothesis of the reality of the two bodies contrasts also with our Cartesian 'legacy in which there is a sharp division between the body and the mind ... [which] is based on the principal assumption that there is no interaction ... between mind and body, and therefore that these two realms or topics can be addressed by separate and distinctive disciplines' (Turner, 32). Rather, my insistence on the reality of the individual body along with the equally real body of the society stems from a premise that human existence is a cognitive or social experience of physical materiality. The basis of the problem is that both existential bodies, that of the individual and that of the society, become conceptualized only within the physical frame of the human body, the individual existentiality. Only the individual human thinks and speaks; the society does not; it instead uses the body of the human being to both conceptualize and express its words and thoughts. Charles Peirce pointed out that Firstness and Secondness, or sensual experience and conceptual awareness, are operative within the human individual. However, Secondness or thought is only arrived at via the mediating factor of group Thirdness; so what we have is that the individual ends up being *a conceptual agent* for both his own and the society's material existentiality. This is the key problem. The individual is not completely free in the sense of being alone in his body, but is only operative with an other embedded within.

These two beings have different existential natures. One lives for seventy years, the other for seven hundred years; one takes up a small amount of space, the other a large amount; one interacts swiftly and is highly adaptive; the other is slow and rejects change. We have the whole team of the everlasting gods, king of whom is Zeus, the 'god who protects the family, the clan and the state,' and we have ourselves as their finite and culpable partners. Both the social body and the human body become existential using the same singular cognitive system – that of the individual. They are necessarily in conflict and as such become defined by us as good or evil. Good can be defined as long-term and evil as short-term; stasis and deviation; society and the individual. But, like the gods, these definitions can change – sometimes the society is evil and the individual is good.

> Flesh and blood is weak and frail,
> Susceptible to nervous shock
> While the True Church can never fail
> For it is based upon a rock
>
>   ...
>
> He shall be washed as white as snow,
> By all the martyr'd virgins kist
> While the True Church remains below
> Wrapt in the old miasmal mist.
> (T.S. Eliot, 'The Hippopotamus,' 1920)

The Source of New Energy

The individual with his finite existentiality is certainly the carrier of both forces of syntax and heteroglossia, but it is not humans who are the ultimate source of new energy. Rather, as previously discussed, it is the gods, those members of our society who are always metaphors of forces beyond human control or cognition. New energy is found within generative energy, that most abstract, chaotic, disorganized of presences. To enter such chaos is to risk being enveloped in its midst. Odysseus knew what he was doing when he lashed himself to the mast and so resisted the Sirens. But we cannot do without them; 'to invite the gods ruins our relationship with them but sets history in motion. A life in which the gods are not invited isn't worth living.

It will be quieter, but there won't be any stories ... [and] the gods get bored with men who have no stories' (Calasso 1993: 387). Without our conversations with the gods, there will be no change and no history; indeed no societies, for all will decay.

Potentiality, the source of the new energy that provides the surety of a future, is forever unknown. It exists outside our daily genres, outside the strictures of habit, in that unknown space between the stability of one heartbeat and the next. Accessible only by the whims of the gods who turn it over to us, it is then grasped and transformed by human beings into the stable codes of the group. In many societies the ultimate source of new energy is forever abstract. As Rabelais pointed out in *Gargantua and Pantagruel* (1534– 52), the subterranean ruler, 'that sovereign Goddess the Egyptians used to call, in their language, Isis, meaning She Who Is Secret, Hidden, Concealed' (1990: 621), this Chaos, is beyond individual cognition or control. Among the Dobe !Kung, one elder explained that 'people have different types of gangwasi. One may have bad gangwasi, another may have good gangwasi ... you have no choice in your gangwasi. You can't control them but must accept what they give you' (Lee 1984: 108). Rabelais, again: 'Have faith in this ... Nor should you believe that rain is caused because the heavens are unable to hold it back and because the clouds are hanging heavy and low. No, it is caused by the command of the subterranean regions' (622). The Australian Aborigines call it the Dreamtime; the Mbuti pygmies call it the forest; Western societies have, in their binary blindness, divided it into heaven and hell, ignoring the fact that both are transformations of the same thing, and where they meet, is life. In all societies, despite the different images, key similarities exist. Potentiality is unlimited, aspatial, atemporal; it is everything that we, as both organic and social beings, are not. This power of uncertainty is most certainly 'only arbitrarily accessible to us, where the powers live that interlock with our fragility, that work with us (but only when they feel like it) to define and permit our existence' (Calasso 1993: 10). Finally, such powers can only be contacted and experienced within activities that move the individual outside the stasis strictures of genre or syntax.

If the gods are the ultimate source of different energy, then to invite them and our haphazard relationships with them into the textual society permits the introduction of the vitalities of instability and variation. Human beings can become very similar and homogeneous. Organically similar to one another, socially homogeneous by the repressive powers of the syntactic and the semantic codes, grouped together within their fragility of birth and death, they must become a society that limits diversity and rejects multiplicity of meanings. After all, to be a society means to be static enough, stable enough to raise organic cells (human beings) to be members of that particular and no other society. Therefore, the textual society must be confined and conceptually limited, where 'truth was the right to possess exclusive knowledge outside of which nothing made sense; therefore knowledge had to be defended against everything that could obscure it' (Veselovsky, in Bakhtin 1984b: 93). A society must have a singular basic ideology or 'logic of being.' The power of this perspective permits it to transform its disorganized or 'uncivilized, natural' physical beings into social beings. But, as has been pointed out, this same stasis will most certainly cause the entropic decay of that society. Stasis metaphors must be swallowed whole, must be accepted without question as singular truth. Stasis metaphors are not meant for usage or transformation but for unquestioning consumption.

A society decays if it is only stasis. There must be that contact with variability, with the power of asociality. Time and time again, from Aztec to Nazi, human beings have sought the stability of a rigid static order, only to find that such reification leads to a society (if one can even call it that) made up of only one level – group reality only, the syntactic logic. All living beings have disappeared and in their place we have frozen automata whom we quite correctly call 'inhuman.' Therefore, human beings, who are born to die, who are therefore the essence of instability, and who, above all, are aware of this fact, are the agents of heteroglossia. They alone, in their desire to overcome their fragility, will contact the gods and thereby access new energy.

Listen to Baqbuc, from the underworld of Rabelais: 'Your philosophers love to tell you that the ancients have already described everything, that there's nothing new left to invent, but they're obviously wrong. That which appears to you out of the sky and which you call natural phenomena, and that which the earth shows you and that which the sea and the rivers contain – all that is nothing, compared to what is hidden underground' (1990: 621). In the pursuit of knowledge, as Bakhtin points out, there were two absolutely necessary things, namely, the guidance of God and the fellowship of men. The chronotope is a logic expressed via codes; the chronotope is the GR level logic of interaction; the code is a cumulative stock, a collection of socially defined horizons to the IRC. The power of the gods is their ability to provoke instability. They alone live within both the world of the unformed and undefined and the world of finite organic beings. They are, like the medieval angels, capable of moving between both worlds; indeed their very nature is as 'action,' and they 'know all things in the Word before they come into existence.' These intermediary beings have contact with the pure energy of chaos before it is caught and defined and named.

Heteroglossia is a means of dialogue with the gods because it moves human minds from the strictures of stasis. Bakhtin's analysis of laughter is one source of instability, for it 'liberates not only from external censorship but first of all from the great interior censor ... Laughter opened men's eyes on that which is new, on the future.' Laughter 'was linked with the procreating act, with birth, renewal, fertility, abundance.' And 'finally it was related to the future of things to come and was to clear the way for them' (1984b: 94, 95). Then, as soon as this free energy is conceptualized, it is trapped in the organizational frame and disappears as open potentiality. It is used and it decays. Laughter is not the only means of accessing new energy. Any action that cracks the spatiotemporal frame of stasis can do this; it is here that violence becomes relevant, and I include all actions that confront stasis – anger, violence, despair, grief. I am rejecting the safety of stasis, the normality of life that we can actually consider as equivalent to Hades, the land of the dead 'who have done with life.'

Pure energy does not spatiotemporally exist; the potentiality to be is outside space and time. The codes of both the syntactic and semantic nodes capture energy within their organizational grids or spatiotemporal frames. Think of language as one such code, where 'Cadmus had brought Greece "gifts of the mind": vowels and consonants yoked together in tiny signs ... the alphabet. With the alphabet, the Greeks would teach themselves to experience the gods in the silence of the mind, and no longer in the full and normal presence' (Calasso 1993: 390). Calasso is here admitting the necessity of stasis, provided by the code, and yet noting that the confinement of energy with the strictures of a spatiotemporal code enables cognition to take place, but the access to pure or aconceptual energy is lost. A code of any form moves energy into a spatiotemporally stable form, the only form in which cognition can exist as a conceptual sign. However, the haphazard and potentially destabilizing contacts with pure energy disappear. That is why access to this energy is only possible by moving outside a spatiotemporal frame.

The Need for Heteroglossia

A society naturally 'consumes' its identity in the daily actions of its spatiotemporal life. Codes, as systems that provide stability over time and space, are used by systems that are unstable over space and time (human beings). The contact between these two opposite forces means that the codes will decay and lose their ability to provide mimesis or exact reproductions of identity. This is natural entropy, the interaction of a means of stability with the experience of instability. To continue to reproduce its stable identity, the textual code must access more energy to replace that which has been lost in use. The amount of energy accessed must replace the amount of energy lost. A society, in this sense, reproduces itself as itself. However, the textual society must not simply reproduce itself, which is why I oppose such mechanical concepts. To repeat yourself as yourself is mimetic. This cannot last, not only because the human body is organic, but because other factors within the textual society (both biological and conceptual) are changing. A society that becomes so rigid that it is able only to reproduce itself and unable to deviate from that self moves outside of history; it is group reality only. What one asks of heteroglossia is the freedom of knowing that there is both an end and a beginning to any social definition of truth. It is between these two spaces, in that indefinable infinite, where the ability to renew life rests. In that space, in that unknown and forever unknowable uncertainty, is certainty of an existence, for a while, for long enough to be a textual society, which means to be an interaction of both stability and variation.

Semantic Binarism as Degenerate Heteroglossia

The term 'binarism' does not in itself mean a dialogical interaction. Semantic binarism, as I have outlined in the previous chapters, is a code system that identifies a single unit by a specific otherness of differentiation and has absolutely nothing to do with the heteroglossic interaction of levels. As Bakhtin pointed out, the 'official feasts of the Middle Ages, whether ecclesiastic, feudal or sponsored by the state, did not lead the people out of the existing world order and created no second life. On the contrary, they sanctioned the existing pattern of things and reinforced it' (1984b: 9). These feasts where variations seemed to exist were actually coded expressions of the binary otherness within a stable semantic code, and therefore, as pointed out, reinforced the definition of the norm. This is not dialogue, which requires not merely a sharing of energy but also a differentiation of energy.

Does our modern world permit the dialogics of variation? Our current society shows signs of extreme instability. It is denying the validity of the semantic binarisms of its previous codes and is thus in a phase of deconstruction and semantic flexibility. On the other hand, it is desperately attempting to remain stable by grasping at any and all metaphoric means of stabilizing meaning. It has a new syntax but is not yet able to articulate and conceptualize it (such an action can take several generations) and is therefore floundering within the semantic collapse of its old terms. It is rejecting variation and heteroglossia and is actually preventing any and all actions of dialogue.

To discuss the reasons for this instability is beyond the scope of this analysis, but it certainly stems from a social text that is undergoing a disruption of energy content and energy organization at both a syntactic and semantic level. We have been moving from a type B to a type A syntactic text since the era of the two world wars. Furthermore, this change is global; it is not merely that human beings all over the world are merging into one syntactic organization but that despite geographic variations, the semantic expressions of that syntax are also becoming similar. Such a syntactic/semantic textual spread entails a complete redistribution of energy and its organization. The catastrophic period of the world wars brought the new syntax into existence, but the semantic conceptualization takes at least one or two generations longer. In this current phase of semantic disruption, groups of people will attempt to regain stasis by reifying their semantic level codes. On the one hand, semantic terms are being rapidly deconstructed; their current meanings are amorphous, flexible, unstable. This is the textual form of individual reality only, where no syntactic form is articulated. On the other hand, stasis is briefly achieved by reifying these semantic level codes and transforming them into forms that are both seemingly stable and also 'other.' Homogeneity of definition provides a certain stability, and men and women become identical, societies become identical, all distinctions become merged. Any reference to 'differences' is seen as evidence of asocial behaviour or thought. However, a text without differentiation cannot last; it will entropically decay. I am not saying that the demise of this homogeneity will be gentle because it is inevitable, but that such uniformity of existence, such stasis of life, cannot last. A first form of the demise of this homogeneity is to split the larger group into smaller homogeneous types. Men and women are no longer identical and equal as members of a single species but become two separate groups, each a homogeneous species in itself. Ethnic groups are no longer understood as variable versions of human beings, but split into smaller sectors that are homogeneous in identity.

Within this era of semantic chaos, individuals will also attempt to find stability, not merely in homogeneity but also in tribalism. Tribalism tries to ensure stability by establishing spatiotemporal boundaries to metaphors of meaning. The concept of definite boundaries is found in the nature of the IRC, the single sign-unit. This IRC is an actual and singular unit of meaning; it is a specific, contextual, and short-term comprehension of an IRS, a sensual impulse. To organize multiple IRS forms (sensual forms of energy, human beings) into one single IRC, one homogeneous sign-unit, is beyond the capacity of any code. It can only be done by strict homogeneity of all these forms; they must all be similar; no deviations in form are permitted. Such totalitarianism of semiosis cannot last. This is why the 1960s attempt to define all human beings as similar has disappeared, and instead the population has become split into smaller groups that are homogeneous in themselves. You are a member of a distinct group, a single IRC unit; this group is homogeneous and thereby seemingly stable. The next step to ensure this stability is to confine and limit the IRC meaning; this is necessary or the energy content will be beyond the organizing capacity. This is done not merely by the easy act of homogeneity but also by using external force to help limit the meaning. As Peirce said about the singularity of meaning of the interpretant, experienced within the confinement of Secondness, 'the next simplest feature that is common to all that comes before the mind, and consequently the second category, is the element of Struggle' (5: 45). The sense of struggle, resistance, opposition are all part of Secondness. 'The idea of other, of "not," becomes a very pivot of thought' (1: 324). Therefore, along with homogeneity of membership, we will find tribalism, which defines itself as other to some other equally homogeneous group; this increases the stability of the homogeneous group by setting it up within the confinement of Peircean Secondness. This is a key error. Secondness, the phase of the IRC sign, is an action and never a form. It is spatiotemporally finite; it is an instant of comprehension and not Thirdness, not habit, not stability. It functions within the Lacanian evasion of meaning, the Bakhtinian action of meaning. To make a sign stable further harms the social text. In this form, difference is defined, not as different amounts and organizations of energy (that is, syntactic and semantic), but within the variations of a similar amount and organization of energy (semantic level only). An easy metaphor is racism, where various physical attributes that should be understood as semantic variations of a single form of energy organization (a human being) are instead understood as totally different forms of energy. Different races are understood to have more or less energy content and a different organization of that energy. This homogeneity is then further stabilized by setting up each form in opposition to another. A similar two-step attempt at stability is found in feminism, where men and women are seen as different forms of existence rather than variables of organization of the human being. Each form is understood, first as homogeneous and second as oppositional. All men are aggressors; all women are victims and are never aggressors. Ethnicity is treated in the same two-step format of homogeneity of type, followed by opposition of behaviour. A final attempt to ensure the stability of these degenerate semantic forms is to attempt to 'validate' their existentiality by denying their nature as semantic metaphors. Their identity as conceptual forms of existence is denied and they are transformed into natural forms of existence. Men are defined as aggressors not merely by socialization but also and above all by nature; the different races are given characteristics defined as genetically natural rather than socially developed. Various forms of behaviour, previously considered social, are now defined as genetic. Reality that is natural rather than social exists outside of the textual reality. What level of existence is this? It is not biological reality, for that is transformable by social interaction. It is generative energy. Therefore, definitions or existences that our modern society considers natural and not social are seemingly properties of the inviolate gods of generative energy. However, this is false generative energy; we must remember that real generative energy has no intentionality of form or function.

Degenerate semantic binarism sets up a fallible and yet dangerous text. The syntactic level is normally stasis, but to set up the semantic level as also made up of stable forms means that both levels of the social text function within stasis. There is no variation, no heteroglossia possible within such a text. It cannot last beyond one generation; the pity is that both its brief life and its demise are so harmful to human beings.

Textual Heteroglossia

The 'rivulets and droplets of social heteroglossia' (Bakhtin 1981: 263) are, by their very imagery, not socialized and closed actions within the individual, but in confrontative interaction. Heteroglossia is dialogical; the individual interacts with both the chaos of the gods and the stasis of the society. To limit conceptual action to the level only of the individual or the group or the gods would change heteroglossia from being a force of interaction with generative energy and confine it to static empty rhetoric. This would result in a situation where 'all events taking place within it (the individual level) acquire one single meaning: death is only death, it never coincides with birth; old age is torn away from youth; blows merely hurt, without assisting an act of birth. All actions and events are interpreted on the level of a single, individual life. They are enclosed within the limits of the same body, limits that are the absolute beginning and end and can never meet' (Bakhtin 1984b: 322). Such singularity of semiosis is not the nature of textuality. Each contact with the other, be they god or human or whatever, permits a different interpretation, a different story, a different perspective of what is real. 'No other woman or goddess had so many deaths as Ariadne. That stone in Argos, that constellation in the sky, that hanging corpse, that death by childbirth, that girl with an arrow through her breast: Ariadne was all of this' (Calasso 1993: 23). This is dialogical heteroglossia. When Adam and Eve lived in the atemporal and monological chronotopic era of the Garden of Eden, they were incapable of differentiation, of awareness of the finite nature of objects, and therefore of their inequality. But when they became aware or conceptual, 'as gods, knowing good and evil' (Genesis 3: 5), then they became subject to death and sorrow but also to life and birth and the generation of history.

We may consider the perspective of Albert Camus, who wrote that 'the spirit of rebellion can exist only in a society where a theoretical equality conceals great factual inequalities' (1956: 20). In the textual society, such inequalities must exist, because inequality in its true nature is diversity. Contrary to many political ideologies, I maintain that unequal interactions are an organic reality and necessity, as the elders are privileged over the young, the hunter is privileged over the prey, and good exists only within evil. In a hunting and gathering band, sharing or equal interaction is vital for its sustenance stability, but within that same social infrastructure there are necessary levels of inequality that permit heteroglossia, and therefore dialogue and therefore history, to all exist. At one time, some members may have more food than others, which they share with those who have less. Such differences and the requirement for sharing permit interaction and thereby a constant sense of social cohesion. Someone may become ill; the illness is understood to come from a more powerful force than the human being. Begging, pleading with this force acknowledges the relationship of the individual to the wider powers of the environment and deprivileges individualism within a society that relies on group cohesion for stability. This unequal distribution of energy is a reality of all organic life. Accepting this permits social history, in the sense that interactions or communication, and therefore the movement of goods and cognition (cf. Lévi-Strauss) can take place and thereby permit the existence of a society. The Bakhtinian analysis of the novel includes this understanding of the relationship of diverse energy and the existence of time. Bakhtin explains the novel as 'a phenomenon multiform in style and variform in speech and voice'; it is 'a diversity of social speech types (sometimes even diversity of languages) and a diversity of individual voices, artistically organized.' Such diversity is vital, for it is via this that 'heteroglossia can enter the novel' (1981: 261, 262, 263). It is this heteroglossia that permits a novel to actually live.

Consider the textual society as a novel, as indeed it is, made up of 'a multiplicity of social voices and a wide variety of their links and interrelationships' with multiple voices, multiple perspectives, all 'artistically organized' (263, 262). This diversity permits heteroglossia as energy to enter the society; energy can only do this within an infrastructure of differentiation. Again, 'the internal stratification of language, of its social heteroglossia and the variety of individual voices in it, (are) the prerequisite for authentic novelistic prose' (264), and for the textual society also.

Consider language as a means of dialogue: it acts as both a unifying force and a force of differentiation. It serves 'to unify and centralize the verbal-ideological world' and, although it seems to exist in active opposition to heteroglossia or diversity, it operates 'in the midst of heteroglossia.' Language is diversified into variations, and 'this stratification and heteroglossia ... insures its dynamics' (270, 271, 272). What we have in the language of the novel and the textual society is a requirement for both stasis and heteroglossia; logic and diversity; organization and rebellion. To return to Camus, 'equality plus inequality.'

This ability to dialogue is the ability to diverge from stasis, to rebel and deviate, for 'rebellion is one of the essential dimensions of man. It is our historic reality' (Camus 1956: 21). Note the word 'historic,' which means currently spatiotemporal. Again and again, Camus reaffirms the necessity for the stability of the long-term logic, the syntactic solidarity of minds. 'In order to exist, man must rebel, but rebellion must respect the limit it discovers in itself – a limit where minds meet and in meeting, begin to exist.' 'The most elementary form of rebellion, paradoxically, expresses an aspiration to order.' The rebel 'attacks a shattered world in order to demand unity from it' (22, 23, 24). Essentially, heteroglossia is a means of actually ensuring the existence of a society. By its action of deviation from the stable spatiotemporal grid or organizational frame of the syntax, heteroglossia in all its varieties, from slight to extreme, adds energy to the social text . This new energy must be organized to be retained, and therefore the syntactic logic is forced to be constantly active. It cannot sleep, it cannot relax its means of retaining energy and the organizational abilities, the cognitive narrative of the society thereby remains alive.

Just as readers, as the source of heteroglossia, are vital to the dialogical text, people who deviate and rebel are vital to the textual society. 'In our daily trials, rebellion plays the same role as does the "cogito" in the realm of thought: it is the first piece of evidence.' This action of deviation 'lures the individual from his solitude. It founds the first value on the whole human race. I rebel – therefore we exist' (Camus 1956: 22). Heteroglossia is a dialogical interaction between levels, between the short-term and the long-term, the single second and the generation. Decentralized and centrifugal forces operate within each other.

There must be both forms of existence in a confrontation that is the true dialogue. As Charles Peirce pointed out, 'to make single individuals absolute judges of truth is most pernicious ... We individually cannot reasonably hope to attain the ultimate philosophy which we pursue; we can only seek it, therefore, for the community of philosophers' (5: 265). The important term is 'community,' and that is the unique nature of the textual society. It is a community, which means a shared cognition, expressed in dialogical and therefore variable form, by individuals.

Heteroglossia is what makes life worth living. The stabilities are empty; we know they are there, we need them, they provide the frame that binds us to the security of our yesterdays and tomorrows. But it is the power to form new concepts, new variations of life, that provides a society with its energy and potentiality to exist as a means of socializing human life and thereby permitting its existence on this earth. The power of heteroglossia, operating within stasis, proves that there is a next time, a next experience, a next heartbeat.

8

Conclusion: Society as Text

Using Peirce's definition of a sign as 'something which stands to somebody for something in some respect or capacity' (2: 228), a society can be analysed as a distinct sign-unit. As a sign, it is an action, rather than an object, for 'thought is an action, and ... it consists in a relation' (5: 399); it is 'an event' (1: 321). As an action, society can therefore be considered organic, which means 'interrelational.' Common terms used in modern analysis, such as the 'production and reproduction of culture,' have provided us with a perspective of society as an object, or even a collection of objects, and led us into analytic frames concerned with various actions of manipulating and manufacturing these differing parts of the society into ideal forms. However, if one understands society as an organic entity, then this mechanistic and functionalist view is no longer tenable. A society is a social *action* of existence. That is why I refer to it as a text, because it exists only in the actions of composition and usage, in the actualities of writing and reading.

As organic entities, societies exist within a biological reality, the given environmental or material realities to which a society is a social adaptation. A variety of social adaptations to the environment may be possible, but a society as text confines this variety and maintains a singular integrity. A desert remains a desert; however, the irrigation adaptations of Egyptian dynastic society permit a distinct and separate text from the adaptations of the industrial methodology in that same environment. These two societies must be considered two different organic entities, two different texts, and cannot be read as simple evolutions or developments of the same text.

The textual society, like an organic cell, is a form of organized energy, and as such, has a finite spatiotemporal reality and a particular organization of that reality. Its spatiotemporal nature is finite in terms of its historic or temporal existentiality and its geographic or spatial existentiality. This spatiotemporal uniqueness or distinctive singularity is as important to the reality of a society as it is to an individual. A nation, a tribe, a village, a committee, can exist only by identifying its distinctiveness. A society's requirement for identifying itself as a singular structure also requires it to maintain and indeed develop *differences* and a sense of otherness, from another society. This requirement is a part of its existence as a sign. However, as discussed, this awareness of otherness is not experienced as a struggle to overcome that other; it is rather a requirement to interact with that which is 'not us.' Because of this organic requirement for distinctiveness, a society cannot exist alone; it must always have a sense of an other, of an entity that is 'not us.' Therefore, there will always be at least two or more societies in the world; there can be no single world society.

The textual society exists within a frame of Secondness, a book cover that clearly identifies its uniqueness. Such a stable identity of the textual reality also acts as a finite horizon to social behaviour, such that an 'effective historical consciousness' recognizes that there is a 'standpoint [which] limits the possibility of vision' (Gadamer 1975: 289). The socio-organic society is not a sum of individuals, each with his own intentionality. Such a collection of people may not be able to function as a society; that is, they may lack the horizons of that shared interactional pattern of the GR syntax and those shared semantic encoding systems. 'Whoever speaks a language that no one else understands does not speak. To speak means to speak "to" someone ... ' For 'speaking does not belong in the sphere of the "I" but in the sphere of the "We" ' (Gadamer 1977: 65). Nor is a society a collection of people led by a leader; that is, consisting of individuals who have given up their unique differential social membrane, their identity as sign-units, and become part of the leader's socio-organic nature. Such a gathering is not a society, but rather an extension of a single individual who has become socially and physically extended beyond his own organic-cognitive structure and has included within his differential identity many 'units' of humanity, many 'bits' of people who were once individuals. The organic society is a hierarchical, multi-leveled and complex interactive system of different amounts and organizations of energy.

It has been suggested by Braudel that at least several hundred people (possibly a minimum of six hundred) are required to ensure the existence of one person as a social entity. A human being cannot reproduce himself, raise himself, interact productively with the environment, use any encoding system for memory (human beings have very little genetically based storage capacity), except within the context of a society. The individual as a sociobiological unit requires a coherent and structured interaction with a stock of individuals over a period of years before being able to 'fend for himself,' if such a state even exists. But we must continue to ask, what is a society? It is still not simply a sum of individuals. Such a conclusion would deny that it, in itself, is real as a long-term entity and would suggest that it is simply an ad hoc creation of the moment. We can come up with the concept that society is a number of units (who can also be individuals as distinct entities) in interaction with each other. This is a superficial although immediately valid analysis, acknowledging meaning to be created within a communal interaction, yet focusing only on the discrete units, on the individual agents of communication and on the individual signs of meaning. I reject such an analysis, which considers only the level of individual reality, as definitive only of a static structure, and insist on a perspective that considers society as active, as organic. A deeper analysis must be that these units and their actions exist within a generative logic, group reality, a pattern of organization that has the capacity to produce, organize, and use such specific units and actions. A society cannot exist within unattached and fleeting individuals; it cannot produce unattached and fleeting images open to any interpretation or usage. A society as a text has a particular organization, which means that its potentiality for making meanings is finite. A society as text operates within a finite cognitive horizon that limits the nature and style of its image content. Braudel defines the internal logic of the 'longue durée' of society as a structure that provides 'both support and hindrances. As hindrances, they stand as limits ("envelopes" in the mathematical sense) beyond which man and his experiences cannot go' (1980: 31). A society as such a structure exists as potential meaning; its actual meanings appear when brought into existential life within the actions of its people operating within their particular logic of organization. As I have noted, the syntactic logic operates within the individual body. Further, the syntax is not a narrative but simply a pattern of organization.

A society is organic because of this definitive membrane or horizon and the equally definitive logic of the organization of the realities within that membrane. The existential expressions of social reality occur within the actions of the particles, cells,units (which we can also call individuals, except that they are not simply biological, but are also social creations), which operate within dialogical interactions to express the reality and life of the society. To be a member of this society you must acquire (because you are not born with) the conceptual infrastructure, the syntactic logic of group reality and the semantic codes of individual reality, to create and use the social metaphors or conceptual images that are meaningful within this society. You must acquire this state of law or habit, as described within Peircean

Thirdness, where 'continuity represents Thirdness almost to perfection' (1: 337), or Popper's Third World, the world of 'objective knowledge, or knowledge in the objective sense, which consists of the logical content of our theories, conjectures' (1972: 73).

As an example, if we use some metaphors that deal with food, we can identify a number of subsocieties or groups within a larger society. Each is functional within its own definitive horizons of reality, for 'artisans dine at nine o'clock [in the morning], provincials at twelve, Parisians at two, business people at half-past two, nobles at three. As for "supper," it is taken at seven in small towns, at eight in large, at nine in Paris and at ten at court' (L.S. Mercier; in Braudel 1981: 328). We can see that the metaphors of a group may seem arbitrary, but once they become social signs that define the specific reality of that group, they are then limited in meaning and usage. They should be understood as differential, but that does not mean that all such images are also prejudicial in the sense that they do not permit the existence of other signs. Prejudice is not a hindrance to understanding but a condition of the possibility of understanding. 'What is necessary is a fundamental rehabilitation of the concept of prejudice and a recognition of the fact that there are legitimate prejudices, if we want to do justice to man's finite historical mode of being' (Gadamer 1975: 246). There is a horizon for every society, a cognitive envelope that defines the reality of that society to itself. Husserl writes of the world, that 'part is perceived ... and part is contextually supplied by our memory' (1970: 13); our actions of perception are not re-actions, but actions, actual creations resting within the logic, the cognitive order that rests in our memory. And Heidegger says that it is our being-in-the-world, by which he means consciously existing within the created signs of the society, 'with its prejudices and presuppositions that makes understanding possible.' For, 'whenever something is interpreted as something, the interpretation will be founded essentially upon fore-having, fore-sight and fore-conception. An interpretation is never a presuppositionless apprehending of something present to us' (1962: 40, 191). A society is a structure for the generation of meaning, but meaning that is operable within a singular, distinct, and knowable perceptual or cognitive horizon. 'We cut nature up, organize it into concepts, and ascribe significances as we do, largely because we are parties to an agreement to organize it in this way' (Whorf 1969: 213). Further, this cognitive horizon is operative within the energy potentialities and limitations of a particular geophysical area and all the flora and fauna within that area (part of biological reality).

Cognition in the society is created via the interaction of individual units, who both share a certain cognitive organization and yet have access to new energy and the power of organizing energy. By this I understand that meaning, which is *reality* – for meaning is not doubt or dreams, but dreams understood as real – is created via the dialogical exchange and transformation of shared cognitive 'bits.' Understanding, as has been well argued by those working in hermeneutics, phenomenology, and post-structuralism, is not achieved by passive reception of the empirical reality, but is an interaction between physical and conceptual units, between individuals, between individuals and units, all acting within a society's cognitive structure, the logic of Peircean Thirdness. This is a dialogue, understood as transformation, even if the interaction takes place only within one's own mind. Knowledge is not, as Popper outlines in his critique of 'the bucket theory of the mind,' simply an act of passively filling one's mind with sense-data from the environment (1972: 61). If you see cognition as a mirror reflection of the world-as-picture, then your definition of thinking will concentrate on proper vision, perception, and indeed, removing all thoughts from the mind. An individual in the textual society does not behave as an isolate being but as an interactive particle or 'bit' within the society. An individual within a society is the agent for the transformation of energy, and as such, is an actual part of the generative cognitive structure of the whole society.

A text is a finite or closed, unique and preserved potentiality to make metaphors of meaning or signs, which operates within a dialogical interaction to produce actual meaning. The text has a confined or limited meaning potential, by reason of its finite content closed within its manuscript structure. Its distinct and unique material content is protected by copyright and is identifiable so that when we quote passages, we can name the text from where those images come. It at first sight seems static and set in its signs content and their format. However, it is never understood in this static form, but is interpreted and reinterpreted within the dialogical interaction of reader and text, such that 'understanding and response are dialectically merged and mutually condition each other: one is impossible without the other' (Bakhtin 1981: 282). Therefore,'a text can begin to speak. When it does begin to speak, however, it does not simply speak its word, always the same, in lifeless rigidity, but gives ever new answers to the person who questions it and poses ever new questions to him who answers it. To understand a text is to come to understand oneself in a kind of dialogue' (Gadamer 1977: 57). Thus, reading is actually a current interpretation that uses the original author's metaphors and creates a current usage or meaning of the original metaphors. In that sense, the text, like the oral myth, has 'around it an aura of meaning which has been put there by all the contexts in which it has occurred in the past' (Lord 1971: 148). The text as existent in a current reality 'incorporates both the prestructuring of the potential meaning by the text and the reader's actualization of this potential through the reading process' (Iser 1974: 11).

A society as a closed and distinct textual system of meaning has identifiable authors who are both its historical or mythic agents of origin and also specific or mythic events in its historical development, which provide it with a unique identity. These original authors of a society are always existent, even if they are social rather than existential facts, as were the mythic gods and medieval heroes. A society will always find an author of its uniqueness and its right to exist; there will always be gods. The metaphoric content of the society as developed over the years may seem as closed as that of the epic text and assume the same power over individual usage. Interpretation includes all members of the society, for 'an essential aspect of the context of any utterance is other utterances and voices' (Wertsch 1985: 64).

Importantly, like the text and the organic entity, the metaphoric stock of a society must be kept active, it must be interpreted and reinterpreted, or rather, as energy, it must be organized and reorganized in the daily interaction of use. 'A society, like a mind, is woven of perpetual interaction' (Bloch 1965: 59). In fact, in order to 'read' society, by which I mean to live currently within its frame, a dialogical interplay between the two levels, between existent logic and current interpretation, is a necessity. Otherwise, entropy sets in and the individual becomes paralyzed within his society, a foreigner, an alien, someone unable to speak and therefore to exist.

The textual society is not simply a haphazard stock of signs that the individual randomly picks up and uses in their pictorial iconic form, but is a selectively collected and preserved *potentiality* of meanings, operating within an equally selective generative system for their specific meaning and usage. With the society, like the text, you cannot randomly remove or add words, chapters, or systems of behaviour and belief, for that would be to deny both the cognitive horizon, the ground logic specific to that society/text, and the necessity of dialogue to create those signs.

I am not saying that society *is* text, society is not identical to a text. A key factor to be remembered is that a society is both an organic and a social entity. As organic, it is an organized content of a specific amount of energy – a cell, finite, differentiated from other cells, and engaged in a continuous organization and reorganization of its energy. And society is also social, because the actions of organization of that energy are socially defined. Therefore a society can be analysed 'as a text,' an organic reality and a social creation that exists only in usage, only within the actions of being written and read.

Removing the study of societies from the grip of analytic fields that concentrate on only one or the other levels as causal of social behaviour and moving it to the analytic base of semiotics, with its understanding of reality as an action, as only existent within interaction, may bring new insights into social structures. To consider that societies are products of the IR level only leads to analyses based around leaders, heroes, villains, and studies of the various methods by which individuals become iconic copies. To consider that societies are caused by the various forces of the group (not as syntactic pattern but as structural systems) reduces the power of the group to various institutional mechanisms of the political, legal, economic, and religious sectors of social interaction. To consider that societies are caused by biological factors leads to, as mentioned, the racism of homogeneous identities and tribalism. And to consider that societies are caused by irrational forces, understood via various metaphors such as gods and aliens, leads to asocial and passive and highly emotive interactions. None of these methods of considering causality in societies is valid because they ignore the generative interaction of the organizational factors of all levels of existence. Semiotics can acknowledge that meaning is dialogically generated and never existent as a cold, static, and unchanging fact; that meaning is not a metaphor related directly to an object, but is deeply embedded in the interactive cognitive interactions of the whole society. Research into societies cannot ignore the powerful organic reality of the socially based syntactic logic that binds and organizes individual interpretations. Semiotics accepts the society as a single coherent system for the generation of meaning. Semiotics can also understand that meaning must have an 'other,' a Secondness that provides a limit to the experience of cognition, and therefore can understand that all societies are finite, and that differences between societies should not be understood as symptoms of dissension and prejudice, but rather as necessary factors to the development of understanding both within the society and between societies. Semiotics can see society not as a temporal collection of images that can be arbitrarily shuffled around, but more deeply, as a multileveled and complex interactive systemic action for the ongoing transformation of energy into various forms of meaning or daily life. And semiotics can help us understand that the production of meaning within a society is not simply by the usage, the introduction, or the discarding of simple images but is a dialogical interaction of multiple forms of energy operating within the boundaries of the text. We can then understand change within a society as able to come about only via a restructuring of the syntactic logic and not via a simple introduction of new images. Forcing Third World people to use different technologies or to use new images in their interactions will not also bring about a change in their society's basic nature. Rather, by alienating their current expressions from their GR level logic, such an action has usually destroyed that logic and left them for many years as a *people* who were not also a *society*. To introduce buying land into a society of indigenous peoples is useless if their textual content does not include both the semantic metaphors of owning land and also the syntactic logic that produces such metaphors as individual buying, owning, and selling. You cannot introduce a new image into a social text without considering all levels.

In summary, a society can be defined as a spatiotemporally closed, socially created systemic and unique formation of various organizations of energy, operative in a dialogical and interactive sense within a long-term and distinct syntactic pattern of cognition, which is created by agents understood as both authors and readers. The cognitive content of a society is 'written, rewritten, and read' or interpreted within this infrastructure. Within the textual confines of a society, knowledge exists as long as the structure exists, and is above all valid only within those confines.

Societies then are specific texts – created by and creative of – human beings. They are not collections of people, but structured actions of cognitively organized energy. There are many further areas of research in this perspective, including such topics as the evolution, development, and demise of societies, the ethics of socio-organic existence, the multi-faceted and hierarchical nature of the various semantic-level codal or 'energy transformation' systems, the function of ritual and myth, and so on. A key aspect of this method is its understanding of society as a semiotic action, a social transformation of multiple forms of energy within the cognitive frames of human individuals. That is why I conpare societies to texts, and urge that they be studied as organic actions of meaning.

Notes

1: The Realities of the Social Text

1 Peirce also used the terms of Presentness, Struggle, and Laws; and Quality, Reaction, and Representation for the three categories of Firstness, Secondness, and Thirdness, thereby defining their key functions. See 5: 41-76.

2 I have used a number of translations of Aquinas' works. The text references are to the location within the original passage and the particular translation. Passage abbreviations are as follows: q. for question; a. for article; c. for body of the article; ad. for reply to the objections. *De veritate* is abbreviated as *De ver*, *Summa contra Gentiles* as *S.C.G.*; *Summa Theologica* as *S.T.*

3 There are variable translations for the three phases (using the Peircean order of Firstness, Thirdness, and Secondness) of *simplex apprehensio, intellectus agens,* and *intellectus possibilis.* In similar order, they include sense-experience, sensible, phantasm; agent intellect, active intellect, and sense (a confusing term found in Mulligan); and possible intellect, receptive intellect, passive intellect, or simply intellect. See Eco's analysis in *The Aesthetics of Thomas Aquinas,* 58–63.

4 Time is discussed in chapters 2 and 4.

5 These nodes and their interactions are examined in chapters 2 and 3.

6 Compare implicate order with group reality and explicate order with individual reality conceptual (IRC).

7 I use the term 'degenerate' rather than 'defective' to suggest the asocial *values* resulting from these forms.

8 The nature of stability is discussed in more detail in chapters 5 through 8.

9 See Colapietro 1989, chap. 1, for a clear analysis of the problems of the Saussurian binary frame.

10 See, for example, Iser 1974; Derrida 1976; Fish 1980; De Man 1983; Clifford and Marcus 1986.

11 See Eco's analysis of deconstructive openness in 1992 and 1994.

12 The analysis of Piaget considers children primarily functional within the sensual node rather than the conceptual.

13 The concept that phylogeny recapitulates ontogeny has led to such false binarisms in social analysis as primitive/civilized and underdeveloped/developed.

14 When I am referring to 'dialogue' and 'dialogical actions' I am referring to interaction between two different organizations of energy. The Bakhtinian use of dialogue sees it primarily as an 'interaction between meanings.' Meanings are IRC, existent on the individual reality level. I am expanding the use of this term to refer to interactions primarily between different forms of energy.

15 The implicate order would be comparable to group reality; the explicate or unfolded order would be comparable to individual reality 'in which the basic notion is one of separate objects' (1987: 174). Implicate order 'may be understood as a particular case of the generative order' (ibid: 184), and the generative order may be comparable to generative energy.

2: The Action of Textuality

1 IR = individual reality; IRS = individual reality sensual; IRC = individual reality conceptual; GR = group reality

2 Interesting comparisons could be made between these nodes and both Lacan's 'phallocentric' points and biological synapses.

3 We must remember that generative energy (GE) is infinite and available to being moved into the group STF via the individual. I am here only discussing the cognitive action, that can take place only within an STF, a finite organization of energy.

4 See analysis on the nature of self-organizing systems in the work of the chemist Ilya Prigogine (1980). I further explore the concepts of equilibrium and disequilibrium and the self-organization of systems in chapter 6, on change in the syntactic logic of social groups, and chapter 7, on the balance of energies within a social text.

5 The nature of otherness in the development of meaning is discussed in more detail in chapter 3.

6 The different patterns of time are discussed in chapter 4.

7 There is a distinct difference between dialogue and discourse. This is clarified throughout the text.

8 I do not consider language to be the only means by which human beings develop and express meaning. It is the most important for the collective, but there are other semiotic systems found within the biological sensual system

(sight, smell, touch, taste, hearing) that are semiotically functional within a nonverbal format.

9 Consider the object as the signifier, the source of external intentionality, and the individual as the signified, the focus of meaning.

10 I suggest this definition merely focuses attention on the nature of deconstruction as an ongoing action; however, actions, even if meant to be continuous, can be abstractly understood by the use of a referent, a metaphoric sign.

3: Otherness in the Production of Meaning

1 IRS = individual reality sensual; IRC = individual reality conceptual

2 The STF is the spatiotemporal frame of a single organic unit. It provides the physical and conceptual horizons of this unit, as defined in space and time. We may consider STF's of individuals or of whole societies.

3 See chapter 2 for a full explanation of the action of textuality (AOT).

4 For an examination of these two forms, see Peirce's analysis of the two degenerate forms of evolution, tychasm or chance changes, and anancasm or mechanical deterministic changes.

5 See chapter 1 for an explanation of 'collapsed realities.'

6 See chapter 1, 13–16.

7 See the dyadic bond analysis in chapter 1 and the Saussurian analysis in this chapter.

8 I emphasize their existential nature; they are not actions of energy but actual and specific systems that are assumed to have energy content.

9 See chapter 1, 9–10, for a discussion of external forms as false generative energy.

10 For a discussion of this frame as a degenerate form of individual reality, see 'Binary Code' in chapter 1, 12–13.

11 Could *présence* be compared with 'deep reality'?

12 The Jungian archetypes can be considered part of biological reality, in that they are universal forms of order (symbolized as archetypes) and common to the organic existentiality of human beings. Writing does not seem to have even the limitations of these symbolic forms of the biological order.

4: Dialogical Time

1 From records of the Virginia Company, in Pearce 1988: 9.

2 President Andrew Jackson, 6 December 1830. Quoted in ibid, 57.

3 See the study by R. Pearce of the European view of Aboriginal peoples in *Savagism and Civilization*, 1988.

4 Something that is existential, that exists within space and time, is a 'spatio-temporal entity,' whether it is material or conceptual.

5 Because Greek adventure time may have been a transitional phase does not mean that other fundamentalist social groups that permit only iconic copies of the group reality are also transitional (eg; ethnic, religious, feminist), but they may be, and it is a factor to consider in their analysis.

6 This is different from early Greek adventure time where the current experience of individual reality is irrelevant to the long-term reality of the group iconic originals.

7 For a more complete discussion of carnival and change see chapters 1 and 6.

8 I would exempt the history of the Annales school from this linearity. With its profound sense of interactions between 'la longue durée,' 'conjunctures,' and the 'event' it is a completely dialogical school.

5: The Pattern of Cognition

1 Aristotle refers to two types of IRS or sensual percepts. One is sense impression from matter and the other is an image, but 'images are like sense impression, except that they are without matter' (*De Anima*, G, 432a: 10).

2 For further analysis, see Eco and Marmo, *On the Medieval Theory of Signs*, 1989.

3 This term is used by Bakhtin to confirm the contextuality of an utterance. 'At any given time, in any given place, there will be a set of conditions – social, historical, meteorological, physiological – that will insure that a word uttered in that place and at that time will have a meaning different than it would have under any other conditions' (1981: 428).

4 I suggest that these two analyses are basically flawed because they suggest that one type of social order (mechanical, bricolage) exists without a metaphysical logic or group reality. However, all societies are organic and dialogic with all four realities.

5 See *Collected Papers*, vol. 2, particularly chapters 2 and 3.

6 See my analysis of this oppositional binarism as degenerate binarism in chapter 1, 8–13.

7 Linkage can be analysed within such terms as metaphor/metonymy, denotation/connotation, and the Peircean triadic frame of icon, index, and symbol.

8 This refers to Io's banishment by her father (Aeschylus, *Prometheus Bound*, 874).

9 This is an enormous topic and has been well researched. See examples in such case studies as Tonkinson 1978, Lee 1984, Stearman 1989, and McElroy and Townsend 1989.

10 Note that invention in the modern industrial society (type A) is not attributed to single isolate individuals but to teams of researchers, whether in the natural or social sciences.

11 Again, this is quite different from the semiotic binarism of the two realities and from Saussure's (and others') semiological binarism and should not be confused with either form. Semantic binarism simply refers to the polarization of forms that an IRC, a sign, can take.

12 See explanations of death, good and bad events in, for instance, Lee 1984 and Keesing 1983.

13 See discussion of this in chapters 1, 6, and 7.

14 These two forces of stability and variation are discussed in chapter 7.

15 See, for example, trances of the Tapirape, the Dobe !Kung, the Plains Sun Dance, the churinga stones of the Aranda of Australia, which are visible manifestations of spirits.

16 See discussion in chapter 1, 8–16.

17 The necessity for social change at this time, due to the increase in population beyond the conceptual/technological organization methods of this time, is explored in more detail later.

18 Morgan 1877. See also Maine 1861.

19 We should recall that Plato was very opposed to books and the idea of mimetic copying as opposed to the dialogical development of a concept.

20 It is interesting to note that, in our current type A syntax, our society is removing the authority of the author and giving it either to the reader or to a discursive interaction between the two.

21 In a semantic sense, stasis is expressed within the forms of owner, storage, and original; variation is expressed within the forms of worker, history, and copy.

22 It should be clear that Lévi-Strauss is not defining the 'savage mind' as an earlier form but a different way of thinking, for 'there are two distinct modes of scientific thought. These are certainly not a function of different stages of development of the human mind but rather of two strategic levels at which nature is accessible to scientific inquiry' (1966: 15).

23 Data from Bernal 1969.

24 For a further discussion, see chapters 1 and 4, under Semantic Discourse, 11–12, and Surrealism, Deconstruction 89–90.

25 Compare with Structuralism.

6: Textual Change

1 See Starr (1984), 'The Marlboro Man: Cigarette Smoking and Masculinity in America.'

7: Two Bodies/Two Powers: Stasis and Heteroglossia

1 Compare such terms as *noumenon* and *phenomenon, ens reale* and *ens rationis.*

2 I stress the word 'until.' The use of technology that uses energy external to the society (gasoline, machine textiles, technology) eventually changes the energy content and usage of that society; this leads to a 'far-from-equilibrium' state and a 'dissipative structure,' leading eventually to syntactic collapse.

3 All references to the gnostic texts come from Pagels 1989.

4 We can find this concept in the many themes of 'media influence' that blame the media for various forms of social behaviour.

Glossary

Action of Intentionality   Introduces a new 'packet' of energy into a spatiotemporally closed organism. This new energy may then be reorganized within the organism, to function within the individual reality conceptual (IRC) node as a sign, a unit-of-meaning/existence.

Action of Textuality (AOT)   The action of comprehension, the semiotic act. This act filters and organizes sensual experience (energy) and transforms it into an experience of comprehension. The AOT is an interaction within three nodes: the individual reality sensual (IRS), group reality (GR) syntax, and individual reality conceptual (IRC).

Actual Conceptual Energy   Particular meaning, a specific spatiotemporally bound unit of energy; located within the action of the individual reality conceptual.

Actual Energy   Energy bound within a spatiotemporal frame; the result of an action of textuality.

Agent of Textuality   Introduces the spatiotemporal horizons within which an action of textuality can take place.

Articulation Point   A point, known as the node, where different realities meet and exchange energy. The new amount of energy is then reorganized within the pattern of organization dominant at that nodal point.

Binary Code   A system of definition/measurement with only two terms. Examples: *gender* is decoded into *male/female*; *human nature* is decoded into *passive/aggressive*. The individual reality conceptual nodal point organizes energy within socially necessary binary codes that function on a polarized scale of social powers. A *degenerate binary code* adds oppositional values to these powers; it considers that binarism is socially harmful rather than necessary.

Biological Reality (BR)   The energy forces of a biological entity. A biological being has a specific and finite amount of energy organized within spatial and temporal limits. It is involved in the thermodynamics of energy gain and loss and the maintenance of stability and variance. It expresses itself via the organizing logic of group reality and the direct experiences of individual reality. The biological reality of a society includes all entities within the environment – air, soil, water, climate, flora, and fauna.

Catastrophe   A system maintains long-term stability by means of its stable and long-term group reality (GR) logic. Ongoing yet limited variations of this logic take place on the level of individual reality. If for some reason an entity or collective either loses its flexibility of adaptation or the variations are beyond the organizing capacity of the GR logic, the syntactic pattern reaches a breaking-point, a catastrophic collapse. In a society, this collapse takes place quickly, over one generation; building a new syntactic pattern takes at least two or more generations.

Code   A system or scale of definition operative at the individual reality conceptual nodal point. It organizes energy into meaningful units; for example, code of law, code of building regulations, code of kinship. The definitions include the name and may also include the description. Without the description, the term is open to multiple interpretations, a factor in many cases of 'interpretation of the law.' For example, the code of law names a particular behaviour (murder) and also describes it. A code scale is finite and measurable; the terms are on a scale of measurement as part of their definition; for example, murder: unintentional/self-preservation/ retaliation/intentional.

	In some cases, codes can have only two key elements: see Binary Code. In others, they can be complex and multi-leveled.
Current Discourse	Interaction taking place only in current time. It may take place without interaction with the syntactic logic of the group reality level; in this case, it is superficial and known as 'idle chatter.'
Dialogue	Interaction between different organizations of energy. Dialogue is only possible within a sense of otherness and differentiation, where different amounts and organizations of energy interact with each other. This can be between organizational levels (individual and group reality) or between individuals/societies who are aware of and accept each other as 'different.'
Discourse	Interaction between similar organizations of energy. Such interaction usually functions to reinforce contact between separate but similarly organized entities. For example, ritualistic greetings between members of a club, followers of a particular political policy. Differences are necessarily ignored and rejected. In a positive form, discourse enforces stasis; in a degenerate form, it prevents heteroglossia and functions as a hidden form of censorship. It can also be understood as monological.
Four Realities	The individual, group, biological, and generative realities. As 'realities' they all, except for the generative, have spatial and temporal frames or horizons. That is, each exists within a specific spatiotemporal frame. In ascending order of both time and space, individual reality has the shortest time span and smallest spatial territory, then group reality and then biological reality. Generative energy is aspatial and atemporal.
Generative Reality/Energy (GE)	Unorganized unfocused energy. It is aspatial, atemporal and infinite. This free energy becomes 'trapped' by being organized within a spatiotemporal frame, a structure that exists for a finite time and within specific spatial boundaries. Spatiotemporal frames are functional within

	biological, group, and individual realities. To access more GE means going outside the horizons of one's existential or spatiotemporal reality and is a dangerous procedure.
Ground Logic	See Syntax.
Group Reality (GR)	The level of order of the collective; existent only as past/future potentiality and expressed within a syntactic pattern of organization. A completely social reality, with no biological content. In order to exist it must express itself within individual reality via the AOT.
Group Reality Syntax (GR Syntax)	The syntax is the pattern of organization found within group reality. See Syntax.
Heteroglossia	Variance, variation. Existent as a force on the level of individual reality. Permits the entity to vary its conception of reality and thereby adapt its behaviour. Each entity must have this ability to vary its interactions with the external world. However, there is a limit on the nature and number of possible variations. If there is either too little or too much variation, the syntactic organization will collapse, destroying the entity (see Catastrophe).
Individual Reality Conceptual (IRC)	The last, the ultimate node of the semiotic act, when cognition appears. Found only within current time within the individual experience. Comparable to Peircean Secondness. Expressed within a variety of codal forms and experienced within the individual as 'meaning,' conception, understanding. Codes can range from simple and binary to complex and multi-leveled.
Individual Reality (IR)	The individual level of experience, functional only within current time and operative within two nodes: sensual and conceptual. Movement between these two nodes is not direct but mediated via the GR syntactic node. That is, individual reality is in direct sensual contact with the external world, but conception is indirect, via the organizing logic of the syntactic action of group reality.
Individual Reality Sensual (IRS)	The first node of the semiotic act, the node of

sensual contact with the external (or aconceptual) world. Existent only within current time. It is totally unconceptual; sensual data at this node, unless transformed into cognition, is 'noise' and is not 'absorbed' into the individual's experience. Comparable to Peircean Firstness.

Node — A point of contact and organization of energy, where different forms of energy meet and are reorganized. The node is an articulation point where different realities meet. There are three key nodes in human cognition: IRS and IRC within the individual reality, and the syntactic node within the group reality. Energy is introduced, lost, and reorganized at these nodal sites.

Otherness — The interaction of shared energy situated at sites that are spatiotemporally and therefore organizationally different from each other. This interaction causes a reorganization of the shared energy. Otherness is necessary for all spatiotemporal and therefore conceptual existence.

Potential Conceptual Energy (PCE) — A finite amount of energy bound within a spatiotemporal frame (STF) by a syntactic pattern; not yet actualized.

Potential Discourse — The habits of meaning within a society, the habits of the syntax as expressed within social rituals and codes that provide boundaries for the expressions of a society.

Potential Energy — Energy potentially available to a spatiotemporal action of framing or holding and organizing that energy.

Semantic — Coded forms of energy, operative on the individual reality level at the IRC node. It is differentiated from syntax, which is a pattern of interaction existent only on the GR level. Semantic entities are actual conceptual realities, encoded in various forms. Semantic actions are exchanges of coded forms and may, in a degenerate fashion, operate only within discourse. See Code; Discourse.

Spatiotemporal Frame (STF) — Energy that is bound within specific spatial and temporal horizons. A spatiotemporal frame permits

	cognitive life in all its forms, chemical, biological and physical, to exist.
Stasis	Stability of interactions. Governed by the group reality level. Each system must have long-term, multiple-generation internal and external stability (see Three Generations). At the same time and functioning with this stability, it must be able to vary those interactions (see Heteroglossia).
Syntax	Other terms for syntax include pattern of cognition, syntactic pattern, logical order, ground logic, group logic. It is a pattern of organization of energy, existent only in past/future time, and expressed within current time by the ongoing regular-periodic (heartbeat) interactions (AOT) with individual reality. It is a long-term pattern and must last for at least three generations in order to maintain social stability. Anything shorter is simply an adaptive variation of a syntax. Within the social domain, there are two key syntactic patterns: A and B. Syntax is comparable in function to Peircean Thirdness.
Syntax A	Cognitive pattern found within group reality. The pattern of conceptual organization is: subject/object ‖ verb. Essentially, the agent and entity of an action operate together.
Syntax B	Cognitive pattern found within group reality. The pattern of conceptual organization is: subject	verb	object. Essentially, the agent is separated from the entity by the verbal action.
Three Generations	The minimum time period for a society to exist. Within this time period, it will have made the syntactic pattern stable, so that it can govern the behaviour and thought of new forms of individual life within the society. It will also have developed the stability of its IRC semantic codes so that the individuals within the society will be able to express themselves and interact with each other. By the third generation, it may be able to conceptually analyse its nature.
Variance	See Heteroglossia.

Bibliography

Aquinas, St Thomas (1954, 1994). *De Veritate:* vol. 1 (questions 1–9) trans. R. Mulligan; vol. 2 (questions 10-20) trans. J.V. McGlynn; vol. 3 (questions 21–9) trans. R.W. Schmidt. Indianapolis: Hackett.

– (1960). *The Pocket Aquinas,* ed. V.J. Bourke. New York: Washington Square.

– (1981). *Summa Theologica.* Vol. 1 (questions 1–119, 1948). Benzinger Bros: Christian Classics.

– (1988). *The Philosophy of Thomas Aquinas,* ed. C. Martin. London and New York: Routledge.

Aristotle. (1928). *Posterior Analytics,* trans. G.R.G. Mure. In *Works,* vol. I.

– (1981). *De Anima: On the Soul,* trans. H.G. Apostle. Grinnell, IA: Peripatetic Press.

Bacon, F. (1960). *The New Organon and Related Writings,* ed. F.H. Anderson, New York: Liberal Arts.

Baggott, J. (1992). *The Meaning of Quantum Theory.* Oxford: Oxford University Press.

Bakhtin, M. (1979). *The Aesthetics of Verbal Creation.* Moscow: Bocharov.

– (1981). *The Dialogic Imagination,* ed. M. Holquist. Austin: University of Texas Press.

– (1984a). *Problems of Dostoevsky's Poetics,* ed. C. Emerson. Minneapolis: University of Minnesota Press.

– (1984b). *Rabelais and His World.* Bloomington: Indiana University Press.

– (1986). *Speech Genres and Other Late Essays by M.M. Bakhtin,* ed. M. Holquist and C. Emerson. Austin: University of Texas Press.

– (1993). *Toward a Philosophy of the Act,* ed. V. Liapunov and M. Holquist. Austin: University of Texas Press.

Barker, E., ed. (1962). *Social Contract: Essays by Locke, Hume, Rousseau.* New York: Oxford University Press.

Barthes, R. (1967). *Elements of Semiology*. New York: Hill and Wang.
- (1973). *Mythologies*. Frogmore: Paladin Press.
- (1974). *S/Z: An Essay*. New York: Hill and Wang.
- (1977). *Image, Music, Text*. Fontana/Collins.
Baudrillard, J. (1975). *The Mirror of Production*. Telos Press.
Benedict, R. (1934). *Patterns of Culture*. Boston: Houghton Mifflin.
Bernal, J. (1969). *Science in History:* Volumes 1–4. Pelican Books/Penguin.
Bernstein, B. (1971). *Class, Codes and Control*. London: Routledge and Kegan Paul.
The Bhagavad Gita (1962). Trans. J. Mascaro. New York: Penguin.
Bierwisch, M. (1980). Semantic Structure and Illocutionary Force. In *Speech Act Theory and Pragmatics*, ed. J. Searle et al, 1–36. Dordrecht: Reidel Press.
Bloch, M. (1965). *Feudal Society*, vol. 1. Chicago: Routledge and Kegan Paul.
Bodley, J. (1988). *Tribal Peoples and Development Issues: A Global Overview*. Mountain View, CA: Mayfield.
- (1990). *Victims of Progress*. Mountain View, CA: Mayfield.
Bohm, D. (1980). *Wholeness and the Implicate Order*. London: Routledge and Kegan Paul.
Bohm, D. and F.D. Peat (1987). *Science, Order and Creativity*. New York: Bantam Books.
Bohr, N. (1935). Can Quantum Mechanical Description of Physical Reality Be Considered Complete? *Physical Review* 48.
- (1958). *Atomic Physics and Human Knowledge*. New York: Wiley.
Bourdieu, P. (1977). *Outline of a Theory of Practice*. Cambridge: Cambridge University Press.
Braudel, F. (1980). *On History*. Chicago: University of Chicago Press.
- (1981). *The Structures of Everyday Life*. London: Collins.
- (1982). *The Wheels of Commerce*. London: Collins.
- (1984). *The Perspective of the World*. London: Collins.
Braverman, H. (1974). *Labor and Monopoly Capital*. New York: Monthly Review Press.
Briggs, J. and F.D. Peat. (1989). *Turbulent Mirror*. New York: Harper and Row.
Calasso, R. (1993). *The Marriage of Cadmus and Harmony*. New York: Knopf.
- (1994). *The Ruin of Kasch*. Cambridge, MA: Belknap Press of Harvard University Press.
Campbell, J. (1968). *The Hero with a Thousand Faces*. Princeton: Princeton University Press.
Camus, A. (1956). *The Rebel: An Essay on Man in Revolt*. New York: Vintage Books.
Castoriadis, C. (1987). *The Imaginary Institution of Society*. Cambridge, MA: MIT Press.
Chomsky, N. (1957). *Syntactic Structures*. The Hague: Mouton.

– (1964). Current Issues in Linguistic Theory. In *The Structure of Language*, ed. J. Fodor and J. Katz, 50–119. New York: Prentice-Hall.

– (1965). *Aspects of the Theory of Syntax*. Cambridge, MA: MIT Press.

– (1972). *Language and Mind*. New York: Harcourt Brace.

Clark, K. and M. Holquist (1984). *Mikhail Bakhtin*. Cambridge, MA: Harvard University Press.

Clifford, J. and G. Marcus, eds. (1986). *Writing Culture: The Poetics and Politics of Ethnography*. Berkeley and Los Angeles: University of California Press.

Colapietro, V.M. (1989). *Peirce's Approach to the Self*. New York: State University of New York Press.

Connerton, P. (1989). *How Societies Remember*. Cambridge: Cambridge University Press.

Davies, P. (1990a) *God and the New Physics*. London: Penguin.

– (1990b). *Other Worlds*. London: Penguin.

Davies, P. and J. Brown, eds. (1986). *The Ghost in the Atom*. Cambridge: Cambridge University Press.

– (1988). *Superstrings: A Theory of Everything?* Cambridge: Cambridge University Press.

Davis, N.Z. (1979). *Society and Culture in Early Modern France*. Stanford: Stanford University Press.

Davis, P. (1993). The Goddess and the Academy. *Academic Questions*, 49–66.

Dawkins, R. (1978). *The Selfish Gene*. London: Granada.

De Man, P. (1983). *Blindness and Insight: Essays in the Rhetoric of Contemporary Criticism*. 2nd rev. ed. Minneapolis: University of Minnesota Press.

– (1984). *The Rhetoric of Romanticism*. New York: Columbia University Press.

Deledalle, G. (1990). *Charles S. Peirce: An Intellectual Biography*. Amsterdam/ Philadelphia: John Benjamins.

Derrida, J. (1973). *Speech and Phenomena and Other Essays on Husserl's Theory of Signs*. Evanston, IL: Northwestern University Press.

– (1976). *Of Grammatology*. Baltimore: Johns Hopkins University Press.

– (1988). *Limited Inc*. Evanston, IL: Northwestern University Press.

Descartes, R. (1960). *Discourse on Method and Meditation*, trans. L.J. Lafleur. New York: Liberal Arts Press.

Dickens, A. and D. Carr, eds. (1967). *Documents of Modern History: The Reformation in England to the Accession of Elizabeth I*. London: Edward Arnold.

Durkheim, E. (1895, 1964). *The Rules of Sociological Method*. New York: Free Press.

Eckhart, Meister. (1941). *A Modern Translation*, trans. R. Blakney. New York: Harper.

Eco, U. (1975). *A Theory of Semiotics*. Bloomington: Indiana University Press.

– (1979). *The Role of the Reader*. Bloomington: Indiana University Press.

– (1988). *The Aesthetics of Thomas Aquinas.* Cambridge, MA: Harvard University Press.

– (1992). *Interpretation and Overinterpretation,* ed. S. Collini. Cambridge: Cambridge University Press.

– (1994). *The Limits of Interpretation.* Bloomington: Indiana University Press.

Eco, U. and C. Marmo, eds. (1989). *On the Medieval Theory of Signs.* Amsterdam: John Benjamins.

Einstein, A., B. Podolsky, and N. Rosen (1935). Can Quantum Mechanical Description of Physical Reality be Considered Complete? *Physical Review* 47.

Eliade, M. (1963). *Myth and Reality.* New York: Harper and Row.

Eliot, T.S. (1954). *Selected Poems.* Faber.

Endicott, K. (1988). Property, Power and Conflict among the Batek of Malaysia. In *Hunters and Gatherers,* vol. 2, ed. T. Ingold et al, 110–28. New York: Berg.

Erickson, C. (1976). *The Medieval Vision.* Oxford: Oxford University Press.

Fish, S. (1980). *Is There a Text in This Class?* Cambridge, MA: Harvard University Press.

Fleischaker, G. (1984). The Traditional Model for Perception and Theory of Knowledge: Its Metaphor and Two Recent Alternatives. *Behavioral and Brain Sciences,* 29: 40–50.

Foucault, M. (1972). *The Archaeology of Knowledge.* London: Tavistock.

– (1973a). *Madness and Civilization.* New York: Vintage Books.

– (1973b). *The Order of Things.* New York: Vintage Books.

– (1977). *Language, Counter-Memory, Practice,* ed. D. Bouchard. Ithaca, NY: Cornell University Press.

Fraser, J.T., ed. (1981). *The Voices of Time.* Amherst: University of Massachusetts Press.

Freud, S. (1938). *The Basic Writings of Sigmund Freud,* ed. A. Brill. New York: Random House.

– (1955). Group Psychology. In *The Standard Edition of Complete Works,* vol. 18. London: Hogarth Press.

Gadamer, H-G. (1975). *Truth and Method.* London: Sheed and Ward.

– (1977). *Philosophical Hermeneutics,* ed. D. Linge. Berkeley: University of California Press.

Geertz, C. (1973). *The Interpretation of Cultures: Selected Essays.* New York: Basic.

Gellner, E. (1974). *Legitimation of Belief.* London: Cambridge University Press.

Godzich, W.(1988). *Writings of the Circle of Bakhtin.* Minneapolis: University of Minnesota Press.

Goethe, J.W. (1963). *Faust,* trans. W. Kaufmann. Anchor

Gould, S.J. (1990). *The Panda's Thumb.* London: Penguin.

Gray, D., ed. (1992). *English Medieval Religious Lyrics.* Exeter: University of Exeter Press.

Grimm, J. (1977). *Grimms' Tales for Young and Old (1819)*, trans. R. Manheim. New York: Anchor/Doubleday.

Grube, G.M.A. (1980). *Plato's Thought.* Indianapolis: Hackett.

Hegel, G. (1967). *The Phenomenology of Mind.* New York: Harper Colophon.

Heidegger, M. (1959). *Introduction to Metaphysics.* New Haven: Yale University Press.

– (1962). *Being and Time.* New York: Harper and Row.

– (1982). *The Basic Problems of Phenomenology.* Bloomington: Indiana University Press.

Holquist, M. (1990). *Dialogism: Bakhtin and His World.* London: Routledge.

The Holy Bible (King James Version [1611] 1958). National Bible Press.

Homer (1967). *The Odyssey*, trans. R. Lattimore. Harper and Row.

Husserl, E. (1970). *The Idea of Phenomenology.* The Hague: Nijhoff.

Ingarden, R. (1973) *The Literary Work of Art.* Evanston, IL: Northwestern University Press.

Ingold, T., D. Riches, and J. Woodburn, eds. (1988). *Hunters and Gatherers*, 2 vols. New York: Berg.

Iser, W. (1974). *The Implied Reader.* Baltimore: Johns Hopkins University Press.

– (1978). *The Act of Reading.* London: Routledge and Kegan Paul.

Jean de Meun and Guillaume de Lorris. *Le Roman de la Rose.* In English: (1983). *The Romance of the Rose*, trans. C. Dahlberg. Princeton: Princeton University Press.

Jung, C.W. (1966). *Collected Works*, 2nd ed. vol. 7; vol. 9, parts 1 and 2. Bollingen Foundation. New York: Pantheon Books.

Kaufmann, W. (1974). *Nietzsche.* Princeton: Princeton University Press.

Keesing, R. (1983). *Elota's Story.* New York: Holt, Rinehart and Winston.

Kenny, A. (1980). *Aquinas.* Oxford: Oxford University Press.

Koestler, A. (1970). *The Act of Creation.* London: Pan.

Koyre, A. (1965). *Newtonian Studies.* Chicago: University of Chicago Press.

Krieger, M. ed. (1987). *The Aims of Representation.* New York: Columbia University Press.

Kuhn, T. (1970). *The Structure of Scientific Revolutions.* Chicago: University of Chicago Press.

Laborit, H. (1977). *Decoding the Human Message.* London: Allison and Busby.

Lacan, J. (1977). *Ecrits*, trans. A. Sheridan. London: Tavistock.

Land, S. (1974). *From Signs to Propositions: The Concept of Form in Eighteenth-Century Semantic Theory.* London: Longman.

Langness, L. (1987). *The Study of Culture.* Novato, CA: Chandler and Sharp.

Le Bon, G. (1960). *The Crowd.* New York: Viking Press.

Le Goff, J. (1988). *Medieval Civilization.* Oxford: Blackwell.

– (1993). *Intellectuals in the Middle Ages.* Oxford: Blackwell.

Lee, R. (1984). *The Dobe !Kung*. New York: Holt, Rinehart and Winston.

– (1988). Reflections on Primitive Communism. In *Hunters and Gatherers*, vol. 1, ed. T. Ingold et al, 252–68.

Lévi-Strauss, C. (1963). *Structural Anthropology*. New York: Basic Books.

– (1966). *The Savage Mind*. Chicago: University of Chicago Press.

– (1975). *The Raw and the Cooked*. New York: Harper Colophon

– (1977). *Tristes Tropiques*. New York: Pocket Books.

Locke, J. (1690, 1975) *An Essay concerning Human Understanding*, ed. P. Nidditch. Oxford: Oxford University Press.

Lord, A. (1971). *The Singer of Tales*. New York: Atheneum.

Lotman, J. and B.A. Uspenskij (1984). *The Semiotics of Russian Culture*. Ann Arbor: University of Michigan Press.

Maine, H.S. (1861). *Ancient Law*. London: J. Murray.

Manchester, W. (1992). *A World Lit Only by Fire*. New York: Little, Brown.

Maritain, J. (1955). *Creative Intuition in Art and Poetry*. New York: Meridian.

Marlowe, C. (1628, 1989). *The Tragical History of Dr. Faustus*, ed. R. Gill. New York: Norton.

Matejka, L., ed. (1976). *Sound, Sign and Meaning*. Ann Arbor: University of Michigan Press.

Maturana, H. (1970). *The Neurophysiology of Cognition*. Portage, MI: Spartan Books.

Mauss, M. (1970). *The Gift*. London: Routledge and Kegan Paul.

McElroy, A. and P. Townsend. (1989). *Medical Anthropology in Ecological Perspective*. Boulder: Westview.

Mertz, E. and R. Parmentier, eds. (1985). *Semiotic Mediation: Sociocultural and Psychological Perspectives*. New York: Academic.

Morford, M. and R. Lenardon. (1977). *Classical Mythology*. New York: Longman.

Morgan, L.H. (1877). *Ancient Society*. New York: Holt.

Morphy, H. (1988) Maintaining Cosmic Unity: Ideology and the Reproduction of Yolngu clans. In *Hunters and Gatherers*, vol. 2, ed. T. Ingold et al, 249–71.

Morson, G.S. and C. Emerson. (1990). *Mikhail Bakhtin: Creation of a Prosaics*. Stanford: Stanford University Press.

Morson, G.S., ed. (1981). *Bakhtin: Essays and Dialogues on His Word*. Chicago: University of Chicago Press.

Motsch, W. (1980). Situational Context and Illocutionary Force. In *Speech Act Theory and Pragmatics*, ed. J. Searle et al, 155–68. Dordrecht: Reidel Press.

Newton, Sir I. (1729, 1947). *Mathematical Principles of Natural Philosophy and His System of the World*, rev. F. Cajori; trans. A. Motte. University of California Press.

Neihardt, J. (1961). *Black Elk Speaks*. Pocket Book ed. Toronto: Simon and Schuster.

Nietzsche, F. (1969). *On the Genealogy of Morals / Ecce Homo*, ed. W. Kaufmann. New York: Random House.

Noonan, J. (1957). *General Metaphysics.* Chicago: Loyola University Press.

Pagels, E. (1989). *The Gnostic Gospels.* New York: Vintage.

Parrett, H. (1983). *Semiotics and Pragmatics: An Evaluative Comparison of Conceptual Frameworks.* New York: Benjamins.

Pearce, R. (1988). *Savagism and Civilization.* Berkeley and Los Angeles: University of California Press.

Peirce, C.S. (1931–58). *Collected Papers*, ed. C. Hartshorne, P. Weiss, and A.W. Burks. 8 vols. Cambridge, MA: Harvard University Press.

– (1955). *Philosophical Writings,* ed. J. Buchler. New York: Dover.

Plato (1973). *Phaedrus and Letters VII and VIII*, trans. W. Hamilton. New York: Penguin.

– (1974). *Republic*, trans. G.M.A. Grube. Indianapolis: Hackett.

Pompa, L. (1990). *Vico: A Study of the New Science.* Cambridge: Cambridge University Press.

Popper, K. (1972). *Objective Knowledge.* Oxford: Clarendon Press.

Pospisil, L. (1978). *The Kapauku Papuans of West New Guinea.* New York: Holt, Rinehart and Winston.

Prigogine, I. (1980). *From Being to Becoming.* San Francisco: Freeman.

Rabelais, F. (1535–54, 1990). *Gargantua and Pantagruel*, trans. B. Raffel. New York: Norton.

Redfield, R. (1960). *The Little Community / Peasant Society and Culture.* Chicago: University of Chicago Press.

Reed, S. (1943). *The Making of Modern New Guinea.* Philadelphia: American Philosophical Society.

Robinson, J. (1968). *An Introduction to Early Greek Writers.* Boston: Houghton, Mifflin.

Sachs, M. (1988). *Einstein versus Bohr.* La Salle, IL: Open Court.

Said, E. (1979). *Orientalism.* New York: Vintage.

Samuel, G. (1990). *Mind, Body and Culture: Anthropology and the Biological Interface.* Cambridge: Cambridge University Press.

Sarup, M. (1992). *Jacques Lacan.* Toronto: University of Toronto Press.

Saussure, F. de. (1966). *Course in General Linguistics*, ed. C. Bally and A. Sechehaye. New York: McGraw-Hill.

Schlipp, P., ed. (1949). *Albert Einstein: Philosopher-Scientist.* New York: Tudor Press.

Searle, J. (1969). *Speech Acts: An Essay in the Philosophy of Language.* Cambridge: Cambridge University Press.

– (1980). The Background of Meaning. In *Speech Act Theory and Pragmatics*, ed. J. Searle et al, 221–32. Dordrecht: Reidel Press.

– (1984). *Mind, Brains and Science.* The 1984 Reith Lectures. British Broadcasting Corporation, London.

Searle, J., and D. Vanderveken. (1985). *Foundations of Illocutionary Logic.* Cambridge: Cambridge University Press.

Searle, J., F. Keifer, and M. Bierwisch, eds. (1980). *Speech Act Theory and Pragmatics.* Dordrecht: Reidel Press.

Sigerist, H. (1970). *Civilization and Disease.* Chicago: University of Chicago Press.

Singer, C. (1959). *A Short History of Scientific Ideas to 1900.* London: Oxford University Press.

Stace, W. (1955). *The Philosophy of Hegel.* New York: Dover.

Starr, M. (1984). The Marlboro Man: Cigarette Smoking and Masculinity in America. *Journal of Popular Culture,* 17, no. 4, Spring, 45–57.

Stearman, A. (1989). *Yukui: Forest Nomads in a Changing World.* New York: Holt, Rinehart and Winston.

Sylvester, D. (1975). *Interviews with Francis Bacon.* London: Thames and Hudson.

Taylor, F.W. (1911, 1977). *Principles of Scientific Management.* New York and London: Harper and Row.

Tejera, V. (1988). *Semiotics from Peirce to Barthes.* London: E.J. Brill.

Thom, R. (1975). *Structural Stability and Morphogenesis.* Reading, MA: N.A. Benjamin.

Tiffany, D. (1989). Cryptesthesia: Visions of the Other. In *American Journal of Semiotics,* 6, no. 2/3, 209–19.

Todorov, T. (1984). *Mikhail Bakhtin: The Dialogical Principle.* Minneapolis: University of Minnesota Press.

Tonkinson, R. (1978). *The Mardudjara Aborigines.* New York: Holt, Rinehart and Winston.

Turnbull, C. (1983). *The Mbuti Pygmies: Change and Adaptation.* New York: Holt, Rinehart and Winston.

Turner, B. (1992). *Regulating Bodies.* London: Routledge.

The Upanishad (1965). Trans. J. Mascaro. New York: Penguin.

Varela, F., and D. Johnson. (1976). On Observing Natural Systems. *Co-Evolution Quarterly,* Summer, 26–31.

Vayda, A., ed. (1969). *Environment and Cultural Behavior.* Garden City, NY: Natural History Press.

Velikovsky, I. (1973). *Earth in Upheaval.* London: Abacus.

Vico, G. (1744, 1948). *The New Science,* trans. from 3d ed. by T.G. Bergin and M.H. Fisch. Ithaca, NY: Cornell University Press.

Voloshinov, V. (1929, 1973). *Marxism and the Philosophy of Language.* New York: Seminar Press.

– (1976). *Freudianism: A Marxist Critique.* New York: Academic Press.

Vygotsky, L.S. (1962). *Thought and Language,* ed. and trans. E. Hanfmann and G. Vakov. Cambridge, MA: MIT Press.

Wellington, J. (1967). *South West Africa and Its Human Issues.* Oxford: Oxford University Press.

Wertsch, J. (1985). The Semiotic Mediation of Mental Life. In *Semiotic Mediation: Sociocultural and Psychological Perspectives,* ed. E. Mertz and R. Parmentier, 49–69. New York: Academic.

Whorf, B. (1969). *Language, Thought and Reality,* ed. J.B. Carroll. Cambridge, MA: MIT Press.

Zeeman, E. (1977). *Catastrophe Theory: Selected Papers 1972–1977.* Reading, MA: Addison Wesley.

Zimmer, H. (1956). *Philosophies of India.* New York: Meridian Press.

Zizek, S. (1991). *Looking Awry.* Cambridge, MA: MIT Press.

Index